"An outstanding book from one of the leading c
world. Rebecca Jones provides a comprehensiv
play in coaching, helping practitioners and schol:
we have come over the past two decades in coac
coaching as an evidenced based discipline. This book is an essential pur-
chase for your coaching library."

Professor Jonathan Passmore, Director Henley Centre
for Coaching, Henley Business School

"Dr Jones has become a leading authority on the measurement of coaching
outcomes, backed by her vast knowledge of the academic literature in the
field. *Coaching with Research in Mind* brings this research base to illuminate
all aspects of the coaching engagement. Wonderful real-life vignettes from
coaching professionals bring it all to life. A vital book bridging the gap between research and practice, which is so desperately needed in our field!"

Brian O. Underhill, Ph.D., Founder & CEO,
CoachSource

"This book corroborates a much needed message – that coaching and research go hand in hand. A must read for academics and practitioners wishing to take an evidence – informed perspective."

Professor Almuth McDowall, Professor of
Organisational Psychology, Birkbeck University of
London

"This excellent book takes the reader on a valuable journey, closely examining
published research and linking it to coaching practice. Not only is it easy to
read, it can inform practice for both trainee and experienced coaches."

Professor Stephen Palmer, Wales Academy for
Professional Practice and Applied Research

"Far too much of coaching is based on supposition, superstition and ritual, with
little or no evidence base. Part of the cure is for coaches to adopt a more eviden-
tial approach to their practice – and this book shows them how!"

Professor David Clutterbuck, EMCC special
ambassador and visiting professor Henley Business
School

Coaching with Research in Mind

How can coaches maximise the effectiveness of their practice?

What can research tell us about how and why coaching 'works'?

How can we use the evidence base to enable others to reach their full potential?

Coaching with Research in Mind brings together cutting-edge research in coaching and psychology, accessibly summarises the findings, and provides a clear and specific breakdown of what research tells us coaches and leaders should be doing and why.

Rebecca J. Jones provides practitioners with the information and guidance they need to apply research in their practice, explaining how coaches can understand coachee characteristics, how they impact the coaching process and how coaches should adapt their practice to accommodate them. The book explains how to identify which principles of the coaching process influence effectiveness and tailor practice to maximise their impact. Jones also explores the impact of environmental factors and assesses how their influence can be limited.

Coaching with Research in Mind will be essential reading for both new and experienced coaches looking to enhance the effectiveness and impact of their coaching, and for managers, leaders and L&D procurers who utilise coaching as a leadership style.

Rebecca J. Jones, PhD, is associate professor of coaching at Henley Business School. She is a world-leading coaching researcher and an executive coach whose passion lies in helping others to achieve goals, realise potential and live life better.

Coaching with Research in Mind

Rebecca J. Jones

Routledge
Taylor & Francis Group

LONDON AND NEW YORK

First published 2021
by Routledge
2 Park Square, Milton Park, Abingdon, Oxon OX14 4RN

and by Routledge
52 Vanderbilt Avenue, New York, NY 10017

Routledge is an imprint of the Taylor & Francis Group, an informa business

British Library Cataloguing-in-Publication Data
A catalogue record for this book is available from the British Library

Library of Congress Cataloging-in-Publication Data
A catalog record has been requested for this book

ISBN: 978-1-138-36317-5 (hbk)
ISBN: 978-1-138-36319-9 (pbk)
ISBN: 978-0-429-43174-6 (ebk)

Typeset in Times New Roman
by codeMantra

For Adam, for always believing in me

Contents

List of figures   xi
List of tables   xii

SECTION ONE
An introduction to coaching   1

1   The evidence-base for coaching   17

2   What outcomes can we expect from coaching?   28

SECTION TWO
The coachee   45

3   Coachee motivation   47

4   Coachee personality   55

5   Coachee goal orientation   64

6   Coachee self-efficacy   74

7   Coachee skills   83

SECTION THREE
The coaching process   93

8   Goal-setting   98

9   Learning through reflection   118

10   Planning for action   148

SECTION FOUR
The role of the organization

165

SECTION FIVE
Conclusion

187

Research in action: Coach biographies   191
Index   195

Figures

2.1 Framework of coaching outcomes   29
8.1 Goal-setting pyramid (adapted from Whitmore, 2017, p. 105)   108

Tables

2.1 Framework of coaching outcomes and summary of
      proposed coaching evaluation criteria (Jones et al., 2016)   30
8.1 Motivational types of values (adapted from Schwartz, 1994)   107
1   Examples of shared assumptions of values, missions and
      goals for learning or coaching culture (adapted from
      Schein, 2010)   170

Section One

An introduction to coaching

The idea for this book was borne out of my experiences with coaches and those interested in coaching. Over the years that I have been researching coaching effectiveness and working as a coach educator, it has become apparent to me that many of the individuals who call themselves coaches or seek to use a coaching style of leadership have a strong desire to incorporate the research evidence into their practice. My own desire to become a researcher stems from a curiosity to dissect how things work and, in particular, how people 'work,' and it is with this curiosity that I continue to design and conduct research that dissects the coaching process. My experience is that those engaged in coaching share this curiosity; however, they can find it challenging to access and sometimes understand how to incorporate this research evidence into their own practice. In addition to the desire to dissect and understand how coaching works, I also have a passion for ensuring that research is read and more importantly used in practice. Coupling these passions, in this book, I bring together my own research and the research of others, which I present in a practical way. Highlighting, for each piece of evidence 'what does this mean in practice?' and consequently answering the question that others frequently ask me 'how can I use this research to make my coaching more effective?'

In this section, I first define what I view coaching to be. This definition sets the context and frames the remainder of the book. I also provide my suggestions as to why coaching has continued to increase in popularity and finally I provide an overview of the remaining chapters, explaining how they fit together with guidance on how I recommend readers to use the book.

What is coaching?

For many years, I must admit that whenever I was asked the question 'what is coaching?' I would feel a degree of frustration. In particular, I was asked this question during my viva – the final exam – for my PhD and many, many times in the reviews that I have received as feedback from reviewers and editors for journal articles. My frustration stemmed from having to answer a question where I perceived the answer to be obvious. A question that did not warrant utilizing precious space in my viva discussion or my journal articles. After all, coaching is a multi-billion global industry, surely we can all agree on what 'it' is? Of course, the answer to this question is that no we cannot. As I developed as a writer and a coach educator, I learned that the term 'coaching' is far from clearly defined, and in fact, for those who perceive it to be clearly defined (such as myself during those early years), our definition rarely matches with those definitions used by colleagues. Now, far from feeling frustrated when asked to define coaching, I am pleased to have the opportunity to share my perspective on what I perceive coaching to be. Although these days, reviewers ask me to clarify my definition less and less, mainly I believe, because I am doing a better job in my journal articles of defining it in the first place! In this section, I explain how I define coaching. This definition informs the remainder of this book but also the research that I conduct, the content of the course that I direct and teach upon, and, of course, my own working practice. This definition has evolved over the years, and I anticipate that it will continue to evolve, as I continue to develop and progress as a researcher, coach educator, and coach.

In essence, for me, coaching is at its most basic level a learning and development tool, with the goal of producing behavioural change. However, the term 'coaching' also describes a leadership philosophy or a way of 'being' that influences how we interact with others at both a personal and professional level. A philosophy where leaders view their roles as supporting others to access their full potential and utilize this to benefit the team and organizational performance. This way of 'being' or philosophy can be described as a coaching mindset. The content of this book is relevant to those who practice coaching as a learning and development tool and those who wish to develop a coaching mindset to understand behavioural change and to enhance their relationships with others.

When considering coaching as a learning and development tool and a coaching mindset, there are five principles that underscore both: openness, unconditional positive regard, non-judgmental attitude, growth mindset, and authenticity. In my view, these principles are fundamental to coaching.

Openness

Openness is one of the five personality traits that scholars generally accept as being universally applicable (Digman, 1990; Saucier & Ostendorf, 1999). Individuals who have a high level of openness tend to be imaginative, cultured, curious, original, and broad-minded (Barrick & Mount, 1991). For me, a high level of openness is fundamental to successful coaching, both as a learning and development tool and in adopting a coaching mindset. To be a coach, you must be curious about human nature to have the desire to learn about others and listen to their stories. You must be broad-minded to avoid passing judgements on others when perhaps they have previously 'failed' to achieve a goal or not worked on agreed actions following a previous coaching session. You must also be imaginative so that you can creatively work with your coachee to overcome challenges and obstacles they have yet to tackle alone. While openness is one of the five personality traits that we tend to exhibit more or less naturally, the good news is that evidence indicates that personality and openness, in particular, is malleable to some extent (Jackson, Hill, Payne, Roberts, & Stine-Morrow, 2012). Therefore, those who tend to have lower levels of openness are able to develop and foster this trait to become more open. The concept of openness is one that we return to in Chapters 4 and 7, as it is so fundamental to successful coaching.

Unconditional positive regard

Carl Rogers described unconditional positive regard in his 1967 text 'A therapist's view of psychotherapy: On becoming a person' as one of the conditions a therapist needs to experience for their client to form a successful psychotherapeutic relationship. Rogers defines unconditional positive regard as feelings of warmth and caring for another 'although [this is] a caring which is not possessive, which demands no personal gratification' (p. 283). This caring is not conditional on the behaviour or actions of the individual; therefore, the therapist or, in this case, coach demonstrates that they care and not that they care if the individual behaves in a particular way. Rogers also uses the word 'acceptance' to encompass what he means with unconditional positive regard. When demonstrating unconditional positive regard or acceptance for another, we accept and care for them as a separate person to ourselves, 'with permission for him to have his own feelings and experiences, and to find his own meanings in them' (p. 283). This means that the coach must be accepting of the individual's expression of 'bad' feelings as much as feelings that one might consider as 'good'. Unconditional positive regard is a fundamental principle of coaching as it creates a climate within the coaching relationship where the coachee feels safe. The coachee feels safe because they experience the coach as someone who feels that the coachee is a person of unconditional self-worth. The coachee is of value regardless of his or her behaviour, feelings, thoughts, or actions. The coach needs to create this safe space to facilitate or enable the coachee to engage in deep reflection. Often, engaging in coaching can lead to insights about the self that are challenging, uncomfortable, alarming, and frequently difficult to accept. Only when working with a coach who is unconditionally accepting of the coachee, can he or she feel secure enough to allow these insights the space they need to be explored. A safe space in the coaching relationship is also necessary to provide sufficient trust between the coach and the coachee so that the coach is able to challenge the coachee when necessary, without encountering excessive resistance. Furthermore, the coach's acceptance of both the 'negative' aspects of the coachee as well as the 'positive' is also necessary for enabling the coachee to be accepting of him or herself.

Non-judgemental attitude

This is the big one and links closely to the notion of experiencing unconditional positive regard for others. Having a non-judgemental attitude is widely accepted as being essential to effective coaching; however, it is notoriously difficult to achieve. Passing judgement on whether a situation or an individual is likely to cause us harm is an inbuilt, evolutionary mechanism that keeps us safe, which is why it is difficult to switch it on and off. Of course, the vast majority of the time, as we interact with colleagues, friends, family, and others in our day-to-day life, most of us, thankfully, are at minimal risk of life-threatening harm from these individuals. Despite this, we may pass judgement on the way in which they behave and draw conclusions or hypotheses on why they may be behaving in these ways. To have a truly non-judgemental attitude, we must practice the ability to stop these involuntary judgements. This means that while we may observe the behaviours of others, we do not attempt to draw any conclusions (either positive or negative) on why they are behaving in that way. This is because, unless we ask the individual in question, we cannot know why they are behaving in a particular way. Instead, we are engaging in mindreading, which, unless you possess the power of telepathy, is unlikely to be a successful tactic in understanding others. Any judgements will be presumptions, based on our frame of reference, influenced by our own life experiences, biases, personality, mood, and emotion at the time. All of these, of course, are likely to be vastly different from those of the individual in question. These presumptions will influence how we respond to that individual within the situation. Abstaining from passing judgement is, of course, extremely difficult to achieve. Having a non-judgmental attitude is a state of being that I attempt to practise and improve every day. Only by observing when I may stray away from being non-judgmental, acknowledging why this may be the case and then letting go of those judgements to maintain an unbiased view of others, is this possible.

Growth mindset

How do you know when a goal or objective that an individual has set for himself or herself is too challenging, unrealistic, or unachievable? That the goal is likely to set them up for disappointment. My answer to this question is that there is no such thing as a goal that is too challenging, unrealistic, or unachievable, and this point encompasses my fourth principle of coaching: a growth mindset. Carol Dweck (2006) explores the concept of a growth mindset and argues that individuals with a growth mindset believe that their abilities are malleable, and therefore, these individuals generally focus on ways to increase their learning, acquire and develop new knowledge and skills, seek challenges, and persist to attain desired results even in the face of failure. Dweck argues that a person's true potential is unknown. That 'it is impossible to foresee what can be accomplished with years of passion, toil and training' (p. 7). Scholars have extensively explored this concept. The impact of coachee growth mindset (also labelled goal orientation) on coaching outcomes is an area I have researched, and I discuss further in Chapter 5. However, it is also important to highlight the role of a growth mindset from the coaches' perspective. I propose that to coach successfully, the coach must hold a growth mindset. Dweck argues that sending a growth mindset message to another person, says to him or her, that you believe "you are a developing person and I am interested in your development". This means that when asked whether an individual has set a goal that is too challenging, they will respond with the answer "there is no such thing as a goal that is too challenging". This is because individuals, who truly hold a growth mindset, appreciate that all individuals have the capacity to learn, develop, and achieve their goals in the right conditions. Of course, it is important to bear in mind the type of goal. When I talk about any goal being achievable, the goal must be something within our control. Therefore, if I were to set a goal to achieve a promotion within six months, this goal would not be in my control as it relies on a number of other factors including the decisions of others. However, I could work back from this goal to understand what else needs to be achieved to secure a promotion (such as gaining relevant skills and experiences, networking with relevant stakeholders, and collecting evidence of my competence) and set these as my goals. The importance of setting the right type of goals is another area that has benefitted from voluminous research and I return to this topic in Chapter 8. The only other constraint that we could place on goal achievement is physical constraint. Therefore, if I set myself the goal to run one mile in five seconds, this goal would be unachievable because it is physically impossible (least of all for a five foot four woman, of some advancing years, with no running experience!). Apart from these exceptions, those who successfully coach others do not seek to confine or restrict the goals that those individuals set for themselves. Clearly, this idea of a growth mindset links to having a non-judgemental attitude. As a coach, it is not my place to pass judgement on whether or not your goal is achievable. It is my role to work with you to enable you to achieve that goal.

RESEARCH IN ACTION: MY STORY

To illustrate a growth mindset in action, I wanted to tell my own story. My story is not one of outstanding success or achievement in the face of great adversity. Instead, it is more of an everyday story, one that you may be able to identify with. A story that despite its lack of 'greatness' is an illustration of the growth mindset in action nonetheless.

As a child, I was always a 'good' student. I worked hard and achieved good grades. Not excellent grades, I was not an A* student, but neither did I have to really worry about failing. I generally sat somewhere in the middle, getting B's most of the time with the occasional A and the occasional C. I had to work hard for those B's, but I was happy to do so. At the age of 11, in the UK, children progress from primary school to secondary school. In the area in which I lived at the time, there were two options for state-funded schools: the general comprehensive secondary school or the grammar school. The grammar school was where the 'smart' kids went. To get into the grammar school, children had to pass an exam called the '11+'. My parents had both gone to grammar schools, my older cousin was at the grammar school, and my best friend at primary school was hoping to go to the grammar school. I sat the 11+ and I failed. I did not get a high enough score to meet the threshold to be able to go to grammar school. My best friend did. At the time, I was devastated. I had to go to a different school to the one that I hoped to attend and I lost contact with my friend. For many years, I must admit that this 'failure' did have an impact on how I viewed myself. Throughout school, I no longer considered myself particularly smart; after all, I wasn't smart enough to go to the school where all the smart kids went.

My subsequent education continued in a similar fashion. On leaving school, in my GCSE exams, I performed as I always had, mainly B's, some C's, one A. At college, I once again got mainly B's for my A levels, and for my undergraduate degree, I graduated with a 2:1. My performance was consistent across all levels. I worked hard, did well enough, but was never top of the class. After leaving university, I worked for a number of years as a manager in recruitment before I decided that I wanted to return to university to complete a postgraduate degree in occupational psychology, with the aim of changing my career. At this stage in my life, I had a four-year-old son, a husband, and a small amount of savings that we used to pay for the cost of the course. Suddenly, studying felt very different for me this time around. It felt extremely important, an investment. It was essential to me that I succeeded. We had sacrificed a lot for me to have this opportunity, and it was important to me that I did as well as I could. I felt that I had to maximize the chances that I could successfully transition into a new career that would create better opportunities for my family and me.

Up until that point in my life, I had considered myself of average intelligence. If I worked hard, I could do well enough. Now I wanted to be better than average. I wanted to reach my full potential and I was prepared to work as hard as it took. Despite this, the very first assignment I submitted for my postgraduate degree was consistent with my previous performance. The grade was OK but not great. I felt bitterly disappointed. Worse than that, I also felt terrified. What if this was all I was capable of achieving? Perhaps with a fixed mindset, I would have resigned myself to this destiny. After all, my performance was in line with my performance at every other similar opportunity in my life so far – why should anything change now? However, instead, I decided that I was going to learn from this experience and understand how I could improve on it. Something in me had shifted; I now had a growth mindset. The stakes felt higher, and I wasn't prepared to accept average anymore. I wasn't prepared to accept that I couldn't do better. This shift had a huge impact on how I approached my postgraduate studies. I believed that if I invested time in understanding *how to learn*, I could learn even better than I had before. I spent time understanding how to effectively learn and study. I spent time developing strategies to ensure that I maximized my grades in both the assignments and exams (which I had always hated and previously always underperformed in). I planned my time meticulously to ensure that every spare minute of the day was spent studying (between working, childcare, and home life). My performance improved. I finished my postgraduate studies with a distinction, the highest grading level that you can achieve. I also decided during the process that I wanted to continue into academia and study for a PhD. I applied for a studentship (a self-funded PhD wasn't a financial option for us) and I was accepted. I believe that the reason I was accepted was not that my original research proposal was exceptional or that my educational attainment to-date had been exceptional. Instead, I believe it was because I adopted the same growth mindset in applying for the studentship that I had adopted throughout my postgraduate studies. I met with my potential supervisor, took on board his feedback and critique of my draft proposal and did everything in my power to write the very best proposal that I could write.

This ethos has stayed with me. My PhD studies were extremely challenging for me. I had to work harder than I had ever worked before to ensure that I could perform to a standard that I felt happy with.

(Continued)

To allow me to reach my full potential. However, I now knew that if I didn't understand something to start with, it didn't mean that I would never understand it. I just had to find a way to learn about it that made sense to me. The way that I learned may sometimes be different from my fellow PhD students, but that was OK.

I wanted to tell my story to illustrate the power of having a growth mindset, as in my experience, when people find out that you have a PhD, they have this assumption that you are a 'smart' person. That you have always done well academically. As I said at the start of this story. This isn't a story of triumph over adversity. Certainly, there are many more compelling stories than mine of academic success in the face of severe challenges. Mine is an average story. However, perhaps, the averageness is what makes it useful.

Authenticity

Authenticity is a term that has gained popularity in recent years, in particular, around the concept of authentic leadership, to the point where it has potentially been overused. Despite this potential overuse, I strongly believe that coach authenticity is a fundamental principle of coaching as, in my experience of researching coaching, practicing coaching and working with others who coach, one of the most important factors that seem to influence positive outcomes from coaching is the authenticity of the coach. Within this book, I will discuss a number of different factors or variables that influence the impact of coaching on outcomes; however, underscoring all of these is the principle that the coach will behave in a way that is authentic to them. I am often asked by my students, 'which is the best coaching approach to use in this situation?' or 'how would you respond to this challenge from a coachee?' The simple answer to these questions is that there is no 'one' single best approach or best technique to use. Instead, my advice is always to respond in the way that feels most authentic to you. As coaching practitioners or individuals who wish to adopt a coaching mindset, we all have our own preferences in how we work, a preferred style of interacting with others and a predilection for one type (or selection) of coaching approach(es). This is what makes you unique and what makes you uniquely able to coach others. To be most effective in your coaching, you must remain true to yourself and do what feels authentic to you. Therefore, I suggest that you bear this in mind as you progress through this book. There may be suggestions in the following chapters on how you could incorporate the evidence-base on coaching into your practice. Some of these are likely to resonate with you, whereas others will not. My advice is to work with those that you feel would fit into your own practice most naturally, those that you feel most comfortable working with and that feel most authentic to you. This does not mean that you have permission not to challenge yourself to work in new and sometimes intimating ways. A core aspect of coaching is providing a supportive challenge to your coachee, and therefore you must be prepared to challenge yourself at times. However, there is a difference between challenging yourself to do something that is a little outside of your comfort zone because you have good reason to believe that it is in the best interests of your coachee, and challenging yourself to work in a way that does not feel authentic to you. It is the latter of these that I suggest you avoid. Only through deep self-reflection can we know where this boundary is.

Authenticity is also important to consider in terms of the other principles I have discussed here, in the sense that an effective coach must authentically or genuinely be open, experience unconditional positive regard for others, be non-judgmental, and have a growth mindset: you cannot fake it! Trust is an absolute cornerstone of effective coaching and a concept I return to in Chapter 9, however, a sure-fire way of breaking trust, or to block the development of trust in the first place, is if the other person perceives that the coach is in any way acting in a manner which is not genuine. We all know, in our gut, when there is something not quite 'right' about another. These feelings often come from an incongruence between the things that an individual may say and what they really believe. This is in a way, one of the greatest challenges of effective coaching, as fostering a consistent and truly unconditional positive regard and a non-judgemental attitude is easier said than done. We are all only human after all, and it is inevitable that at times you may feel frustrated, annoyed, or even dislike an individual whom you are coaching. It would be unrealistic to set standards for ourselves as coaches where this never happens. Therefore part of being non-judgmental and accepting is acknowledging that we may not always fully achieve the non-judgmental and accepting attitude towards others for which we strive for. Engaging in reflective practice, such as working with your own coach or coaching supervisor, can be one way in which the coach or an individual wishing to adopt a coaching mindset can continue to develop and improve in achieving these conditions for effective coaching.

Therefore, to summarize, in defining coaching, those who coach or who have a coaching mindset are open, they are characterized by holding others in unconditional positive regard, they have a non-judgemental attitude, a growth mindset, and they behave in a way that is authentic to them. These five principles underscore every aspect of coaching. You may notice that empathy does not appear in my list of principles that make up the foundations of coaching. Empathy demonstrates an understanding of another's experience as if it was their own. For me, if the coach is genuinely demonstrating the other five principles listed here, then we can create the conditions for effective coaching. I believe that it is more important that the coachee experiences unconditional acceptance for their feelings from the coach rather than "I understand how you feel". If we are not careful, feelings of empathy can spill over into a space that is unproductive, where the understanding of the coachee's experience is so high that they become mixed with the coach's own experiences. On the other hand, in demonstrating acceptance for the feelings of the coachee, the coach allows the coachee to experience these as an individual, completely separate from the coach and in the safe space created in the coaching relationship, in order for the coachee to work on self-acceptance.

These five principles are fundamental, in my view, to an effective coaching relationship, and consequently, an individual who wishes to coach others or develop a coaching mindset, should strive to develop these principles within themselves. In addition to these five principles, coaching as a learning and development tool or as a mindset can also be defined as consistently incorporating the following six features:

Coaching is goal focused

While there are many different types of approaches to coaching, a core element that is consistent across all types of coaching is the focus on a specific goal, which the coachee selects or defines. The coachee leads coaching, and therefore, the goal must always be dictated by the coachee. I have already touched on the importance of goals in relation to holding a growth mindset. I discuss this area in more detail in Chapter 8.

Coaching enables behavioural change through raising awareness and reflection

The most powerful tools at a coach's disposal are the ability to enable insight and raise awareness. Learning through reflection is a fundamental feature of coaching and is the basis of almost all coaching approaches, tools, and techniques. I explore the role of reflection in coaching in detail in Chapter 9.

A trusting relationship between the coach and coachee is essential

To allow the coachee the safe space needed to engage in deep self-reflection, the coachee must feel a high degree of trust with their coach. This is because deep self-reflection can often be uncomfortable, challenging, or even painful, which is generally why many of us do not naturally practise it alone. The trusting relationship between the coach and coachee enables the coachee to explore their goals and the barriers to achieve these goals at a deeper level than they can achieve on their own. I discuss the role of trust in coaching in detail in Chapter 9.

The coaches' role is to provide a supportive challenge

An essential aspect of successful coaching is supportive challenge. Generally, a coachee brings a goal to coaching that they have been unsuccessful in achieving alone. Therefore, it can be assumed that for whatever reason, this goal is challenging for the coachee to achieve. Given this, it is unlikely that the coach will enable the coachee to achieve this goal without providing some degree of challenge to the coachee's current pattern of behaviour. In order for that challenge to be successful, the coach must provide it in a supportive way and within the confines of the trusting coach/coachee relationship. Otherwise, the coachee will likely meet the challenge with resistance and potentially disengagement.

The coach is not a subject expert

My students often debate this notion in my classroom. How important is it that the coach has some knowledge of the coachee's role, industry, or organization? For me, the answer to this is "not very important". However, of course, the reality is that often coaches work or specialize in an industry where they have previously worked and, therefore, do have technical or subject expertise. This in itself is not a problem, and some clients may see this experience as advantageous. However, in its purest sense, the coach does not need to have subject expertise, as the way in which coaches enable behavioural change is not by providing subject relevant advice.

The coach does not provide advice

The lack of importance of coach subject expertise is evident in my final feature of coaching, which is that the coach does not provide advice. The role of the coach is to enable behaviour change through facilitating reflection and self-awareness, not through advising the coachee on what to do. Occasionally, it may be appropriate to provide advice when specifically asked by the coachee; however, this should be an exception and not the norm.

Therefore, in the context of this book, I define coaching in the following way:

> The aim of coaching as a learning and development tool or a coaching mindset is to enable behavioural change in others. Coaching is goal focused and enables behavioural change through raising the coachee's self-awareness and capacity for learning through reflection. This is achieved via a trusting relationship between the coach and coachee, where the coaches role is to provide a supportive challenge to the

coachee. The coach is not normally a subject expert and does not provide advice to the coachee. Individuals who coach others, are characterised by being open, holding others in unconditional positive regard, have a non-judgemental attitude, a growth mindset and they behave in a way that is authentic to them.

The continued popularity of coaching

In 2015, the opening chapter of my doctoral thesis started with the following quotation from John P. Campbell from the Annual Review of Psychology of Personnel Training and Development published in 1971:

> voluminous, non-empirical, non-theoretical, poorly written, and dull, faddish to the extreme

In this quotation, Campbell shares his views on the limitations of training and development research at the time. Fast forward 40 years, Salas and colleagues (Salas, Tannenbaum, Kraiger & Smith-Jentsch, 2012) conclude their review of the training and development research, with the remarks that the field has come a long way since Campbell made these comments. Salas et al. describe current training research to be 'empirical in nature and theoretically based' (p. 95). In my thesis, I conclude that research in training has successfully made the transition from one which the scholarly community viewed as faddish, non-empirical, and non-theoretical to a credible, scientific discipline. I go on to write that this transition from 'fad' to 'science' is highly significant to my thesis, proposing that coaching, as a more recent addition to the training, learning, and development toolbox, could easily be described with Campbell's quotation. In my thesis, I argued that the popularity of coaching in practice, despite the underdeveloped body of coaching literature, means that coaching as a profession is in danger of being viewed by many as a 'fad'.

While less than five years have passed since I made this argument, in my view, the evidence-based for coaching has developed in leaps and bounds. The popularity of coaching in practice also shows no sign of waning. Our coaching programmes at Henley Business School continue to be oversubscribed, and based on their coaching survey in 2016, the International Coach Federation (ICF) estimated that there were 53,300 professional coach practitioners worldwide (ICF, 2016) in an industry said to be worth $2 billion globally (Dunlop, 2017). With this growth showing no sign of abating, coaching continues to be in high demand.

The changing nature of the workplace may provide a potential explanation for the continued growth in coaching. It is widely accepted that the current business environment is dynamic, volatile, uncertain, complex, and ambiguous (Bennett & Lemoine, 2014). Businesses compete on a global scale and competitive advantage now relies much less on the uniqueness of the product or service. Instead, the role of employee talent has become increasingly important (Park & Jacobs, 2011). Organizational competitiveness is instead more reliant on the knowledge, skills, and abilities of the organizations' human resources. Furthermore, if the business environment is dynamic and volatile, to retain any competitive advantage, the employee's talent must also adapt in line with the environmental demands. The role of training, learning, and development is to equip employees with the requisite knowledge, skills, and abilities to meet dynamic and adapting organizational objectives. Couple the provision of instructional training with today's web-enabled working environment, the challenge for employees is no longer how to access the information they need to improve and perform their job more effectively, instead the challenge is how to make sense of the wealth of information that is readily available at their fingertips (Kraiger, 2014).

These factors offer a potential explanation for the rise in the popularity of coaching. Swart and Harcup (2013) propose that coaching helps managers to expand their insight and develop their sense-making abilities. If the biggest challenge to employees in today's organization is not how to access information but instead how to filter this information into what is relevant, then coaching may provide a solution to this challenge. Kraiger (2014) proposes that the prevailing trend in learning and development places the learner central to the process. In addition to this, learners are responsible for making sense and constructing their own knowledge, often from disjointed information. Coaching is a learning and development approach that places the learner at the centre of the learning experience. Coaching provides the employee with the time, mental space, support and guidance the employee may need to make sense of the information available to them and explore how to apply it most effectively in their unique situation. Coaching provides a tailored approach to help individuals to understand themselves, ensuring that they have the capability to move with and adapt to a dynamic working environment. Therefore, in this challenging, volatile business environment, coaching provides an adaptable learning and development solution to facilitate sense-making. This context helps to explain why the use of coaching has seen such a meteoric increase in recent years.

Aim of the book and overview of the contents

While coaching continues to grow in popularity in practice, the demand for demonstrating the hallowed 'return-on-investment' from coaching continues to increase. While in this book, I avoid attempting to put a figure on the return-on-investment from coaching, for reasons that I will explore in more detail in Chapter 2, the primary aim of this book is to translate the flourishing evidence-base around coaching into practical steps that those who coach can follow to enhance the impact of their coaching. The evidence-base for coaching has been growing steadily in parallel with the practical application of coaching. However, often, the research evidence is not easily accessible for those who practise coaching, either sitting behind journal paywalls or written in a manner that is tailored for an academic rather than a practitioner audience. Many coaches are unable to access the up-to-date evidence on what makes coaching effective. In this book, I bring together the research evidence and translate this in a way that is easy to apply in practice. In Chapter 1, I provide further detail on the evidence on which the remainder of this book is based. I clarify how this differs from other coaching texts that are available and highlight why it is important to consider the quality and rigour of research when deciding what to incorporate into your practice. In the following chapters, within each chapter, I then focus on a different aspect of coaching. Starting in Chapter 2, I explore what outcomes we can expect from coaching and how you can measure these outcomes in your own practice when seeking to evaluate the impact of your coaching. In Section two, I turn to the coachee and discuss the evidence around the factors present in the coachee that influence coaching effectiveness. Section two includes Chapter 3 which explores the role of coachee motivation; Chapter 4 which explores coachee personality; Chapter 5 which explores coachee goal orientation; Chapter 6 which explores coachee self-efficacy and Chapter 7 which explores coachee skills. In Section three, I focus on what the coach can do to enhance their impact in coaching. This includes in Chapter 8 an exploration of goal-setting; Chapter 9 is learning through reflection; and Chapter 10 is planning for action. In Section four, I focus on what the evidence suggests should be done once coaching is complete to maximize effectiveness, therefore this section explores the role of the organization. Finally, in Section five, I draw some conclusions, highlighting the key practical implications from the book and turn to my assessment of what's next for the future of coaching.

In each chapter, you will find a series of questions that I seek to address through translating the research evidence into recommendations for practice. These questions are the ones that I am frequently asked when teaching, at public speaking events or through social media. In each section, I provide a summary of the evidence related to each topic explored as well as examples to illustrate how this translates into practice. Each chapter concludes with a summary section, highlighting the key points made throughout that chapter and with a reference list of works that I have cited within that chapter. The interested reader may wish to seek out these original sources to read the evidence first hand. You will also find in each chapter, a research in action section, which includes vignettes from a number of highly successful and experienced coaches. These coaches kindly agreed to be interviewed on their experiences of how the evidence discussed in this book has translated into practice in their experience. At the end of the book, you will find the coach biographies with further details on each of the coaches interviewed for these vignettes.

I hope that this book will become a helpful resource for those who are interested in enhancing the impact of their coaching. Readers can have the confidence that the recommendations I provide come from good quality research evidence rather than my recommendation alone. As outlined at the start of this chapter, the book is written with two audiences in mind: the coaching practitioner who either works externally or internally to the organization and the individual who wishes to adopt a coaching mindset when working with others. At many points throughout the book, I explicitly draw out where the evidence base may be slightly different for these separate ways of applying coaching. The book is intended to be viewed as a whole, as for me, the key to maximizing effectiveness is to consider every element of the coaching process. However, I have structured the book in a way so that readers can easily dip in and out of sections based on their needs and particular area of interest.

This chapter in summary

- Coaching is a learning and development tool, with the goal of producing behavioural change
- Coaching is also a way of 'being' that influences how we interact with others at both a personal and professional level, called a coaching mindset
- There are five fundamental principles that underscore what it means to be a 'coach':
  - Openness – coaches must be curious, broad-minded, and imaginative
  - Unconditional positive regard – demonstrates to the coachee that the coach is a person of unconditional self-worth
  - Non-judgmental attitude – while we may observe the behaviours of others, we do not attempt to draw any conclusions (either positive or negative) on why they are behaving in that way
  - Growth mindset – it is impossible to foresee what another can accomplish in the right conditions
  - Authenticity – you must remain true to yourself and do what feels authentic to you
- Coaching incorporates six features:
  - Coaching is goal-focused
  - Coaching enables behavioural change through raising awareness and reflection
  - A trusting relationship between the coach and coachee is essential
  - The coaches role is to provide a supportive challenge
  - The coach is not a subject expert
  - The coach does not provide advice
- Coaching provides a tailored approach to help individuals to understand themselves, ensuring that they have the capability to move with and adapt to a dynamic working environment.

References

Barrick, M. R., & Mount, K. M. (1991). The big five personality dimensions and job performance: A meta-analysis. *Personnel Psychology, 44*, 1–26.

Bennett, N., & Lemoine, J. (2014). What VUCA really means for you. *Harvard Business Review, 92*, 27–42.

Campbell, J. P. (1971). Personnel training and development. *Annual Review of Psychology, 22*, 565–602.

Digman, J. M. (1990). Personality structure: Emergence of the five-factor model. *Annual Review of Psychology, 41*, 417–440.

Dunlop, C. W. (2017). The success and failure of the coaching industry. *Forbes Community Voice*. Retrieved from https://www.forbes.com/sites/forbescoachescouncil/2017/10/05/the-success-and-failure-of-the-coaching-industry/#518980fd6765

Dweck, C. (2006). *Mindset: How you can fulfil your potential.* New York: Random House.

International Coach Federation. (2016). ICF global coaching study. Retrieved from https://coachfederation.org/research/global-coaching-study

Jackson, J. J., Hill, P. L., Payne, B. R., Roberts, B. W., & Stine-Morrow, E. A. (2012). Can an old dog learn (and want to experience) new tricks? Cognitive training increases openness to experience in older adults. *Psychology and Aging, 27*(2), 286–292. doi:10.1037%2Fa0025918

Kraiger, K. (2014). Looking back and looking forward: Trends in training and development research. *Human Resource Development Quarterly, 25*(4), 401–408.

Park, Y., & Jacobs, R. L. (2011). The influence of investment in workplace learning on learning outcomes and organizational performance. *Human Resource Development Quarterly, 22*, 437–458.

Rogers, C. (1967). *A therapist's view of psychotherapy: On becoming a person.* Wiltshire, UK: Redwood Press.

Salas, E., Tannenbaum, S. I., Kraiger, K., & Smith-Jentsch, K. A. (2012). The science of training and development in organizations: What matters in practice. *Psychological Science in the Public Interest, 13*(2), 74–101.

Saucier, G., & Ostendorf, F. (1999). Hierarchical subcomponents of the big five personality factors: A cross-language replication. *Journal of Personality and Social Psychology, 76*, 613–627.

Swart, J., & Harcup, J. (2013). 'If I learn do we learn?': The link between executive coaching and organizational learning. *Management Learning, 44*(4), 337–354. doi:10.1177/1350507612447916

Chapter 1

The evidence-base for coaching

Coaching: An enduring classic or passing fancy?

Any readers who have children (or nieces or nephews), of a certain age will be sure to know what I mean when I mention the words "fidget spinner". For those who have no idea what I am talking about, the fidget spinner was a 'toy' that become the craze for all kids in 2017. I use the word 'toy' with caution, as the fidget spinner didn't do anything except spin, and therefore the play opportunities were somewhat limited! My two boys had about five each in a rainbow of colours, and it is safe to say that once they had spun the spinner around for two minutes, it would be discarded and forgotten. The fidget spinner is just one example of a recent toy fad. Fads are not, however, confined to toys. Another area that can succumb to 'faddish' trends is management. A Google search returns numerous blog posts and websites detailing those management trends consigned to the unfortunate label of fad. These management trends were ones that almost every organization attempted to embrace at the time; however, they soon went out of fashion and fell by the wayside. Examples include six sigma, matrix management, and management by walking around, to name a few. In Section one, I discussed how, when I first began researching coaching effectiveness, I was concerned that coaching may be the next management fad. Let me explain the reasoning behind my concern.

Management fads exist because people are looking for that magical secret to success. The secret that will explain how to get rich quick and there are many, many, who are all too keen to offer their miracle solution. Some management trends may be based on solid empirical evidence (I can 'prove' that this works), some based on direct experiences (I did this and it worked for me), and others on ideas and theories (I believe that this will work). None of these bases is problematic in their own right. The problem arises if the author does not make it clear to the reader, which of these is the basis of their idea. Without knowing whether the approach is based on evidence, experience or is simply a theoretical idea, the reader is unable to make his or her own judgement on the trustworthiness of the approach. Indeed, a further complication is when the approach is based on either an idea or experience yet is presented as being based on evidence, whether this is explicit or implied. The reality is that many management trends are based on an individuals' experience or ideas alone and when implemented on a larger scale do not stand the test of time. The impact of the approach does not generalize across different contexts. In essence, it does not work. Robust empirical testing would have established this; however, in the absence of robust empirical testing, organizations plough ahead, embracing the trend and find out for themselves that the approach is simply a fad or passing fancy and not an enduring classic.

So how does this relate to coaching? For many years, organizations have implemented coaching on a global scale based on a weak body of evidence (Grant, Passmore, Cavanagh, & Parker, 2010). The bulk of this historic evidence-base for coaching, consisted of coaching books that were generally written by practicing coaches and provided details of the approaches or methods they have used in their own coaching practice that have worked for them (I did this and it worked for me). Or research studies, also often conducted by practicing coaches, the majority of which were based on self-reported feedback from the coaches giving their view of the impact of coaching (I think my coaching works) and the coachees who have experienced coaching (I enjoyed receiving coaching). Now, let me be clear that every body of evidence has to start somewhere, and coaching, as a brand new technique to behavioural change, had to start from a base of nothing and build up from there. Those early researchers have, therefore, made an invaluable contribution to coaching that we can continue to build upon today. The problem arises, when individuals make claims about the impact, effectiveness and dreaded return on investment of coaching that are simply unsubstantiated. Back in 2015, this was my appraisal of the state of the coaching profession. The profession was rife with uncorroborated claims on the impact of coaching which meant that many non-supporters were highly sceptical about what coaching could achieve. In a critique of the evidence-base of coaching, Briner (2012) highlighted that a simple online search identified many coaches who were making strong and precise claims to the impact of their coaching. Examples included: coaching increases leadership capacity; coaching positively impacts the bottom line; coaching has helped hundreds to find more fulfilling work; and coaching is a proven way to achieve goals more effectively. Briner (2012) pointed out that none of the websites from which these claims were taken included any indication of the evidence on which the claims were based, and furthermore, a search of the literature (at the time) demonstrated that neither was there a large quantity of good quality evidence to support any of these claims. Therefore, back in 2015, in coaching, we have an example of an intervention that was growing in popularity in practice, which organizations were widely implementing based on unsubstantiated claims of impact. These claims appeared to be based on, at worse, theoretical ideas, and at best, accounts of individuals' own coaching experiences. The danger, therefore, was that if the reality of the impact of coaching did not live up to these expectations, then surely coaching was destined to become another management fad, a passing fancy.

Why does this matter?

The lack of evidence-base for coaching is important because in my view, coaching <u>does</u> work and, therefore, does not deserve to be confined to the discard heap of other management fads. In my view, coaching *can* transform peoples' lives. Coaching *can* positively impact the bottom line and increase leadership capacity. However, my word is not enough. Neither for that matter is the word of the thousands of other coaching practitioners or hundreds (or thousands?) of coaching authors. We need to show that coaching can achieve these outcomes through an accumulation of well-designed, well-executed, rigorous, high-quality evidence. Evidence that will tell us when coaching works, why it works, and how to make it work even better. Notice that I do not use the word 'prove'. We will never be able to prove that coaching works. Unfortunately, that isn't how we roll as researchers in the behavioural sciences. Humans are complex, tricky subjects to research, and as such, we can never be 100% sure that our findings will 100% translate across different contexts. However, with good quality research, we can have some degree of confidence that our findings are due to our intervention (in this case, coaching) and not due to chance. When our findings are replicated time and time again across different conditions and contexts, our confidence in these findings can grow, allowing us to draw firmer conclusions in relation to the evidence-base of coaching.

I hope that I have managed to convince you that the evidence-base for coaching was problematic and explained why we should be concerned with this. I personally want to be involved in a well-respected profession, a profession recognized as positively contributing to people's lives. For me, the route to achieving this is by building the evidence-base for coaching and using this evidence in practice, so that we can be confident that coaching will become an enduring classic that is here to stay.

What does good quality research look like?

While I have argued that historically, we could have described the research on coaching effectiveness as weak and lacking in scientific rigour, the good news is that there has been a vast improvement in the quality of research conducted on coaching in recent years. Additionally, there is a wealth of excellent quality research in related fields of scholarship, which we can apply to coaching, to help us understand coaching better. In this book, I draw together coaching research and related research from the fields of management, leadership, organizational behaviour, and work psychology. Given my focus on quality in research, throughout the book, I make it clear to the reader, what my appraisal is of the quality of the research in each of the areas I discuss. This is so that the reader is able to make their own informed judgement as to whether they can feel confident in the evidence-base of my practical recommendations. In order for the reader to be able to make that assessment, it is important to provide some further details on what good quality research 'looks' like.

The general measure of quality in research is scientific rigour. According to Chen (2015), scientific rigour encompasses high standards of and consistency among theory and hypothesis development, study design, measurement, analytical approaches, and evidence-based conclusions drawn from the research. A research article should always provide sufficient information on the sampling, study design, procedures, measures, analyses and results, to ensure that the reader can sufficiently understand what was done and what was found (Chen, 2015). As a rule, the article should be detailed enough to allow another researcher to accurately replicate the study. It is important to stress here that the question of good quality research is not a quantitative versus qualitative divide. For readers not familiar with these terms, a rudimentary explanation is that the terms refer to the type of data collected in the research: quantitative research involves the collection of numerical data, whereas qualitative research does not. Regardless of the type of data collected, good quality research is essential. When assessing the quality of qualitative research, Arino, LeBaron, and Milliken (2016) argue that the reader needs to be reassured that the researcher is using rigorous analytical tools that are consistent with the philosophical assumptions and methodological principles. Therefore, qualitative researchers have an obligation to make a convincing empirical case that the data warrant the findings they report.

The question of research study quality is such an important one, that Dr Gil Bozer, my colleague, and I developed a system for assessing study quality (Bozer & Jones, 2018). We wanted an approach that could be used to rate the quality of both quantitative and qualitative studies to systematically assess studies and acknowledge that not all research is of equal value. To do this, we suggest ranking studies on four criteria: explicit theoretical underpinning, consistency of evidence, directness of the intervention, and directness of outcome.

Explicit theoretical underpinning

When ranking a study based on explicit theoretical underpinning, we are assessing the degree to which the researcher engages with and discusses the relevant established theory that they test in the study. A theory is the explanation of why something occurs and when we should expect it to occur.

Without a theory, our findings are relatively useless as we are unable to explain why we found what we did and when we should expect to find it again. A good quality research study should either test established theory or seek to develop theory and, therefore, should include an explicit discussion of this. Even in research areas where there is an absence of established theory for the researcher to test, the researcher should make this clear to the reader and consequently position the study as aiming to develop a new theory. Consequently, an explicit discussion of theory would indicate a higher quality study.

Consistency of evidence

When assessing quality, we can classify a body of research, rather than individual studies, in relation to the consistency of evidence. Consistency of evidence refers to the degree to which findings in a particular area are consistent across multiple studies. So, for example, where there is a high level of consistency, multiple studies testing similar constructs would all draw similar conclusions. On the other hand, a low level of consistency is where multiple studies test similar constructs; however, the studies all result in different findings, and therefore, the researchers draw very different conclusions when comparing these studies to one another. Inconsistency in findings across studies that are large and unexplained would mean that we rate the evidence in this area as lower quality than evidence where the findings demonstrate higher levels of consistency across studies. This is because inconsistency of findings is likely to indicate that we need to conduct more research to understand fully the phenomena in question, as it may be that there are other variables influencing the results not yet identified and tested.

Directness of the intervention

We can also assess the study quality in relation to the directness of the intervention. The directness of the intervention refers to whether the researcher investigates coaching only or whether, in the research project; the researcher has coupled coaching with another intervention such as providing 360-degree feedback. Coaching is frequently utilized in practice and research as one element in a combination of developmental methods delivered together or in sequence. For example, leadership training plus coaching or one-to-one coaching combined with team coaching. When conducting research, it is important that we control as many of the variables that we can to isolate the impact of coaching and consequently understand the conditions across which our results can generalize. If we conduct a research study in which coaching is provided following the discussion of a 360-degree feedback, then any results drawn from that study can only be generalized to coaching when provided in conjunction with a 360-degree feedback. Therefore, to draw confident conclusions on the direct impact of coaching on outcomes, research that directly investigates coaching will lead to findings that we can have greater confidence in generalizing across contexts. Therefore, we would assess research studies that test a 'direct' intervention (i.e., coaching provided on its own) as higher quality than research studies that combine different interventions and, therefore, have a low level of intervention directness.

Directness of outcome

Our final criteria for quality is the directness of the outcome, which refers to the way in which the outcome of the research is measured. The outcome of the research is the variable that we are interested in when assessing impact: what outcomes can we expect coaching to have a positive impact on? For the directness of outcome, the highest level of quality is for objective outcomes and external ratings of performance. We can consider outcomes assessed by objective means, such as sales performance, as having high levels of reliability, as there is minimal likelihood that these outcomes are influenced by bias. This means that there is a minimal chance that the research or researcher has inappropriately influenced the objective outcome. The second type of outcome that we would assess as high quality is ratings of the coachee's performance from an external source, such as the coachee's supervisor or peers. Although external ratings of performance can be problematic in that they are somewhat subjective, there is a low risk of bias due to factors such as the placebo effect (a positive change experienced simply due to participating in the research rather than as a direct effect of the intervention) as the raters are once removed from the research experiment.

Frequently, researchers collect outcome data from the coachee, described as self-report data, which we suggest is rated as moderate quality. This is because while the coachee themselves may be best placed to identify changes in outcomes at certain levels, such as affective or emotional outcomes following coaching, it could also be argued that it is difficult for the coachee to disassociate his or her perception of the impact of coaching from factors such as the placebo effect. Another possible risk of bias may occur when coachees perceive that it is in their personal interest to report positively on the coaching outcomes after they have devoted time and effort engaging in coaching and their organizations have sponsored and coordinated the coaching.

Finally, we suggest classifying research that utilizes outcomes measured from the coaches' perspective as having a low directness of outcome and, therefore, a lower quality. This is because the coach is potentially less likely or able to offer a fully objective assessment of outcomes following coaching that they have provided. Further, there might be job-related measures, such as skill-based and performance outcomes, that are not suitable to be assessed by the coach due to a lack of opportunity to observe changes in the coachee from this perspective. Another potential bias in the coaches' effectiveness ratings might derive from their self-interest to demonstrate their professional success as reflected by positive coaching outcomes.

In the remaining chapters of this book, I will refer to these four criteria of research study quality to provide the reader with my view on how confident we can be of the quality of the research and, therefore, the generalizability of the findings in each area.

Bringing it all together

Briner, Denyer, and Rousseau (2009) argued that evidence-based management is a process individuals use to make managerial decisions. They suggest that managers make decisions based on four elements: evaluated external evidence, practitioner experience and judgements, stakeholders such as employees, preferences, or values and the context including organizational actors and circumstances. Briner et al. (2009) argue that the strength and influence of each of these elements will vary depending on the decision in question, however, in all cases; the manager should make the choice to place more or less emphasis on various elements in a mindful, conscious fashion. In this book, I will provide you with a summary of the evaluated external evidence related to coaching effectiveness. I will dissect the implications of this evidence in relation to recommendations for your practice. Finally, I will provide information on the quality of the evidence so that you can make your own, mindful, and conscious choice as to whether you wish to incorporate that evidence into your own practice. For coaching to become an enduring classic, a respected profession, we as coaches have an obligation to ensure that our practice is evidence-based. This means taking into consideration our own experiences and judgements, our stakeholders, the context and circumstances, and, of course, the evaluated external evidence.

RESEARCH IN ACTION: COACH EXAMPLE

This particular example of when I have integrated evidence from multiple sources into my own practice is around personality profiling. I was working with a coachee who had gone through a particular personality tool, one that classifies people according to a personality 'type'. Quite quickly, in the first coaching session, it became apparent that the coachee was referring to themselves and others through the lens of this personality profiling tool. I found this situation quite tricky as my own research and my own experience had led me to be sceptical about the reliability, validity, and usefulness of type measures of personality. I wondered whether it was worth engaging with

(Continued)

the fact that the coachee was looking at the world through the lens of this personality tool – was this the biggest thing right now to tackle in the session?

The organization had endorsed this particular personality typing system. They had put the coachee through it, a lot of their colleagues had completed it, and it was a common vocabulary in the organization. When I started to gently ask about it, it was quite clear that the coachee was really committed to this particular method. They had gone on to do further training and had got the practitioner certificate. I have also found in cases like this, that HR or the organizational background very much sets the direction. For example, because the organization has endorsed and mandated these tools, people really buy into them. Usually, the research base never tends to come up when I ask around the reasons for the decision to endorse a particular tool. Usually, it is something that someone has used historically, and they have just brought it in for their team or it tends to be centrally mandated from HR and rolled out to the rest of the organization. This has a very powerful effect on people. They don't tend to question whether it is valid or reliable. It's just assumed that it is. Just like my organization gives me a laptop and the laptop works, why wouldn't my organization give me a personality assessment that works?

My personal interest over the last couple of years has been in evidence-based practice. While there are still plenty of gaps in the evidence around coaching practice, the field of personality assessment is an area where there is a reasonable evidence base in terms of the research literature. From my own reading of the evidence on personality profiling, I have found that the trait approach, in particular the Big Five, seems to be the best that we have at the moment. It's not perfect, there are a few criticisms. However, comparing it to type approaches and the Jungian-based models, I am convinced that the Big Five demonstrates better predictive validity and reliability. The research also demonstrates all sorts of interesting things are happening around the Big Five and heritability, with twin studies and being able to predict things like susceptibility to mental health issues. None of this type of research is being conducted with type approaches to personality like MBTI or Insights Discovery. Even just looking at the number of citations in research papers a year, it is clear that the research psychologists just aren't using these type models of personality.

I have also drawn on my own personal experience as evidence in relation to this topic. About eight years ago, a manager said to me, 'let's be frank, the reason that we don't get on that well is that I am an x, y, z and you are an a, b, c according to this typing model and that's just the way it goes'. There are two sides of this as a personal experience that struck me. One was that I didn't like being labelled and the other was that it seemed very final, well what do we do with that information?

So I am sitting there, having the coaching conversation with all this in the back of my mind, thinking, well there is a potentially more accurate model to describe personality. I am questioning, when and how is it appropriate or is it even appropriate to introduce that into the conversation? I am conscious that my coaching sessions are not a platform for me to spread ideas that I like. I often reflect on whether my actions are in the best service of the coachee or is this just the method that I quite like and I'm most comfortable with? I reflected on this and I came to the view that in this particular instance, the coachee was using the type of personality profiling in a way that was affecting how they were seeing the world. This personality type lens was leading the coachee to make a number of assumptions about themselves and others which meant that it needed to be brought up so that these assumptions could be questioned and explored.

As a practitioner, I do tend to draw on a variety of sources of evidence; however, I do also question does it matter what the evidence says? If, for example, the personality profile gives people insight or opens a conversation that might not have happened otherwise, perhaps in these instances, the validity of the tool doesn't matter too much. They can have a place. However, when the reliability and validity of a tool become really important, is when people start to use the information they have gained from the tool to make assumptions about themselves and others. I feel that this is when it is important to understand how accurate this information is and how useful it is. I suppose the question to ask is: Is the tool leading to insight or is it leading to assumptions?

For details of the coaches who were interviewed for the 'research in action' vignettes, see page 191.

Resources

Science for Work is an independent, not-for-profit foundation with the aim of summarizing the findings and implications of research evidence for practice in brief blogs that can be read in less than five minutes: https://scienceforwork.com/

The Coaching Academic is my own podcast series that is aimed at translating research into practice. In each brief episode, I take a piece of cutting-edge research and translate how you can use the findings in your own practice. The podcast can be found on iTunes and SoundCloud.

Google Scholar is Google's search engine for scholarly literature. While many journal articles do sit behind a paywall, a number don't and you can access this by keyword searches on Google Scholar: https://scholar.google.com/

This chapter in summary

- Historically, coaching was based on a weak evidence-base, lacking in scientific rigour and characterized by unsubstantiated claims on the impact of coaching
- Recently, the quality of coaching research has improved, and we can learn much about coaching from research in a related field such as management, leadership, organizational behaviour, and work psychology
- The quality of both quantitative and qualitative research can be assessed in terms of four criteria:
  - Explicit theoretical underpinning – does the researcher explain why they found what they did and when the findings will generalize?
  - Consistency of evidence – are the findings consistent across similar studies – are similar results reported across similar studies?
  - The directness of the intervention – does the researcher test the impact of coaching on its own or has coaching been combined with another intervention?
  - The directness of the outcome – how is the impact of coaching measured? Outcomes less likely to be influenced by bias (such as objective performance) is rated as higher quality than outcomes where the risk of bias is greater (such as ratings by the coach)
- Evidence-based practice involves making decisions based on four elements:
  - Evaluated external evidence
  - Practitioner experience and judgements
  - Stakeholders
  - Context
- This book allows the reader to make an informed and mindful assessment of the relevant evaluated evidence upon which they may wish to base their practice.

References

Arino, A., LeBaron, C., & Milliken, F. J. (2016). Publishing qualitative research in academy of management discoveries. *Academy of Management Discoveries, 2*, 109–113. doi:org/10.5465/amd.2016.0034

Bozer, G., & Jones, R. J. (2018). Understanding the factors that determine workplace coaching effectiveness: A systematic literature review. *European Journal of Work and Organizational Psychology, 27*(3), 342–361. doi:10.1080/1359432X.2018.1446946

Briner, R. (2012). Does coaching work and does anyone really care? *OP Matters.* Retrieved from https://www.cebma.org/wp-content/uploads/Briner-Does-Coaching-Work-OP-Matters-2012.pdf

Briner, R. B., Denyer, D., & Rousseau, D. M. (2009). Evidence-based management: Concept cleanup time? *Academy of Management Perspectives, 23*(4), 19–32. doi:10.5465/amp.23.4.19

Chen, G. (2015). Editorial. *Journal of Applied Psychology, 100,* 1–4. doi:10.1037/apl0000009

Grant, A. M., Passmore, J., Cavanagh, M. J., & Parker, H. (2010). The state of play in coaching today: A comprehensive review of the field. In G. P. Hodgkinson & K. J. Ford (Eds.), *International review of industrial and organizational psychology* (Vol. 25, pp. 125–168). West Sussex, UK: Wiley-Blackwell.

Chapter 2

What outcomes can we expect from coaching?

The challenge of evaluating coaching

Evaluating coaching is hard. It's complicated. Really complicated. For me, this is because the strength of coaching as a learning and development tool is also its downfall when it comes to evaluation. One of the biggest advantages of coaching as a learning and development tool, one of the reasons why it has continued to be so popular, is because the coachee leads and directs the focus of the coaching conversation. This means that the coachee can tailor the support they receive based on their needs. They are able to dictate the goals and objectives that they discuss during coaching to receive targeted, tailored, bespoke development, that is 100% fitted to their needs. Coaching in this sense is like a made-to-measure suit and the coach is the tailor. Based on the coachee's requirements, the coach has a selection of styles from which the coachee can select; the coach has access to a range of fabrics in different colours and finishes, all of which the coach can adjust to ensure the perfect fit. This tailoring means that coaching, as an approach, is adaptable and flexible to provide a seamless match to the requirements of the coachee. These requirements may change over time for the individual coachee and will most definitely differ between coachees. In evaluation terms, this is where the problem arises. If each coachee has a different set of requirements, a different set of goals they seek to achieve, how can we evaluate the impact of coaching in a way that is consistent across multiple coachees, coaches, and organizational contexts? This has been the greatest challenge of my career as a researcher to-date and is a challenge that unfortunately continues to perplex me.

The variation in coaching outcomes is problematic for a number of reasons. First, knowledge builds through an accumulation of an understanding of a topic over time. An essential element of the scientific process is the replication of results in the same as well as different contexts and conditions. If the replication of results is not being provided, for example, if different outcome measures are used in different research studies, then we have no way of knowing whether any given finding was a one-off due to a unique characteristic of that particular study or an outcome that can be generalized across the wider context. Furthermore, if multiple studies use different outcomes, then we cannot group outcomes to establish a theme upon which we know coaching can have an impact. While it is true that the outcomes from coaching can vary widely from coachee to coachee, the first step in attempting to measure the broader impact of coaching is to find a way in which we can classify the vast range of outcomes to provide a framework across which we can group outcomes. In our 2016 paper, my co-authors and I sought to address this challenge and consequently provided a framework of coaching outcomes, which we subsequently tested in our meta-analysis on coaching effectiveness (Jones, Woods, & Guillaume, 2016). The reasoning behind this approach was that while the individual outcomes from coaching may vary, by providing a structure into which different types of outcomes can be grouped, we can begin to create an understanding of which types of outcomes coaching can positively impact on and whether the impact of coaching differs for different types of outcomes.

A framework of coaching outcomes

To develop our framework of coaching outcomes, we utilized existing frameworks of training outcomes as a start point (see Kirkpatrick, 1996; Kraiger, Ford, & Salas, 1993). We proposed that the potential outcomes of coaching can be separated into four groups: affective, cognitive, skill-based, and results outcome criteria. This is presented in Figure 2.1 and further expanded in

Figure 2.1 Framework of coaching outcomes.

Table 2.1 Framework of coaching outcomes and summary of proposed coaching evaluation criteria (Jones et al., 2016)

Outcome criteria	Description	Measurement methodology
Affective outcomes *How does the coachee feel?*	Attitudes and motivational outcomes (e.g. self-efficacy; well-being; satisfaction).	Self-report questionnaires
Cognitive outcomes *How does the coachee think?*	Declarative knowledge; procedural knowledge; cognitive strategies (e.g. problem-solving).	Recognition and recall tests Free sorts Probed protocol analysis
Skill-based outcomes *What does the coachee do?*	Compilation and automaticity of new skills (e.g. leadership skills; technical skills; competencies).	Behavioural observation in the workplace (e.g. multi-source feedback questionnaire) Skill assessment
Results *What does the coachee achieve?*	Individual, team and organizational performance	Financial results; objective or goal achievement; productivity

Table 2.1 (Jones et al., 2016). This framework of outcomes is one that I return to throughout the book. Whenever I discuss the results of research studies, I will do so using the language described here to provide the reader with a guide as to where individual outcomes fit within the overall framework.

Affective outcomes from coaching

Affective outcomes describe outcomes that we would understand as being outcomes felt by the coachee or experienced internally by the coachee, therefore, how does the coachee feel? These include outcomes such as changes in attitudes, motivation, satisfaction, confidence, resilience, or stress. While the coachee is likely to be acutely aware of changes in outcomes within this group, others around them may not be able to detect a change in these types of outcomes, although a change in an affective outcome may also result in a change in another outcome that others may more easily detect. For example, a coachee who experiences an increase in motivation will be able to identify that they feel more motivated. This increased motivation may result in changes in his or her behaviour at work such as working in a more proactive manner. Colleagues of the coachee may notice the change in work behaviours rather than being able to directly observe the change in motivation.

Kraiger et al. (1993) identify affective outcomes as likely outcomes of training, and we argue that affective outcomes are relatively more important in coaching than training (Jones et al., 2016). This is because many of the valued outcomes of coaching, reflected in the types of goals coachees set to address in coaching, represent affective outcomes. For example, to test the impact of coaching, I conducted a field experiment where I provided 84 employees with four one-hour coaching sessions each. During the first coaching session, the coachees discussed with me the goals they wished to explore during the subsequent sessions. Of these goals, 38% were focused on addressing an affective outcome and included goals such as 'To become more emotionally resilient and avoid taking on others problems' and 'To develop self-confidence, particularly in high-risk meeting scenarios'. A further reason why affective outcomes are relatively more important in coaching than training is that there may also be an indirect impact of coaching on affective outcomes from simply engaging in the coaching process. For example, the process of setting goals that are of value to the coachee, regardless of the focus of the goal set, is likely to increase motivation, while the process of working towards a challenging goal with a valued outcome is likely to create a positive impact on reactions such as positive emotion and job satisfaction (Locke & Latham, 1990).

In the context of the existing coaching literature, in our 2018 paper, Gil Bozer and I report that affective outcomes are the most frequently assessed outcome (Bozer & Jones, 2018), with 93 out of 117 studies exploring affective outcomes[1]. We suggest that this is likely to be for two key reasons. First, affective outcomes are very easily assessed by utilizing self-report questionnaires. Second, due to the transient nature of many affective outcomes (such as mood and emotion), coaching has the potential to have a positive impact at the affective level, even following a brief coaching intervention. Some examples of affective outcomes from the coaching literature include perceived coaching effectiveness (Jones, Woods, & Hutchinson, 2014); self-efficacy (Baron & Morin, 2010); work well-being (Jones, Woods, & Zhou, 2018); career satisfaction (Bozer, Sarros, & Santora, 2014); stress (Bright & Crockett, 2012); intention to leave/quit (Ladegard & Gjerde, 2014); depression (Grant, 2014); resilience (Grant, 2014); anxiety (Grant, Curtayne, & Burton, 2009); and organizational commitment (Luthans & Peterson, 2003).

As affective outcomes are experienced internally by the coachee, they are generally measured using self-report questionnaires. In relation to our criteria for assessing study quality, the directness of outcome assessment would be moderate. This is because we can assume that there is a moderate risk of bias when measuring outcomes at this level as self-report measures may be influenced by other factors, such as the placebo effect. Having said this, there are many reliable and valid measures of a range of affective outcomes that can be utilized that would ensure that these risks are minimized. My recommendation though is that any research study or coaching evaluation project should measure a range of outcomes that fall within each of the four outcome groups within our framework. This would ensure that the evaluation is of high quality in relation to the directness of outcomes.

Cognitive outcomes from coaching

Cognitive outcomes are a group of outcomes that we can also describe as knowledge and understanding or the coachee's mental process or mental actions. In other words, how does the coachee think? Examples of cognitive outcomes from coaching can include gaining new declarative knowledge (facts and pieces of information), procedural knowledge (knowing how to do something), and cognitive strategies (such as problem-solving, decision-making, or reflective thinking). As with affective outcomes, Kraiger et al. (1993) identify cognitive outcomes as likely outcomes of training. In comparison with the anticipated cognitive outcomes from training, we propose that the development of certain cognitive outcomes from coaching is more likely than others. For example, new declarative knowledge (i.e. obtaining new facts and pieces of information) is the cognitive outcome least likely developed through coaching. As the aim of coaching does not include providing instruction to the coachee, it is unlikely that coaching will result in obtaining new facts or knowledge in the same way that might result from training. Instead, coaching is concerned with assisting the coachee in the process of making sense of existing knowledge. This process may involve the coachee making new associations between existing knowledge to address barriers or blockers to behaviour change, therefore applying existing knowledge in new ways. Consequently, through the process of making sense of his or her existing knowledge, the coachee may develop new procedural knowledge in relation to understanding how to do something better or new cognitive strategies in terms of solving problems or making decisions. A final example of a cognitive outcome from coaching is enhanced capacity for reflection. We consider reflective thinking, self-awareness, or self-insight a cognitive outcome as this explains a way of thinking or a mental process. While enhancing reflective capacity may not frequently be a selected goal of coaching, by engaging in the coaching process, which achieves change through the mechanism of raising awareness and self-reflection, an indirect outcome of engaging in coaching is the enhancement of this cognitive outcome. For example, by working with a coach to decrease stress, the coach may use a range of behavioural techniques that include raising the coachee's awareness of themselves on topics such as the factors in his or her life that are leading to the current stress levels, current strategies for handling stress and why this may be problematic or unsustainable. In exploring the topic of stress, the coachee's capacity to think reflectively and understand him or herself (in this case in relation to stress) is enhanced, a cognitive strategy that can then be applied to different contexts other than stress.

In our 2018 paper, Gil and I demonstrated that cognitive outcomes are the least frequently evaluated outcome from coaching, with only 13 of the 117 studies testing cognitive outcomes[i]. This could be partially due to the challenging nature of accurately capturing the development of new mental models and problem-solving strategies following coaching. In my field experiment, of the goals set by the 84 coachees, just 11% directly focused on cognitive outcomes. Examples of goals focused on cognitive outcomes from this participant group were 'To improve knowledge and understanding of law relevant to role' and 'to gain more subject specific knowledge in communications'. Other examples of cognitive outcomes explored in the coaching literature include self-reported learning following coaching (Ammentorp, Jensen, & Uhrenfeldt, 2013); solution-focused thinking (Grant et al., 2017); problem-solving (Gyllensten & Palmer, 2006); self-insight or self-awareness (Bozer, Sarros, & Santora, 2013); knowledge (Taie, 2011); and learning agility (Trathen, 2007).

In relation to the quality assessment of directness of outcome, this is likely to differ based on the type of cognitive outcome assessed and the methodology used. For example, researchers generally measure self-insight using self-report questionnaires, and, therefore, as with affective outcomes, we would classify the directness of this outcome as moderate quality. Assessments of knowledge, whether declarative or procedural could be conducted using knowledge style tests (for example on topics such as problem-solving or decision-making ability) which could be objectively scored. While we would rate this type of assessment as higher quality than self-report assessments, in practice, I have rarely seen this type of assessment of cognitive outcomes from coaching due to the complexity of creating a suitable measure.

Skill-based outcomes from coaching

Skill-based outcomes are a group of outcomes that we can also describe as our expertise or abilities to complete certain tasks, so what does the coachee do? Compared to affective and cognitive outcomes, skill-based outcomes are more easily detected by others. Skill-based outcomes are often the focus of coachee goals and may include the development of skills such as leadership skills, assertiveness, communication, delegation, or time-management skills. Coaching is able to promote skill acquisition and skill enhancement through the discussion of actions the coachee can take to target skill acquisition and the planning of activities that will subsequently target the development and improvement of newly acquired skills. For example, during the coaching process, the coach may discuss with the coachee potential opportunities in which they are able to practise the skills developed during coaching, agree on actions for the coachee to follow between coaching sessions and in subsequent sessions, reflect on the completion of these actions in relation to skill acquisition, providing feedback to guide next steps.

Following affective outcomes, skill-based outcomes are the next most popular group of outcomes assessed in the coaching literature with 57 of the 117 studies exploring outcomes of this type[i] (Bozer & Jones, 2018). Likewise, in my field experiment, skill-based outcomes were the focus of 37% of the goals set by coachees. Examples of skill-based goals with this sample include 'To develop informal networking skills' and 'To improve prioritisation skills'. Some examples of skill-based outcomes from the coaching literature include leadership skills (Williams, 2016), networking skills and career planning (Spurk, Kauffeld, Barthauer, & Heinemann, 2015), and safety-oriented communication skills (Kines et al., 2010).

In terms of the quality assessment of skill-based outcomes, previous studies have generally used a combination of self-reported measures (where coachees identify whether they perceive the skill to have changed following coaching) and others ratings of the skill (where the manager or colleagues of the coachee rate whether they perceive a change in the skill). We can classify studies that utilize others ratings of the skill as being of higher quality compared to self-report measures of skill-based outcomes. However, it is also worth bearing in mind that it is important to ensure that those rating the skill have sufficient exposure to the coachee to accurately assess whether the skill has been developed. For example, a manager who does not work closely with a coachee on a daily basis may not be able to detect whether a change in a given skill has taken place.

Result outcomes from coaching

The final group of outcomes we can expect from coaching is results, so what does the coachee achieve? We can further differentiate results into individual-, team-, and organizational-level results. Results is a broad group of outcomes that include any type of outcome where the coachee's behavioural change has had an impact. Therefore, examples at the individual level might include performance at work or financial indicators such as increased sales. By aligning individual goal setting to team or organizational-level goals and objectives, achieving results outcomes at the individual level may also impact the performance of the team and the organization.

While outcomes at the results level are arguably most important from an organizational perspective, these are one of the least frequently explored in the coaching literature, with only 17 out of 117 studies investigating outcomes within the results group[i] (Bozer & Jones, 2018). This is likely because assessing the results level outcomes is highly complex. It is often very difficult, if not impossible to isolate the impact of coaching on results outcomes, as a vast range of factors such as the economic context and the behaviour of the wider team, often influence outcomes at this level. In my field experiment, I found that only 11% of the goals set by coachees directly focused on results outcomes. Examples of results-focused goals with this sample include 'To create a business case for the organization to fund an external qualification' and 'To have clear and focused goals for a future career with an action plan'. Both of these goals can be classified as results as achieving these goals will result in a tangible outcome (i.e. a business case for the qualification and a career development action plan). Other examples of results outcomes explored in the literature include goal attainment (Sonesh et al., 2015); retention (Gardiner, Kearns, & Tiggemann, 2013); productivity (Olivero, Bane, & Kopelman, 1997); productivity quality (Parker-Wilkins, 2006); sales performance (Libri & Kemp, 2006); safety performance (Kines et al., 2010); promotion (Feggetter, 2007); selection success (Andrews & Jones, 2020) and sickness records (Duijts, Kant, van den Brandt, & Swaen, 2008).

In terms of quality of research, we can rate research that utilizes objective measures of results outcomes, such as productivity metrics or sales performance, as the highest level of quality as the influence of bias on the outcomes due to the research is likely to be low. We can also rate others ratings of performance as high quality, with self-ratings of performance considered moderate quality.

What do we know about the general effectiveness of coaching?

'Does coaching work?' was one of the first questions I sought to address as a researcher and our 2016 paper directly explores this (Jones et al., 2016). To answer this question, we adopted a meta-analytic approach to our research. Meta-analysis is a particularly useful technique as it allows the researcher to review a whole body of research evidence and draw conclusions (based on statistical analysis) that allow us to objectively determine what the effect is of the intervention being examined (in this case coaching) and what factors or moderators may also influence that effect. Effect size is of particular importance because this tells us the size of the difference in the outcomes from coaching. For example, most coaching practitioners would hope that their coaching intervention generated a large improvement in performance for the coachee, in research terms, this would translate into a large effect size. The other benefit of using meta-analytic techniques is that the researcher can 'control' for other factors that can influence results from research, for example, small sample sizes and reliability of outcome measures. Therefore, meta-analytic results are likely to give us a clearer, more robust answer to the question 'does coaching work?'

Following a comprehensive review of the coaching literature, a total of 17 studies met our criteria to be included in our meta-analysis (i.e. that explored workplace coaching with a working sample of coachees (i.e. not students) and the research design included either pre and post measures and/or a control group (data collected at one point in time only or qualitative data were not included). We set out to understand whether coaching works and if so what kind of effect size can we expect from coaching (i.e. what is the magnitude of change that a coachee would experience from coaching).

In the meta-analysis, we were able to test for all of the outcomes in our framework apart from cognitive outcomes as there were not enough studies identified in our analysis that utilized cognitive outcome measures. We found that coaching had a positive impact on all three outcomes assessed (affective, skill-based, and results); however, interestingly it was the results outcome where coaching had the greatest impact (or the largest effect size). This contrasts with meta-analytic results on the impact of managerial training interventions which has demonstrated that the impact on results is often smaller than other types of outcomes. This is often attributed to potential training transfer issues, in that learning gained in the training room does not effectively transfer or translate back into the workplace (Powell & Yalcin, 2010). In our meta-analysis, we suggest that the high impact of coaching on results is perhaps indicative of the fact that the individualized nature of coaching actually promotes the transfer of learning from coaching back to the coachee's workplace. Therefore, in comparison with training, it is easier for the individual to take learning from coaching and apply this to their day-to-day working lives. This finding is really important in terms of answering the question 'does coaching work?' Not only do our findings provide clear evidence that coaching does work, furthermore the largest effect was for changes in performance which is arguably (at least from an organization's perspective) one of the most important outcomes.

What about return-on-investment?

Noticeable in its absence from our framework of coaching outcomes is return-on-investment. You can easily find statistics on the return-on-investment from coaching in coaching research papers, in coaching textbooks, and most definitely on many websites of coaching practitioners. However, I do not believe that it is possible to calculate the return-on-investment from an intervention such as coaching and furthermore, I believe that attempting to do so can be damaging to the profession of coaching.

Return-on-investment is the gain or loss generated on an investment relative to the amount of money invested. To calculate return-on-investment, you must have the net profit available to you that has arisen from the investment. I have yet to work with a coach or coaching client where the impact of the coaching has been so clear-cut that there would be any degree of confidence in the net profit directly generated from and attributed to coaching. No coachee exists in a vacuum; therefore, the impact of coaching is always going to be in conjunction with everything else in that individual's life at the time. Even in a controlled experiment, we cannot minimize the impact of other variables to the degree that we could accurately put a figure on the impact of coaching. In addition to this, there are very few coachees where we have access to a financial-based outcome that we can directly attribute to the individual and the individual alone. The exception to these could potentially be a sole trader who works alone and owns their own business or an individual working in sales who has their own sales performance targets. By coaching these individuals and measuring company profit and sales performance respectively, we would have a net profit figure upon which to calculate return-on-investment. However, I would strongly advise against this. Without matching our coachees to a control group who are the same in every other characteristic, one still could not be confident that any change in financial performance was due to the coaching and not due to other factors such as changes in the economic climate or peaks and troughs in sales.

In addition to being practically challenging if not impossible to calculate return-on-investment, I also feel strongly that it is damaging to do so. Let me take some previous claims of the return on investment as examples. Figures cited range from a 529% return-on-investment from Anderson (2001) to a return of 5.7 times the original investment from McGovern et al. (2001). Let us take a moment to understand what these authors are claiming. If an organization was to invest £5,000 on a coaching intervention, then they could expect a return-on-investment (i.e. growth in business directly attributed to the coaching intervention and the coaching intervention alone) of £26,450 according to Anderson and £33,500 according to McGovern et al. Now I don't know what type of coaching those guys have been doing but those figures certainly don't match up to my experience! This is why return-on-investment is dangerous. Vastly exaggerated statistics such as these can only lead to scepticism and doubt on the impact of coaching. Instead, surely it is preferable to provide accurate data on the coaching outcomes that we have evidence for?

The popular alternative to return-on-investment is the notion of return-on-expectation. Practitioners often use this method as an approach to demonstrating the organizational value of training and this approach has similarly been applied to coaching. The idea with return-on-expectation is that any development intervention should start with the end in mind, outlining what qualifies as a successful result at the end of the intervention. This principle represents good practice and given the focus on goals, a practice most coaches will be applying automatically. What may be less automatic is the explicit conversation with the organization regarding what success should look like following coaching. My advice in relation to evaluating coaching is that measuring return-on-expectation is not enough. Understanding expectations is an important start point of any coaching intervention, and I would certainly encourage practitioners to assess this at the end of the intervention. However, even more useful is identifying what success looks like to both the coachee and the organization and measuring the impact on these criteria in addition to whether expectations have been met. Therefore, if the coachee wants to see a decrease in stress, let us measure stress before and after coaching to understand the impact on this variable. If the organization wants to see coachees who are more adaptable at work, let us measure adaptable performance before and after coaching, from multiple perspectives, to see whether there is an actual change. This way, we can supplement the return-on-expectation data with additional data that directly targets the outcomes of interest.

Recommendations for practice: evaluating coaching

Based on my experience of evaluating coaching for research purposes and also when consulting with organizations, I have a number of specific recommendations to ensure that your coaching evaluation accurately captures the real changes that occur as a result of coaching and provide you with useful evidence upon which to further inform your practice.

Start with the end in mind

As discussed in the context of return-on-expectation, evaluation must be aligned with coachee goals. Sounds obvious but is rarely implemented in practice. If the coachee wants to improve work-life balance, then measure work-life balance. If the coachee wants to improve sales performance, then measure sales performance. In my first research projects, I anticipated that coaching would have a general positive effect on a range of outcomes such as performance, job satisfaction, and organizational commitment. While when speaking with coachees, they would often comment on general positive outcomes from coaching such as these, when measuring outcomes, general outcome measures often do not accurately capture the change that has taken place, particularly when a robust measurement methodology (such as pre and post-coaching measurements or comparison to a control group) are used. Therefore, in my experience, these kinds of general outcomes do not accurately capture the variation in outcomes experienced by a large group of coachees, each working towards their own set of unique goals and objectives. For those working with organizational clients, it is also important to consider what the client wants from the coaching programme. So, for example, if a client is interested in using coaching to develop proactivity and adaptivity in the workforce, then aligning the evaluation measures with these outcomes is likely to give you data that is useful for your client; however, it also accurately captures the impact of your coaching. Therefore, evaluation must be planned even before the coaching has begun.

Measure a range of outcomes

In addition to ensuring that the outcomes that you measure are aligned with the coachees' goals, wherever possible, measure a range of outcomes, ideally from each of the four types of outcomes in the coaching outcome framework (affective, cognitive, skill-based, and results). For example, if your coachee wishes to improve the performance of their team and is receiving coaching on their team leadership skills, you might decide to evaluate the impact of your coaching by measuring team performance, such as team sales performance (which would be a results outcome), you could also measure your coachee's team leadership skills (a skill-based outcome), you could measure team reflection (a cognitive outcome) and team psychological safety (an affective outcome). By evaluating your coaching at all four levels you are more likely to capture some useful data related to the impact of your coaching as you may find that while the data show a positive change in some areas (such as affective or cognitive outcomes), changes in other areas may take longer to develop or take impact (such as skills or results). Capturing evaluation data in this way will also give a fuller picture of the diverse impact of your coaching.

Use a scientific approach

The majority of evaluation that takes place in real-life organizational settings unfortunately tends to rely solely on questionnaires given to coachees after coaching has been completed. The problem with this approach is that there is no baseline measure from which to draw a comparison to determine whether any changes are as a result of the coaching. Therefore, it is essential that you collect some information on whichever outcomes you decide to measure before the coaching has started. Ideally, you would also aim to collect the same data from a group of individuals who are as similar as possible to your coachees who will not be receiving coaching, this group would form a control group which you could also compare any changes to. In reality, accessing a control group is very difficult; however, it may be worth considering particularly if you are working on a larger scale coaching intervention. Another way of providing a scientific, robust approach to your evaluation would be to incorporate evaluation data from a range of sources. Therefore, rather than solely relying on self-reported data from your coachees, you could also collect data from relevant others to measure the wider impact of the coaching. When selecting who to capture data from and what to measure, it is once again important to consider the relevance of the measure (i.e. specific measures are better than general measures) and whether the person has the ability to accurately detect changes in the coachee. For example, if you decide to capture performance data from the coachee's line manager, you need to be sure that the coaching was targeted at improving performance and that the coachee's line manager works closely enough with the coachee to detect any changes in this measure. Using the same example as previously, if your coachee wishes to improve the performance of his or her team, it would be appropriate in this instance to capture the coachees own views of the team's performance (before and after coaching) as well as the teams own rating of their performance (also before and after coaching).

Select your measurement tools wisely

Building on the idea that evaluation should utilize a scientific approach is the recommendation that you consider the measurement tools you use wisely. Unfortunately, all too often, I work with organizations that have created their own questionnaires to evaluate coaching. Creating a measurement tool that accurately measures a psychological construct takes many stages of development. Without following these stages, there is the danger that the tool will not accurately measure what it sets out to measure (i.e. how can we be sure that my definition of a construct such as trust is the same as your definition?). There is also the challenge that the measure may not be reliable so that each time the measure is used a slightly different results is obtained, even when we might expect it to be unchanged (consider how useful a set of scales might be that give a different weight for the same item each time it is weighed?). To avoid these potential pitfalls in evaluation, my recommendation would be to use measures that have been developed with the explicit purpose of evaluation in mind, ideally those developed by researchers. You can access measures such as these through resources such as texts on coaching evaluation and also through many research papers that can often be accessed for free online through Google Scholar. In this book, in the remaining chapters, you will also find useful resources in the reference lists where I have detailed the research papers that include questionnaires that have been used in coaching evaluation.

Resources

In one of my research studies (Jones et al., 2018), I developed two self-report questionnaires that coaches can use to evaluate their coaching practice. These questionnaires should be used following coaching to assess the impact of coaching on two key areas: personal effectiveness and work well-being. The questionnaires are as follows:

As a result of working with my coach, I believe that:
Work well-being items (affective outcome)
I feel more satisfied in my job
I feel less frustrated
I feel happier at work
I enjoy my job more
I feel less stressed at work
I am more motivated
I feel more engaged
Personal effectiveness items (skill-based outcome)
I am able to prioritize more effectively
I am able to plan more effectively
I am more organized
I behave more assertively
I am more flexible in the way I work to meet organizational objectives

---

Note: Response scale: 1 = strongly disagree to 5 = strongly agree.

This chapter in summary

- The ability to tailor the developmental challenge to the coachee is one of the key strengths of coaching as a developmental approach; however, this is also what makes evaluating coaching so challenging: coaching is not a one-size-fits-all approach
- We can expect coaching to result in four different types of outcomes:
  - Affective outcomes (how does the coachee feel?)
  - Cognitive outcomes (how does the coachee think?)
  - Skill-based outcomes (what does the coachee do?)
  - Results outcomes (what does the coachee achieve?)
- The research evidence shows that coaching positively impacts on affective, skill-based and results outcomes; however, the impact is the greatest on results outcomes
- Attempting to measure return-on-investment from coaching is at best extremely difficult and at worst damaging to the profession of coaching
- When evaluating your own coaching practice:
  - Start with the end in mind – align outcomes to the objectives of coaching
  - Measure a range of outcomes – ideally from all four outcomes (affective, cognitive, skill-based and results)
  - Use a scientific approach – always measure outcomes before and after coaching, ideally use a control group and where possible capture data from other sources as well as the coachee
  - Select your measurement tools wisely – do not be tempted to create your own questionnaires. Use tools developed by researchers to ensure your evaluation is reliable and valid

Note

1 Multiple studies tested multiple outcomes.

References

Anderson, M. C. (2001). Executive briefing: Case study on the return on investment of executive coaching. Retrieved from https://10eighty.co.uk/web/wp-content/uploads/2012/09/MetrixGlobal-coaching-roi-briefing.pdf

Andrews, H., & Jones, R. J. (2020). Can one-to-one coaching improve selection success and who benefits most? The role of candidate generalized self-efficacy. *Unpublished manuscript.*

Ammentorp, J., Jensen, H. I., & Uhrenfeldt, L. (2013). Danish health professionals' experiences of being coached: A pilot study. *Journal of Continuing Education in the Health Professions, 33*, 41–47. doi:10.1002/chp.21157

Baron, L., & Morin, L. (2010). The impact of executive coaching on self-efficacy related to management soft-skills. *Leadership & Organization Development Journal, 31*(1), 18–38. doi:10.1108/01437731011010362

Bozer, G., & Jones, R. J. (2018). Understanding the factors that determine workplace coaching effectiveness: A systematic literature review. *European Journal of Work and Organizational Psychology, 27*(3), 342–361. doi:10.1080/1359432X.2018.1446946

Bozer, G., Sarros, J. C., & Santora, J. C. (2013). The role of coachee characteristics in executive coaching for effective sustainability. *Journal of Management Development, 32*(3), 277–294. doi:10.1108/02621711311318319

Bozer, G., Sarros, J. C., & Santora, J. C. (2014). Academic background and credibility in executive coaching effectiveness. *Personnel Review, 43*(6), 881–897. doi:10.1108/PR-10-2013-0171

Bright, D., & Crockett, A. (2012). Training combined with coaching can make a significant difference in job performance and satisfaction. *Coaching: An International Journal of Theory, Research and Practice, 5*(1), 4–21. doi:10.1080/17521882.2011.648332

Duijts, S. F. A., Kant, I., van den Brandt, P. A., & Swaen, G. M. H. (2008). Effectiveness of a preventive coaching intervention for employees at risk for sickness absence due to psychosocial health complaints: Results of a randomized controlled trial. *Occupational and Environmental Medicine, 50*(7), 765–776. doi:10.1097/JOM.0b013e3181651584

Feggetter, A. J. W. (2007). A preliminary evaluation of executive coaching: Does executive coaching work for candidates on a high potential development scheme? *International Coaching Psychology Review, 2*(2), 129–142.

Gardiner, M., Kearns, H., & Tiggemann, M. (2013). Effectiveness of cognitive behavioural coaching in improving the well-being and retention of rural general practitioners. *Australian Journal of Rural Health, 21*(3), 183–189. doi:10.1111/ajr.12033

Grant, A. M. (2014). The efficacy of executive coaching in times of organisational change. *Journal of Change Management, 14*(2), 258–280. doi:10.1080/14697017.2013.805159

Grant, A. M., Curtayne, L., & Burton, G. (2009). Executive coaching enhances goal attainment, resilience and workplace well-being: A randomised controlled study. *The Journal of Positive Psychology, 4*(5), 396–407. doi:10.1080/17439760902992456

Grant, A. M., Studholme, I., Verma, R., Kirkwood, L., Paton, B., & O'Connor, S. (2017). The impact of leadership coaching in an Australian healthcare setting. *Journal of Health Organization and Management, 31*(2), 237–252. doi:10.1108/JHOM-09-2016-0187

Gyllensten, K., & Palmer, S. (2006). Experiences of coaching and stress in the workplace: An interpretative phenomenological analysis. *International Coaching Psychology Review, 1*(1), 86–98.

Jones, R. J., Woods, S. A., & Guillaume, Y. R. F. (2016). The effectiveness of workplace coaching: A meta-analysis of learning and performance outcomes from coaching. *Journal of Occupational and Organizational Psychology, 89*, 249–277. doi:10.1111/joop.12119

Jones, R. J., Woods, S. A., & Hutchinson, E. (2014). The influence of the Five Factor Model of personality on the perceived effectiveness of executive coaching. *International Journal of Evidence Based Coaching and Mentoring, 12*(2), 109–118. doi:10.1111/j.1744-6570.2003.tb00152.x

Jones, R. J., Woods, S. A., & Zhou, Y. (2018). Boundary conditions of workplace coaching outcomes. *Journal of Managerial Psychology, 33*(7/8), 475–496. doi:10.1108/JMP-11-2017-0390

Kines, P., Andersen, L. P. S., Spangenberg, S., Mikkelsen, K. L., Dyreborg, J., & Zohar, D. (2010). Improving construction site safety through leader-based verbal safety communication. *Journal of Safety Research, 41*(5), 399–406. doi:10.1016/j.jsr.2010.06.005

Kirkpatrick, D. L. (1996, January). Great ideas revisited. *Training & Development, 50*, 54–59.

Kraiger, K., Ford, J. K., & Salas, E. D. (1993). Application of cognitive, skill-based, and affective theories of learning outcomes to new methods of training evaluation. *Journal of Applied Psychology, 78*, 311–328. doi:10.1037/0021-9010.78.2.311

Ladegard, G., & Gjerde, S. (2014). Leadership coaching, leader role-efficacy, and trust in subordinates: A mixed methods study assessing leadership coaching as a leadership development tool. *The Leadership Quarterly, 25*(4), 631–646. doi:10.1016/j.leaqua.2014.02.002

Libri, V., & Kemp, T. (2006). Assessing the efficacy of a cognitive behavioural executive coaching programme. *International Coaching Psychology Review, 1*(2), 9–18.

Locke, E. A., & Latham, G. P. (1990). *A Theory of Goal Setting and Task Performance.* Englewood Cliffs, NJ: Prentice Hall.

Luthans, F., & Peterson, S. J. (2003). 360-degree feedback with systematic coaching: Empirical analysis suggests a winning combination. *Human Resource Management, 42*(3), 243–256. doi:10.1002/hrm.10083

McGovern, J., Lindemann, M., Vergara, M., Murphy, S., Barker, L., & Warrenfeltz, R. (2001). Maximizing the impact of executive coaching: Behavioral change, organizational outcomes, and return on investment. *Manchester Review, 6*(1), 19.

Olivero, G., Bane, K. D., & Kopelman, R. E. (1997). Executive coaching as a transfer of training tool: Effects on productivity in a public agency. *Public Personnel Management, 26*, 461–469. doi:10.1177/009910260970260040

Parker-Wilkins, V. (2006). Business impact of executive coaching: Demonstrating monetary value. *Industrial and Commercial Training, 38*(3), 122–127. doi:10.1108/00197850610659373

Powell, K. S., & Yalcin, S. (2010). Managerial training effectiveness: A meta-analysis 1952–2002. *Personnel Review, 39*, 227–241. doi:10.1108/00483481011017435

Sonesh, S. C., Coultas, C. W., Marlow, S. L., Lacerenza, C. N., Reyes, D., & Salas, E. (2015). Coaching in the wild: Identifying factors that lead to success. *Consulting Psychology Journal: Practice and Research, 67*(3), 189–217. doi:10.1037/cpb0000042

Spurk, D., Kauffeld, S., Barthauer, L., & Heinemann, N. S. R. (2015). Fostering networking behavior, career planning and optimism, and subjective career success: An intervention study. *Journal of Vocational Behaviour, 87*, 134–144. doi:10.1016/j.jvb.2014.12.007

Taie, E. S. (2011). Coaching as an approach to enhance performance. *Journal for Quality and Participation, 34*(1), 34–38.

Trathen, S. A. (2007). *Executive coaching, changes in leadership competencies and learning agility amongst Microsoft senior executives.* PhD Dissertation. School of Education. Colorado State University. Fort Collins, Colorado.

Williams, J. S. (2016). *An investigation of goal-focused and process-oriented approaches to executive coaching using random assignment and switching replications designs.* PhD Dissertation. Alliant International University. San Diego, California.

Section Two

The coachee

The importance of the coachee

> To her question of what I planned to do, I replied that I would get a job on the streetcars. She rejected the proposal with: 'They don't accept colored people on the streetcars.'
>
> I would like to claim an immediate fury which was followed by the noble determination to break the restricting tradition. But the truth is, my first reaction was one of disappointment. I'd pictured myself, dressed in a neat blue serge suit, my money changer swinging jauntily at my waist, and a cheery smile for the passengers which would make their own work day brighter.
>
> From disappointment, I gradually ascended the emotional ladder to haughty indignation, and finally to that state of stubbornness where the mind is locked like the jaws of an enraged bulldog.
>
> I would go to work on the streetcars and wear a blue serge suit. Mother gave me her support with one of her usual terse asides, 'That's what you want to do? Then nothing beats a mind but failure. Give it everything you've got. I've told you many times "Can't do is like Don't Care." Neither of them have a home.'
>
> Translated, that meant there was nothing a person can't do, and there should be nothing a human being didn't care about. It was the most positive encouragement I could have hoped for.
>
> (I know why the caged bird sings, Maya Angelou, 1969, pp. 284–285)

The above extract is taken from the first autobiography of the inspirational writer and activist Dr. Maya Angelou and describes her decision to pursue her first paid job as a conductorette on the streetcars in San Francisco in the early 1940s. As a result of persistence and determination, Dr. Angelou became the first person of colour to be a conductorette on the San Francisco streetcars. What was it that gave Dr. Angelou the desire, determination, and resilience to persist in this quest? Was it her upbringing? Was it her experience? Was it something about her personality or her values? Almost certainly it was a combination of all of these factors that when put together made her the unique character that she was. Stories such as these have always fascinated me and for as long as I can remember, I have had a burning curiosity to understand what makes people different from one another and how these differences influence the lives that we lead.

This curiosity has led me to question why do individuals make certain choices in life. Why are we motivated and driven by different forces? Why one person's love is another person's loath? Why do some individuals thrive and others falter? A curiosity to understand the answers to these questions is what drove me to study Psychology at college and then continue along this path with my degree and beyond. The complexity of the human mind continues to fascinate me and the more I learn on this subject, the more I realize that there is still so much that we do not know and may never know. Despite this, as leaders and coaches, we can benefit from a wealth of research on individual differences to inform how best to enhance our coaching practice and enable behavioural change in others. As mentioned in earlier chapters of this book, I believe that one of the strengths of coaching is the ability to tailor the coaching approach to the individual coachee. Despite this, I rarely see the coachee discussed in the literature in the context of understanding what the coachee brings to the coaching conversation and how this is likely to impact the effectiveness of coaching. It is almost as though it is assumed that all coachees will engage equally in the coaching process, develop, and change in the same way and therefore benefit equally from coaching. Coachees often seem to be treated as one homogenous group: passive in their 'receipt' of the coaching experience. I am sure that you will have many examples of working with a variety of individuals where you know that this is not the case. The evidence certainly indicates that this is not the case. In the chapters in this section, I will outline what we know in terms of how coachee characteristics interact with coaching to influence coaching outcomes. I will discuss this evidence from the perspective that while you may not be able to influence the characteristics of the coachee as they arrive at coaching, you can work with these characteristics to tailor your coaching approach to ensure that it is as effective as possible. Forewarned is forearmed!

In the chapters in this section, I will explore five coachee individual difference variables: coaching motivation (Chapter 3), personality (Chapter 4), goal orientation (Chapter 5), self-efficacy (Chapter 6), and coachee skills (Chapter 7). In each chapter, I will explain what we know about how this variable is likely to influence the effectiveness of coaching based on the evidence and then provide some specific recommendations for your own practice. As always, I will highlight the quality of the research and use the framework of coaching outcomes discussed in Chapter 2 when describing the types of outcomes explored in the research I discuss.

Chapter 3

Coachee motivation

'You can lead a horse to water but you can't make him drink'[1] the proverb goes, which accurately describes this first chapter on coachee individual differences. The reason coaching motivation is the first individual difference discussed is no accident – in my opinion, it is the most important factor that influences how effective coaching will be. If an individual is not motivated to be coached, does not want to be coached, or is not interested in changing their behaviour then they won't! This is despite the fact that there are many instances where individuals are referred to coaching by their organization to 'fix' poor performance. In my experience, coaching is likely to make at best, a marginal impact on behaviour change with these individuals, regardless of what the coach does.

On that depressing note, let me explain why. Motivation to learn or training motivation has been widely investigated in the broader learning and development literature. A generally accepted definition provided by Salas and Cannon-Bowers (2001) describes training motivation as the 'direction, effort, intensity, and persistence that trainees apply to learning-oriented activities before, during, and after training' (p. 479). Research has consistently shown that trainees' motivation to learn predicts the level of attention and effort the trainee gives during the training process. This subsequently affects the skills gained from the training, the degree to which these skills are retained following completion of the training, and the willingness to apply newly acquired knowledge, skills, and abilities on the job (e.g. Martocchio & Webster, 1992; Quiñones, 1995).

In our 2018 systematic literature review (Bozer & Jones, 2018), Dr. Gil Bozer and I included motivation to learn as one of the seven theoretical influences that explain how coaching works. We found a number of studies in the coaching literature that explored motivation to learn; however, these studies often utilized a range of terminologies such as receptivity to coaching, readiness to be coached or commitment to the coaching relationship. In our view, all of these concepts can be adequately classified according to the definition of training motivation provided by Salas and Cannon-Bowers (2001), and consequently, we called this 'coaching motivation': broadly described as the motivation to be coached or the direction, effort, intensity, and persistence that *coachees* apply to learning-oriented activities before, during, and after coaching.

The majority of studies on the topic of coaching motivation, investigate it qualitatively, where coaches, coachees, and HR professionals have been interviewed on the factors they believe are important influences of positive outcomes from coaching. Findings generally indicate that individuals who enter into coaching with a high level of coaching motivation will experience more positive outcomes following coaching. This is because individuals actively regulate their motivation, emotion, and learning processes. Gully and Chen (2010) describe this process in the context of the training literature, detailing how learners decide what to pay attention to and determine how much effort to devote to the learning task. Learners can actively engage themselves (or disengage themselves) from learning and they are responsible for applying and transferring skills from their learning to the work environment.

For example, a coachee may not be motivated to receive coaching because perhaps they do not believe that coaching will have an impact on their behaviour, they might not perceive that they have the time to invest in coaching or perhaps they have been referred to coaching, which they view as a 'punishment' for poor performance. This low level of coaching motivation will have a negative impact on their subsequent behaviour during coaching. On the one hand, while the unmotivated individual may be able to disengage themselves and not pay attention to the training room, in relative terms, this is much more difficult in coaching. It is harder for a coachee to not pay attention during coaching as the coachee is working one-to-one with the coach, the nature of the coaching conversation itself forces the coachee to pay attention. However, the degree of coaching motivation can still influence the nature in which the coachee responds to the coaches' interventions, for example, the coachee may hold back in responding to questions, not providing fully honest or deep answers. The level of coaching motivation may also influence the level of effort the coachee expends in any follow-up actions after the coaching, consequently influencing whether any changes discussed in coaching manifest into actual changes when they return to work. Consequently, coaching motivation can also influence the degree to which any learning gained in coaching is transferred back to the coachee's work environment, therefore, are they motivated to make any changes following coaching to how they behave on a day-to-day basis? Conversely, coachees who have a high level of coaching motivation are likely to fully engage in the coaching process, responding honestly and with deep consideration to the coaches' interventions. They are more likely to proactively engage in follow-up tasks and actions and be motivated to apply their learning to their work environment. These actions combined are likely to lead to a greater impact of coaching.

Examples of evidence supporting the impact of coaching motivation on coaching outcomes include a study by MacKie (2015). MacKie found that coaching motivation (which he called coaching readiness) had a positive impact on skill-based outcomes as reflected in improved transformational leadership behaviour (when these behaviours were rated by the coachee themselves and others who worked with the coachee such as their line manager, peers, and subordinates). The positive impact of coaching motivation was also evidenced by Bozer, Sarros, and Santora (2013), who found that coaching motivation explained the relationship between coachee mastery goal orientation and coaching effectiveness. This means that coachees who had a mastery goal orientation (i.e. were likely to set goals oriented towards learning or mastery rather than performance in comparison to others) experienced more positive outcomes from coaching because these individuals were also more motivated to learn. In terms of the quality of research on coaching motivation, the overall rating is relatively high as the evidence consistently suggests that coaching motivation is an important antecedent of coaching outcomes. However, there is only a moderate level of confidence in relation to the directness of outcome as the majority of outcomes are predominately self-reported at the coachee level rather than from third-party or objective sources.

RESEARCH IN ACTION: A COACH'S EXPERIENCE

This particular example came to mind because I had been particularly struck by the way the coachee showed up for the work. What was noticeable was the energy that he brought to the work that we did together. It was very apparent from the word go, that this person was curious and interested in getting as much as possible from coaching. This motivation to engage with coaching also meant that he was very quick to share, to demonstrate vulnerability, and be open to challenges from me.

The coachee's motivation became clear in relation to the dedication with which he pursued his individual reflection and completion of activities between coaching sessions. There was never an occasion where he didn't come back with detailed updates on progress he had made or actions he had completed between our sessions. He was very methodical, and he had a particularly high level of diligence in doing whatever was discussed in coaching very thoroughly. He was prepared to be challenged and to stretch himself. This was with no pushing from me, I wasn't marking the homework, so to speak. Often you get clients who say "thank you for sending that through but I haven't managed to read

(Continued)

that" and that's fine because it's just a different style and type of intervention. This was certainly not the case with this coachee.

Because of his consistent completion of work between our sessions, it meant that we were able to follow a process in each session where we would review the work he had completed and either build on that work or we would move on to something else that had cropped up. One of the things that helped was that this individual was clearly a natural reflector in learning style but also very pragmatic. So, with this individual, there was rarely a challenge for him to put something into practice from the reflective experience. I was able then to say, "OK, well you've got that far but what about this?" I could push him further in terms of his reflective practice as opposed to "well I did that and it worked and that was ok", instead the next step is "well what does that mean then?" I really don't think that this reflective challenge can work as well if the individual is not really motivated and doesn't have the energy and curiosity that comes from that motivation. One of the outcomes of this incredibly high motivation to learn, including how he showed up to coaching and the subsequent actions between sessions, was, at a basic level, we were able to do more together, we could hit the ground running.

In terms of anything I did as the coach to help foster this high motivation, I think part of it was around the contracting process. The chemistry meeting was very much part of the contracting process and in this, I outlined my approach, which is to make it clear that we can work in whatever way feels appropriate, so demonstrating an ability to be flexible. The coachee also selected me from a number of coaches, from my profile. My profile detailed my background and probably helped to build my credibility as someone who would be a good match for him in relation to my experience, having worked in the specific area and with some of the same challenges that he was facing. So there is something to do with the credibility of my background in terms of why I was chosen that may have made a difference to his motivation and then this also created a sense of an initial rapport, as there was the shared assumption that the challenges he was facing were challenges that I understood while making it clear that as a coach, I wasn't making assumptions that my answers were his answers. During the coaching process, to help maintain the high level of motivation he was demonstrating, I felt that I went with what the coachee had to offer. This meant noticing his strengths and the preferred ways of learning and being able to adapt my coaching to match that.

For details of the coaches who were interviewed for the 'research in action' vignettes, see page 191.

Recommendations for practice

The implications of the evidence related to coaching motivation highlight that a coachee who enters the coaching relationship with a high level of motivation to be coached is more likely to experience positive outcomes as a result of coaching than a coachee with a lower level of motivation. The good news is that there are actions that you can take to enhance the level of coaching motivation prior to the start of coaching and maintain this beyond the coaching conversation. First, you can give credibility to the coaching process and yourself as a coach. If coachees believe that coaching will have a positive impact on helping them to achieve their goals and they have confidence in your ability to facilitate this goal achievement, they are more likely to feel motivated. This includes demystifying the coaching process by providing clear and specific information regarding what the coachee can expect prior to coaching. The use of chemistry meetings prior to the start of the coaching can help the coachee to get to know you, ask any questions they may have, understand the expected outcomes of coaching and help to build motivation towards the coaching itself. Likewise, providing written information about the coaching process and yourself as a coach can help to build motivation, again by providing credibility to coaching and yourself as a coach by demonstrating your expertise in the area. It may be useful to provide coachees with information regarding the evidence to indicate that coaching works, why coaching works, and the type of outcomes that can be expected. This is not to say that a hard sales pitch based on testimonials of 'coaching changed my life!!' or 'coaching helped me achieve 500 times my normal performance output!' are going to help coachees to feel more motivated. In fact, they are likely to do the opposite by taking away any credibility due to over-exaggerated claims about what can be achieved. However, a balanced and authentic account of what can be expected from coaching and what you need the coachee to contribute to this process is likely to provide reassurance of the credibility of the intervention.

The importance of managing expectations prior to coaching is often discussed in the context of the coaching contract. O'Broin and Palmer (2010) argue that regardless of whether a written contract is adopted in coaching, a psychological contract exists between the coach and coachee that influences the coaching relationship. This psychological contract concerns mutual reciprocal obligations. O'Broin and Palmer (2010) suggest that there should be an alignment between the coach and the coachee in relation to:

- Goals – there must be a clear mutual agreement about the goal of the work and the desired coaching outcome
- Tasks – there needs to be a mutual understanding of how the coaching work will take place and the tasks or roles of each party
- Bonds – mutual empathy and respect need to exist

O'Brion and Palmer (2010) suggest that in the process of explicitly discussing and agreeing on the goals and tasks of the coaching, the conditions of clarity and transparency, which are a prerequisite to trust and respect, are created. I would extend this argument and suggest that the process of discussing and agreeing on these elements also positively contribute to coaching motivation by managing expectations. It is hard to feel motivated in an ambiguous context and certainly, if expectations are not met, then it can be highly demotivating. These factors combined emphasize what an important part of the coaching process the contracting stage is. I will return to the importance of effective contracting in relation to the coaching relationship in Chapter 9.

It is also possible to continue to influence coaching motivation once the coaching starts. This is important to ensure that the coachee continues to stay motivated and therefore expends the required effort to implement changes following the coaching sessions when they return to work. Motivation can be encouraged by ensuring that the actions the coachee decides on are led by the coachee. This should be a given in coaching (as the conversation should be fully led by the coachee and not the coach) however it is worth restating here. A key enabler of motivation generally is autonomy, in particular the freedom to decide how to work to accomplish goals (Hackman & Oldham, 1980), as autonomy is central to developing a sense of personal responsibility. When individuals have control over their work they are more likely to feel motivated. Therefore, it is important that the coachee decides what they are going to do following coaching to help them to achieve their goals: they need to experience autonomy over these decisions. A further influencing factor for maintaining motivation is feedback on progress towards goal achievement (Locke & Latham, 2002). When individuals are working towards a goal, to enable them to stay motivated towards achieving that goal, they need to receive feedback on how they are progressing. This does not necessarily mean that someone else needs to tell them how they are progressing (although feedback could come in this form), rather, it is important that coachees have the opportunity to take stock and assess how they are progressing towards their goal, therefore they provide their own feedback. Often, when we are working towards achieving a goal, it is easy to lose sight of how far we have come. The coaching process can provide an excellent format for enabling the coachee to reflect and review their progress towards achieving their goal, gaining feedback on how they are progressing, consequently enhancing their motivation to persist in applying the content of their coaching sessions to their daily lives. The role of goal-setting in coaching is discussed further in Chapter 8.

In relation to enhancing coaching motivation for leaders who adopt a coaching mindset, the line between coaching motivation and motivation generally is less clear-cut. However, you can aim to foster a strong motivation to learn within your team, which should subsequently enhance openness to a coaching style of leadership. Fostering a strong motivation to learn is likely to include designing opportunities to learn into the average working day. For example, in meetings, ensure that learning is a scheduled agenda item – what can we learn from this experience and how can we apply this learning in the future? Encourage a culture where learning is valued over performance. To do this, learning needs to be rewarded, and learning from failures and mistakes needs to be encouraged. Changes in practice based on learning should be communicated to reinforce how the team and wider organization are learning together and making enhancements based on learning. Individuals should also be given autonomy over their learning. What goals are important to them and what actions do they want to take, to what schedule, to achieve these goals. The leader as a coach can also provide the opportunity for individuals to reflect on their progress towards goal achievement to gain that all important feedback necessary for maintaining motivation to learn. The organizational culture is discussed in more detail in Section four.

This chapter in summary

- The coachee's motivation to be coached indicates the direction, effort, intensity, and persistence that they will apply to learning-oriented activities before, during, and after coaching. Coaching motivation can be enhanced by:
  - Give credibility to the coaching process and yourself as coach by providing information (either in writing or in chemistry meetings) on what to expect in coaching and examples of the expected outcomes from coaching
  - Foster motivation and trust by using the contracting stage to agree on goals and tasks in coaching
  - Maintain motivation by ensuring the coachee has autonomy over actions they pursue towards goal achievement and provide the opportunities for the coachee to reflect (to give their own feedback) on their progress towards goal achievement
  - Motivation to learn can be enhanced by leaders by creating a learning culture where opportunities to learn are incorporated into day-to-day working lives.

Note

1 In fact, in my experience, if the horse doesn't want to go to the water you can't lead him there either, as I learnt one afternoon spending two hours trying to 'encourage' a stubborn horse into his stable box. Let's just say that the horse got his way in the end.

References

Bozer, G., & Jones, R. J. (2018). Understanding the factors that determine workplace coaching effectiveness: A systematic literature review. *European Journal of Work and Organizational Psychology, 27*(3), 342–361. doi:10.1080/1359432X.2018.1446946

Bozer, G., Sarros, J. C., & Santora, J. C. (2013). The role of coachee characteristics in executive coaching for effective sustainability. *Journal of Management Development, 32*(3), 277–294. doi:10.1108/02621711311318319

Gully, S., & Chen, G. (2010). Individual differences, attribute-treatment interactions, and training outcomes. In S. W. J. Kozlowski & E. Salas (Eds.), *SIOP organizational frontiers series. Learning, training, and development in organizations,* (pp. 3–64). New York: Routledge/Taylor Francis Group.

Hackman, J. R., & Oldham, G. R. (1980). *Work design.* Reading, MA: Addison-Wesley.

Locke, E. A., & Latham, G. P. (2002). Building a practically useful theory of goal setting and task motivation: A 35 year odyssey. *American Psychologist, 57,* 705–717. doi:10.1037//0003-066X.57.9.705

Mackie, D. (2015). The effects of coachee readiness and core self-evaluations on leadership coaching outcomes: A controlled trial. *Coaching: An International Journal of Theory, Research and Practice, 8*(2), 120–136. doi:10.1080/17521882.2015.1019532

Martocchio, J. J., & Webster, J. (1992). Effects of feedback and cognitive playfulness on performance in microcomputer software training. *Personnel Psychology, 45*(3), 553–578.

O'Broin, A., & Palmer, S. (2010). Building on an interpersonal perspective in the coaching relationship. In S. Palmer & A. McDowall (Eds.), *The coaching relationship: Putting people first,* (pp. 34–54). Hove, UK: Routledge.

Quiñones, M. A. (1995). Pretraining context effects: Training assignment as feedback. *Journal of Applied Psychology, 80*(2), 226–238. doi:10.1037/0021-9010.80.2.226

Salas, E., & Cannon-Bowers, J. A. (2001). The science of training: A decade of progress. *Annual Review of Psychology, 52*(1), 471–499. doi:10.1146/annurev.psych.52.1.471

Chapter 4

Coachee personality

Personality has been a hot topic of research for over a century. As such, we have a great deal of evidence that appears to link personality with important outcomes such as work performance and learning (Barrick & Mount, 1991). In relation to measuring personality, while a number of different personality scales are available, the five-factor model has generally been accepted as the most reliable and valid method of understanding personality (Digman, 1990). The five-factor model describes personality in terms of five basic dimensions: neuroticism versus emotional stability, extraversion versus introversion, openness to experience, agreeableness versus antagonism, and conscientiousness. Extraversion is most frequently associated with traits such as being sociable, gregarious, assertive, talkative, and active. Neuroticism generally consists of traits such as being anxious, depressed, angry, embarrassed, emotional, worried, and insecure. Agreeableness is most frequently associated with traits such as being courteous, flexible, trusting, good-natured, cooperative, forgiving, soft-hearted, and tolerant. Conscientiousness consists of traits such as being careful, thorough, responsible, organized, achievement-oriented, hardworking, and persevering. Finally, openness to experience is commonly described with traits such as being imaginative, cultured, curious, original, broad-minded, and artistically sensitive (Barrick & Mount, 1991).

Research into the influence of coachee personality on coaching outcomes is relatively limited, this is despite a wealth of research on the importance of personality on learning outcomes (for example see Campbell, Castaneda, & Pulos, 2010; Cellar, Miller, Doverspike, & Klawsky, 1996; Dean, Conte, & Blakenhorn, 2006; Kappe & van der Flier, 2010; Komarraju, Karau, Schmeck, & Avdic, 2011; Studer-Luethi, Jaeggi, Buschkuehl, & Perrig, 2012; Woods, Patterson, Koczwara, & Sofat, 2016). The research that has been conducted in this area has indicated that coachee personality may be an important factor to consider when understanding the effectiveness of coaching. For example, Stewart, Palmer, Wilkin, and Kerrin (2008) found that coachees who were higher in conscientiousness and openness and lower in neuroticism were more likely to report that they had successfully transferred learning from coaching to their workplace. In an early study (Jones, Woods, & Hutchinson, 2014), I found a significant positive relationship between Extraversion and perceived coaching effectiveness, in that, extraverted coachees were more likely to report that they perceived coaching to be effective. We suggested that this relationship may be explained by the extraverts' preference for an interactive learning environment such as learning through talking and doing. However, these early studies could be considered relatively low in quality (yes – I am including my own research in this assessment!), as both are reliant on cross-sectional data, with little consistency over the coaching intervention applied (therefore, a low directness of the intervention) and both use coachee reports of outcomes (therefore have a low directness of outcomes). Therefore, we must be tentative in relation to drawing conclusions from these findings.

More recently, I have further investigated the role of coachee personality on coaching effectiveness with a more rigorous research design (Jones, Woods, & Zhou, 2019). In a field experiment, 53 participants were provided with four, one-hour telephone coaching sessions and compared with 31 participants in a control group who did not receive coaching. We collected data over three time points to assess the impact of coaching on performance change, utilizing a results-based outcome in the form of self and supervisor-ratings of performance. In this study, we found that out of the Big Five the only personality characteristic to influence outcomes from coaching was openness. We found that coachees who were high in openness experienced a greater impact on performance following coaching. We explained this finding as individuals high in openness tend to exhibit higher motivation to learn and prefer novel learning techniques (Chamorro-Premuzic & Furnham, 2008), which is particularly important in coaching as coaching involves the use of novel and creative approaches to learning. For example, we suggest that a core component that defines coaching is that coaches may draw upon a wide range of psychological and behavioural tools, techniques, and approaches to work with the coachee to achieve their goals (Bono, Purvanova, Towler, & Peterson, 2009). Consequently, the coach has a great deal of flexibility to tailor the 'content' of the coaching intervention towards the needs of the coachee. The types of tools, techniques, and approaches used by coaches can vary from those that may be considered more 'conventional' or familiar within an organizational setting, such as reflective questioning and discussion of psychometric results, to those that may be less familiar in an organizational context, such as visualization, storytelling, drawing, constellations, or the use of Lego or other 'toys'. Consequently, for coaching to be effective, it is important that the coachee is open to novel and often creative methods of learning during the coaching intervention (Stokes, 2018). If the coachee is resistant to novel or creative approaches, they are unlikely to be motivated to engage in these interventions as they may feel uncomfortable with these approaches or may not perceive them to be a worthwhile use of their time.

The experimental research design, directness of intervention, and directness of outcomes used in this study mean that we can have greater confidence in the validity of the findings. These findings suggest that out of the Big Five openness is the key characteristic that seems to influence outcomes from coaching.

RESEARCH IN ACTION: A COACH'S EXPERIENCE

What I have noticed, over the course of my practice, is that there is a connection between the readiness the coachee has to embark on the various activities I tend to use in coaching, which involves different forms of learnings, and the outcome that results from them being ready and courageous enough to try this. In coaching, I invite my coachee to do a number of things. For example, one would be to engage with role plays within the coaching session. I would play the role for example of an employee or his or her boss and I would invite the coachee to play with me as if I was really the boss or the employee. The more the coachee is ready to embark on this, to really try this out, the more he or she will get out of this session. Another example would be doing some emotional work. By that I mean that sometimes, I've noticed that some coachees have difficulties in accessing certain emotions and I'm thinking in particular about anger. Although this is not therapy, it is still important, if you want as an executive or as a human being to be effective, to be able to access the different emotions that we have and sometimes we don't necessarily feel these. Anger, for example, is really necessary as it allows you to set your limits, your boundaries. If you don't have access to anger, you might just say yes to everything to please everyone because you do not have an emotional connection with your own boundaries and your own sense of importance. Therefore, even when somebody asks you to do something that would be abusive, you might just say 'yes' because you are not in contact with your anger. Anger allows you to question this. To say: "I can't believe that he is even asking this! This is incredible! It's not right! I should say no!" But, if we don't feel anger, then we won't do this. So to address this, I might use activities where I will engage my coachee to contact their anger. So let's say their boss has asked them to do something that is really not fair and really unacceptable by any reasonable standards, I would ask them to speak to their boss as if their boss was right there with them, but contacting anger as they speak to their boss to try this out. So they would say something typically like "No, I disagree with you. I think it is unacceptable" and they might say something like this without any emotion. In this case,

(Continued)

I would now challenge them. I would say "I didn't hear any anger. I didn't sense any anger here. Would you try this out contacting some anger now" and they would try. Typically, if they are not in contact with their emotion, they would fail initially. So I would push them on this. I might demonstrate this, I would show them. I would then invite them to try this out. Activities such as this type of emotional work or role play might feel a bit strange and might feel a bit uncomfortable for the coachee. To help the coachee to feel more comfortable with this, I might do a number of things; however, in particular, I would be conscious about when I would introduce these types of activities. First of all, in any coaching session, we would discuss what the situation is, what's going on for the coachee, what is working, what is not working, what is the challenge here, what is preventing them from doing what they want to do. However, at some point, it becomes evident that we can only go so far in trying to describe the situation as it is. At some point, it seems like almost a logical progression, to say rather than describing how you are going to speak to that person, just speak to me as if I was that person. That may be more impactful and may come naturally in the process. At that point, often the coachee also realizes that it is necessary. The person often realizes that there is something that they could learn from this type of activity, so they understand it rationally. Some coachees might be more ready to try this form of learning than others. However, in my experience, those who are not willing to try will reap fewer benefits than those who are eager and courageous enough to try this.

For details of the coaches who were interviewed for the 'research in action' vignettes see page 191.

Recommendations for practice

While personality characteristics are thought to be relatively stable, evidence indicates that personality and openness, in particular, is malleable to some extent (Jackson, Hill, Payne, Roberts, & Stine-Morrow, 2012). Therefore, those who tend to have lower levels of openness are able to develop and foster this trait to become more open. This has important implications for those wishing to enhance the impact of coaching effectiveness. On the one hand, we could argue that coaching may be best reserved for those who score higher on the openness personality trait. However, if we do not want to limit our coaching provision to these individuals, it is important to consider how we can foster openness in others to ensure that we can enhance the impact of our coaching intervention. One of my first recommendations in this respect is to raise awareness with the coachee of the importance of openness. This can be done by explicitly discussing this trait at the start of the coaching process, ideally by including an assessment of this (see further resources at the end of this chapter for an example of a free online personality assessment) and explaining why it is important to be open for the coaching to have a positive impact. The coach can also provide information to the coachee about what to expect in the coaching process, including information on how coaching raises awareness through a range of processes such as creative experiments, challenge, and manipulation of metaphor. This will ensure that coachees are prepared when these processes are used by the coach, understand why the processes are being used, and understand the role they play as the coachee (in relation to their level of openness) in the impact of these processes. For those coachees who are instinctively less open, having an expectation about what the coaching process might involve will help them to prepare for these novel learning approaches. At the start of the coaching process, the coach could also aim to equip the coachee with some tangible prompts that they can use in the coaching conversation in instances where they may initially feel resistance to the coaching approach. For example, the coachee could be encouraged to say: "tell me a little more about what that might look like?" or "I'm not sure I feel comfortable with doing that, is there another option" when they feel some resistance towards any of the interventions suggested by the coach. This will enable the coachee to experience a higher level of autonomy over the coaching process, which, as we have already explored, is likely to enhance their coaching motivation. Finally, when coaching an individual low in openness, our findings indicate that you should be cautious when introducing interventions during the coaching session that may be considered to be particularly unusual or novel. These coachees may need a little more time to adjust to the style of learning and development used in coaching and consequently 'build up' to more novel or creative coaching interventions.

RESEARCH IN ACTION: A COACH'S EXPERIENCE

Most of the time people do openly engage in coaching activities; however, I believe that this is partly because I use a selection process at the beginning. First of all, I convey the fact that while the coachees select me, I also select them in a way, as I want to make sure that they are ready to embark on this process as it will require some work. I try to have a sense of whether or not they will be willing to do this work. I would typically have a conversation before we start the coaching process, the purpose of which is twofold. First, it is for us to get to know each other. For me to understand their expectations of this process, what do they hope to get from the coaching? Second, it is also so that

(Continued)

I can take this opportunity to explain how I work. I will explain my overall philosophy. Therefore, the coachee knows that we are going to look at their reality from multiple perspectives, from the physical all the way to the spiritual. Then they have a sense that they will be engaged in their development in very different ways than they may have previously be used to. I guess that's what they sign up for as well. They know that this is my approach. When I do this, I would also explain what I expect from the coachee. So this would take place at the beginning, and typically most of the time, as the coachee has initiated the process, they have called upon me because they want to be coached, they are already motivated to engage and be open to the process and they know what is involved.

If, however, I get the impression that they are not going to be willing to do this work, that instead they expect some magical process that won't involve any effort on their part, then I would not engage further in the coaching process. There may be a situation, for example, where the HR person or a Director has asked someone to be coached. At that time, I want to make sure that the coachee is going to understand that first of all, this coaching process is going to be entirely confidential and I am here to serve the coachee before I even serve the organization, even though the organization is paying for the coaching, I am clear with the fact that my first commitment is to that coachee. Typically, once I have explained that, they can see that they can only benefit from the process, and therefore I address some of their concerns. However, I still try to get a sense of what they want to get from this, if it's just "Yes, my boss asked me to do this. I don't really believe that I have a problem or that I need to change anything, but they've asked me to do this" I would say "I think probably then, if you don't need this then let's not do this then. If everything is fine then we shouldn't do any coaching" I'm not going to push them.

However, most of the time people are ready to be open during coaching, although of course there are some different levels of readiness to go outside of their comfort zone. Of course, we also don't ever really know what is going to happen, and if the person is really going to be fully open. Sometimes, there may be some surprises. Some people, which I didn't necessarily expect will go further, will go even deeper than I was expecting and the other way around.

For details of the coaches who were interviewed for the 'research in action' vignettes, see page 191.

Low coachee openness may be less of an issue for the leader as a coach because as a general rule, the leader as a coach is using less creative or novel coaching tools and techniques than the independent coach. By definition, the leader as a coach is incorporating a coaching mindset into their everyday leadership rather than engaging in specific coaching interventions. However, the leader as a coach may still experience resistance from the employee who is low in openness, if the approach of leadership differs or is a change to that which has been experienced previously. Furthermore, while the leader as a coach may be less likely than the independent coach to use creative or novel coaching tools and techniques, these may be used to great effect by the leader as a coach during one-to-one's to facilitate learning, and therefore, the leader as a coach may need to be mindful of the level of openness within individual members of their team and tailor approaches accordingly. Consequently, I would recommend that the leader as coach gathers data from the team in relation to their personality profile. If you are aware that you have members of your team who are low in openness and you are planning on shifting your style of leadership, it may be more effective to transition into a new coaching style of leadership gradually rather than abruptly to allow these individuals time to adjust. For individuals low in openness, it may be useful to provide explanations as to why you are engaging in certain activities (such as facilitating reflection in one-to-one's), as raising their understanding of what to expect in these activities and why they might be helpful to their learning and development is likely to increase motivation to engage in these activities (which is likely to be lower in individuals low in openness at the outset) and is likely to reduce barriers or resistance that may be present due to the 'newness' or novelty to the approaches. Raising understanding of what to expect and how activities generate learning is a good approach to adopt as best practice generally, as while individuals low in openness may particularly benefit from this approach, similar benefits may also be seen even within those employees higher in openness.

Resources

Online personality questionnaire based on the five-factor model: http://www.personal.psu.edu/~j5j/IPIP/ipipneo120.htm

This chapter in summary

* Coachee's who are high in openness tend to experience more positive outcomes following coaching primarily because they are more likely to be open to novel approaches to learning
    * Aim to raise awareness of the importance of openness prior to the start of coaching by assessing personality and discussing the implications of the coachee personality with them during the initial session

- Provide information on what to expect in relation to coaching interventions and discuss with the coachee how they can respond if they do not feel comfortable engaging with a specific coaching intervention

References

Barrick, M. R., & Mount, K. M. (1991). The big five personality dimensions and job performance: A meta-analysis. *Personnel Psychology, 44*, 1–26. doi:10.1111/j.1744–6570.1991.tb00688.x

Bono, J. E., Purvanova, R. K., Towler, A. J., & Peterson, D. B. (2009). A survey of executive coaching practices. *Personnel Psychology, 62*(2), 361–404. doi:10.1111/j.1744–6570.2009.01142.x

Campbell, J. S., Castaneda, M., & Pulos, S. (2010). Meta-analysis of personality assessments as predictors of military aviation training success. *International Journal of Aviation Psychology, 20*, 92–109. doi:10.1080/10508410903415872

Cellar, D. F., Miller, M. L., Doverspike, D. D., & Klawsky, J. D. (1996). Comparison of factor structures and criterion-related validity coefficients for two measures of personality based on the five factor model. *Journal of Applied Psychology, 81*(6), 694–704. doi:10.1037/0021–9010.81.6.694

Chamorro-Premuzic, T., & Furnham, A. (2009). Mainly openness: The relationship between the Big Five personality traits and learning approaches. *Learning and Individual Differences, 19*, 524–529. doi:10.1016/j.lindif.2009.06.004

Dean, M. A., Conte, J. M., & Blankenhorn, T. R. (2006). Examination of the predictive validity of big five personality dimensions across training performance criteria. *Personality and Individual Differences, 41*, 1229–1239. doi:10.1016/j.paid.2006.04.020

Digman, J. M. (1990). Personality structure: Emergence of the five factor model. *Annual Review of Psychology, 41*, 417–440.

Jackson, J. J., Hill, P. L., Payne, B. R., Roberts, B. W., & Stine-Morrow, E. A. (2012). Can an old dog learn (and want to experience) new tricks? Cognitive training increases openness to experience in older adults. *Psychology and Aging, 27*(2), 286–292. doi:10.1037%2Fa0025918

Jones, R. J., Woods, S. A., & Hutchinson, E. (2014). The influence of the Five Factor Model of personality on the perceived effectiveness of executive coaching. *International Journal of Evidence Based Coaching and Mentoring, 12*(2), 109–118. doi:10.1111/j.1744–6570.2003.tb00152.x

Jones, R. J., Woods, S. A., & Zhou, Y. (2019). The effects of coachee personality and goal orientation on performance improvement following coaching: A controlled field experiment. *Applied Psychology: An International Review.* https://iaap-journals.onlinelibrary.wiley.com/doi/abs/10.1111/apps.12218

Kappe, R., & van der Flier, H. (2010). Using multiple and specific criteria to assess the predictive validity of the big five personality factors on academic performance. *Journal of Research in Personality, 44*, 142–145. doi:10.1016/j.jrp.2009.11.002

Komarraju, M., Karau, S. J., Schmeck, R. R., & Avdic, A. (2011). The big five personality traits, learning styles and academic achievement. *Personality and Individual Differences, 51*, 472–477. doi:10.1016/j.paid.2011.04.019

Stewart, L. J., Palmer, S., Wilkin, H., & Kerrin, M. (2008). The influence of character: Does personality impact coaching success? *International Journal of Evidence Based Coaching and Mentoring, 6*(1), 32–42.

Stokes, P. (2018). The skilled coachee. In B. Garvey, P. Stokes, & D. Megginson (Eds.), *Coaching and mentoring: Theory and practice.* London, UK: SAGE Publications.

Studer-Luethi, B., Jaeggi, S. M., Buschkuehl, M., & Perrig, W. J. (2012). Influence of neuroticism and conscientiousness on working memory training outcome. *Personality and Individual Differences, 53,* 44–49. doi:10.1016/j.paid.2012.02.012

Woods, S. A., Patterson, F. C., Koczwara, A., & Sofat, J. A. (2016). The value of being a conscientious learner: Examining the effects of the Big Five personality traits on self-reported learning from training. *Journal of Workplace Learning, 28*(7), 424–434. doi:10.1108/JWL-10-2015-0073

Chapter 5

Coachee goal orientation

This was an individual who I had been coaching for a little while. He arrived for our session and described how his chief executive was going to be away at the next meeting of shareholders, so he would have to do the financial analysis briefing for the shareholders. This coachee had a long track record of success with his company, he was pretty well-liked, and he had good relationships with the executive team. However, he was very nervous about handling this shareholders' meeting as he had chaired this meeting once previously and had received feedback from his chief executive who suggested that he hadn't done it very well. Following this, he had also had feedback from the markets that had been less than satisfactory. So this was the issue that my coachee wanted to talk about in this session.

At the start of this session, he was very much thinking about avoiding failure. He was talking about what had gone wrong for him in the past and wanted to concentrate on how he could avoid those sorts of things going wrong again. So I listened for quite a long time and then I asked him, because he was clearly a very experienced man, "when have you enjoyed doing presentations in the past?" At this question, he brightened up and he said that he very often enjoys presenting to his team. He reflected and said that he thought that one of the things that he thought was tricky about talking to the shareholders was that they didn't really understand the area very well so he felt that he had to work quite hard to ensure that everyone understood the context as well as the content. So then I asked him whether presenting to the shareholders reminded him of any other situations that he had been in when he had successfully talked to people who were in a similar state, people who didn't know much about the business. My coachee thought for quite a while and then his face lit up and he smiled, you could see him reliving this experience and he said: "well every year I am responsible for taking Japanese students around our businesses, explaining to them what we are doing". He explained that this was something that he really enjoyed doing, in particular, he really enjoyed educating the students about the organization. What was interesting was listening to him, I could see him become a different person, from being very stuffy and very preoccupied with delivering the message to the shareholders and avoiding failure in doing this, to being enormously interested in his students and communicating with them. So I asked him "is there anything there that you can apply to this forthcoming challenge?" My coachee suggested that he could see his shareholders as the equivalent to his Japanese students, he could view the meeting as an education for the shareholders, as a sort of assignment. So this is what he did. It worked incredibly well and he had very good feedback from the shareholder meeting. My coachee said some months later that he often thinks about his Japanese students when covering for his boss, and it really made all the difference in how he approached these tasks.

With this coachee, he came into our coaching session and focused on the fact that he had to chair the shareholders meeting, that he didn't want to do it, it had gone badly before and his main objective was that he didn't want it to go wrong again. Consequently, he was fixated on how to avoid that failure. Because I had worked with this individual over a number of sessions, I already knew that he had previously had huge amounts of media training, he was very skilful at presenting and I knew that he had done that sort of work successfully in other contexts. So I wondered, what was stopping him making the connection between his training, skills, and experience and this upcoming challenge himself? While he was clearly very competent, his focus on failure was limiting his ability to draw on his skills to apply them to this challenge. In this instance, he needed that third party to open his mindset to stop viewing the upcoming shareholder meeting in this very fixed way. To move away from messages such as "I'm no good at presenting to shareholders, I don't enjoy it, I did a terrible job last time and I need to avoid doing that this time" and to shift to seeing this as an opportunity to develop. This shift in mindset was what helped him. In the end, he not only avoided failure, but he went beyond that to chairing the meeting successfully and learning how to apply his existing skills in this new context.

For details of the coaches who were interviewed for the 'research in action' vignettes, see page 191.

We have already touched on the importance of a growth mindset in Section one of this book when I explored this from the perspective of the coach. The mindset has also been explored from the perspective of the coachee; however, in this research, it is often referred to as goal orientation. Dweck's (2006) theory of goal orientation suggests two different goal orientations that individuals pursue in achievement settings, namely, performance goal orientation and learning or mastery goal orientation. Individuals who are learning or mastery goal-oriented believe that their abilities are malleable and, therefore, generally focus on ways to increase their learning and/or task competence, acquire and develop new knowledge and skills, seek challenges, and persist to attain desired results in the case of failure. In contrast, individuals who are performance goal-oriented hold the belief that ability is fixed, and therefore, they focus on the outcomes of their performance and do not strive to learn but rather to demonstrate their current ability (Button, Mathieu, & Zajac, 1996).

In a training and learning context, learning or mastery goal orientation is considered to be a major individual motivational factor that influences the allocation of effort to learn, perform, and facilitates training transfer (Fisher & Ford, 1998). That is, trainees with a learning or mastery goal orientation are more likely to make sustained efforts (Hertenstein, 2001), seek feedback (VandeWalle & Cummings, 1997), possess high self-efficacy or self-belief (Kozlowski et al., 2001), and have greater performance in training interventions (Bell & Kozlowski, 2002). Within the coaching research, studies have investigated coachee goal orientation as an antecedent of coaching effectiveness, and, overall, the studies within this domain can be rated as high quality as there is strong evidence to indicate that coachee goal orientation is relevant to understanding coaching outcomes. This variable has been investigated using primarily quantitative research designs with a greater number of studies utilizing outcomes measured by third-party or objective sources. Specifically, research has indicated that coachee learning or mastery goal orientation is positively related to skill-based outcomes as reflected in improved self-reported job performance (Bozer, Sarros, & Santora, 2013) and self-reported professional development focus (Scriffignano, 2011). The positive link between learning or mastery goal orientation and coaching outcomes is consistent with the underlying assumption in coaching that individuals have the ability to change and achieve their goals (Ennis, Otto, Goodman, & Stern, 2012). A learning or mastery goal orientation indicates that a coachee is more likely to hold the belief that they are able to change, this belief will then influence the individual's focus on their goal, likelihood to seek challenging goals and persistence towards desired results, even in the face of failure.

Coachee's goal orientation was one of the variables we investigated in our field experiment mentioned in Chapter 4 (Jones, Woods, & Zhou, 2019). In this study, we used a trichotomous framework to measure goal orientation: mastery, approach, and avoid goals. As before, approach goals (like performance goals) are focused on attaining competence in relation to others and mastery goals are concerned with competence or mastery of a task. In this framework, avoid goals are focused on avoiding incompetence in comparison to others. (Elliot, 1999). Theory suggests that while all types of goals direct employees towards successful behaviour, they do so in different ways (Ferris et al., 2011). Ferris et al. (2011) suggest that self-regulatory resources focus an individuals' behaviours towards achieving their goals and therefore improving job performance. However, the nature of the goal (either approach or avoid) places different demands on these self-regulatory resources. For example, approach goals involve the individual utilizing their self-regulatory resources to achieve that goal, whereas avoid goals involves the individual utilizing their self-regulatory resources to block every path that may lead to failure (Schwarz, 1990). Avoid goal orientation has also been shown to interfere with the cognitive and motivational mechanisms that promote learning by increasing anxiety and fear of failure (Middleton & Midgley, 1997).

In our field experiment, we found that there was a positive interactive effect between coaching and avoid goal orientation. This meant that while coachees with all types of goal orientation benefitted from coaching, coachees high in avoid goal orientation benefitted the most. To explain this finding, we proposed that the intrapersonal focus of learning through the reflection in coaching allows individuals high on avoid goal orientation to effectively explore and extend their goals beyond the avoidance of failure and consequently enable the greater application of self-regulatory resources to goal achievement behaviours. Limiting goals to those that are directed to the avoidance of failure (rather than competence or mastery) means that individuals with a high avoid goal orientation tend to be oriented towards failure, threats, and losses rather than success, opportunities, or gains. For example, research by Neff, Hsieh, and Dejitterat (2005) found that self-compassion was negatively associated with avoid goal orientations, and therefore, individuals high in avoid goal orientation tended to demonstrate less self-compassion. A further challenge related to this is that individuals who struggle to demonstrate self-compassion may be inclined to ruminate rather than reflect. Reflection can be described as self-attentiveness that is motivated by curiosity or an epistemic interest in the self (Trapnell & Campbell, 1999), whereas rumination can be described as self-attentiveness that is motivated by perceived threats, losses, or injustices to the self and is associated with negative outcomes such as higher stress and reduced sleep quality (Cropley, Rydstedt, Devereux, & Middleton, 2015). Evidence from the coaching literature indicates that an important outcome from coaching is increased self-efficacy or self-belief (Baron & Morin, 2009, 2010; Grant, 2014; Libri & Kemp, 2006; Tooth, Nielsen, & Armstrong, 2013). Therefore, as a result of receiving coaching, individuals are more likely to have an enhanced sense of their own abilities to achieve their goals. Consequently, those individuals who are high in avoid goal orientation may particularly benefit from working with a coach, as the coach can facilitate learning from reflection, directly address the negative consequence of low self-compassion by exploring the consequence of negative self-talk (Palmer & Szymanska, 2019) and subsequently enhance their belief in their own ability to achieve their goals. It may also be the case that when working with a coach to set goals, individuals who may automatically set avoid goals may be able to reassess these goals to convert them into mastery goals, the achievement of which are more likely to be linked to other positive outcomes. The process of receiving coaching will also foster increased levels of self-belief in relation to their ability to pursue and achieve goals oriented away from failure and towards the achievement of competence or mastery.

Recommendations for practice

With regard to the implications for enhancing the impact of your coaching, the first recommendation is to ensure that when you are working with your coachee to set goals, ensure these goals are mastery goals rather than performance/approach or avoid goals. It can be helpful to explain to coachees why the wording of their goals is important so that they are able to use this information in the future when setting their own goals. Understanding the impact of the type of goals we set ourselves on our performance can help us to maximize the impact of goal-setting on our motivation to change. As a general rule, mastery goals are focused on achieving mastery or assessing achievement against one's own standards of performance, performance or approach goals are measured against others and avoid goals are measured against failures. Therefore, if a coachee wanted to work on their confidence in dealing with a difficult member of their team, they might formulate one of the following three goals:

> I want to stop feeling so anxious when communicating with difficult employees (avoid goal)
> I want to be better than my peers at communicating with difficult employees (approach/performance goal)
> I want to understand how to be a better communicator when dealing with difficult employees (mastery goal)

These slight variations in the way that the goal is worded will influence the nature of the attention and effort the coachee expends in attempting to achieve the goal. By focusing on a mastery goal and therefore understanding how to be a better communicator, not only will the coachee automatically achieve the avoid goal and possibly the approach goal along the way (as once they have a better understanding of how to communicate effectively they are likely to feel less anxious and once they have a better understanding of their communication skills they will be in a position to put this into practice and therefore improve in this respect relative to others), the coachee will likely go beyond achieving these goals by focusing on their own learning and development in relation to this skill.

Coaches can also consider the design of effective coaching relative to the coachee's goal orientation. For example, in our paper, we theorized that coachees high in avoid goal orientation benefitted the most from coaching as they are able to work with a coach, using facilitated reflection, to regulate their attentional and motivational resources in a way that positively influences their performance (Jones et al., 2019). For example, by engaging in effective reflection to enable learning from experience rather than engaging in rumination which may lead to higher levels of anxiety and worry. Therefore, as a coach, it is useful to understand the goal orientation of your coachees before the start of coaching. By gathering data on goal orientation, you will be better informed as to the potential areas of development the coachee may need prior to the coaching conversation. While the coaching conversation would still be led by the requirements of the coachee, this additional information will help to raise the coaches' awareness of potential barriers to behaviour change that you can then support the coachee to overcome. For example, a coachee high in avoid goal orientation may be automatically limiting their potential by formulating goals that fixate on avoiding failure. An example might be 'I do not want to mess up this presentation'. Setting a goal focused on failure first orientates the coachees' attention towards failure. This means that their attention will be geared towards considering what it would feel like to fail, the impact of this failure elsewhere in their role and all the possible ways in which they might fail. Ironically, by orienting their attention towards failure, they have reduced attentional capabilities that can be used to considering how not to fail. A further negative consequence of a focus on failure is that the coachee is automatically limiting their own potential. Even if the coachee achieves their goal, they have simply avoided failure rather than potentially achieving full mastery or competence (i.e. 'I want to learn how to deliver engaging and confident presentations). By orientating a goal in this way, the coachee will free up their attentional resources to focus on the various avenues towards success (i.e. what are all of the different methods and sources that I can use to learn about delivering engaging and confident presentations? What do I need to do to apply this new learning?). Furthermore, the process of focusing on positively oriented goals is likely to reduce feelings of anxiety and rumination that tend to accompany a fixation on failure and the consequent negative impact of this anxiety and rumination (such as higher stress and reduced sleep) which are unlikely to help the coachee to achieve their goal. While measures of goal orientation do exist (i.e. Elliot & Church, 1997), these have been created for research purposes and are therefore not particularly user-friendly in their raw format. An alternative way to assess the goal orientation of your coachee is based on their self-formulated goals. The wording of these goals should indicate whether the individuals are oriented towards mastery or learning, performance in comparison with others or in avoiding failure.

As with the recommendation for coaches, the first recommendation for the leader as a coach is to review the wording of employees' self-set goals to gather information from your team regarding individual goal orientations. It is useful to understand whether your employees have a tendency to set mastery, approach, or avoid goals. Once you have this information, you are able to use this to tailor the focus of your attention, based on the needs of your individual employees. If you have members of your team who are high in avoid goal orientation, as detailed above, the most important recommendation is to work with these individuals so that they are able to reorient their goals away from avoid towards a more optimal form of goal orientation (such as low avoid and high mastery) that is likely to have positive benefits for the individual and the organization. Wang, Wu, Parker, and Griffin (2018) present a study in which they demonstrate how goal orientation can be changed if employees perceive that such a change is desirable and feasible. To test this, Wang et al. (2018) took a sample of 132 MBA students in an Australian university who completed a goal orientation change programme as an optional element of the MBA course. The goal orientation change programme ran over three months and consisted of multiple sessions. The researchers found that after the three-month programme, participants significantly reduced their avoid goal orientation and that this change was particularly noticeable among participants who perceived a high level of support from the programme facilitator. This study suggests that leaders and coaches working with employees should explore with their coachees their goal orientations and discuss with them the fact that goal orientations are malleable and some types of goal orientations are more favourable than others. The leader or coach can then work with the coachee to realign goals to ensure that they are aligned with a mastery or learning goal orientation rather than avoid orientation. Wang et al.'s (2018) findings also have important implications in relation to the role of the supportive relationship in facilitating goal orientation change as they found that a strong supportive relationship from the facilitator was important in changing goal orientation. Therefore, if a coachee wishes to change their goal orientation, a supportive relationship between themselves and the coach or the employee and the leader as a coach is going to be even more important. The importance of a supporting, trusting relationship in coaching is discussed further in Chapter 9.

A further consideration for the leader as a coach is whether the working environment facilitates and rewards an optimal form of goal orientation (i.e. low avoid and high mastery). The working environment can either help or hinder goal orientation change dependent on whether it is one that actively encourages and rewards learning or actively encourages and rewards competition, creating a subsequent fear of failure. I discuss the important role of organizational culture in detail in Section four.

This chapter in summary

- Goal orientation describes the types of goals individuals set. Goals can be classified as either:
  - Approach goals (or performance goals) are focused on attaining competence in relation to others
  - Mastery goals (or learning goals) are concerned with competence or mastery of a task
  - Avoid goals are focused on avoiding incompetence in comparison to others
- Coachees high in avoid goal orientation benefit the most from coaching as the process of coaching is likely to directly address the negative consequences of this goal orientation (i.e. high levels of rumination versus reflection, low self-compassion, and low self-belief). The coach can also work with the coachee to reframe these avoid goals into mastery goals
- Evidence suggests that generally, mastery goals lead to greater improvements in performance, and therefore, it is important that coaches work with coachees to ensure that goals set during coaching are mastery-oriented goals

References

Baron, L., & Morin, L. (2009). The coach-coachee relationship in executive coaching: A field study. *Human Resource Development Quarterly, 20*(1), 85–106. doi:10.1002/hrdq.20009

Baron, L., & Morin, L. (2010). The impact of executive coaching on self-efficacy related to management soft-skills. *Leadership & Organization Development Journal, 31*(1), 18–38. doi:10.1108/01437731011010362

Bell, B. S., & Kozlowski, W. J. (2002). Goal orientation and ability: Interactive effects on self-efficacy, performance, and knowledge. *Journal of Applied Psychology, 87*(3), 497–505. doi:10.1037/0021–9010.87.3.497

Bozer, G., Sarros, J. C., & Santora, J. C. (2013). The role of coachee characteristics in executive coaching for effective sustainability. *Journal of Management Development, 32*(3), 277–294. doi:10.1108/02621711311318319

Button, S. B., Mathieu, J. E., & Zajac, D. (1996). Goal orientation in organizational research: A conceptual and empirical foundation. *Organizational Behavior and Human Decision Processes, 67*(1), 26–48. doi:10.1006/obhd.1996.0063

Cropley, M., Rydstedt, L. W., Devereux, J. J., & Middleton, B. (2015). The relationship between work-related rumination and evening and morning salivary cortisol secretion. *Stress and Health, 31*(2), 150–157. doi: org/10.1002/smi.2538

Dweck, C. (2006). *Mindset: How you can fulfil your potential.* New York: Random House.

Elliot, A. (1999). Approach and avoidance motivation and achievement goals. *Educational Psychologist, 34*(3), 169–189. doi:10.1207/s15326985ep3403_3

Elliot, A. J., & Church, M. A. (1997). A hierarchical model of approach and avoidance achievement motivation. *Journal of Personality and Social Psychology, 72*(1), 218–232.

Ennis, S. A., Otto, J., Goodman, R., & Stern, L. R. (2012). *The executive coaching handbook: Principles and guidelines for a successful coaching partnership*, (5th ed.). Wellesley, MA: The Executive Coaching Forum.

Ferris, D. L., Rosen, C. R., Johnson, R. E., Brown, D. J., Risavy, S. D., & Heller, D. (2011). Approach or avoidance (or both?): Integrating core self-evaluations within an approach/avoidance framework. *Personnel Psychology, 64*, 137–161. doi:10.1111/j.1744-6570.2010.01204.x

Fisher, S. L., & Ford, J. K. (1998). Differential effects of learner effort and goal orientation on two learning outcomes. *Personnel Psychology, 51*(2), 397–420. doi:10.1111/j.1744-6570.1998.tb00731.x

Grant, A. M. (2014). The efficacy of executive coaching in times of organisational change. *Journal of Change Management, 14*(2), 258–280. doi:10.1080/14697017.2013.805159

Hertenstein, E. J. (2001). Goal orientation and practice condition as predictors of training results. *Human Resource Development Quarterly, 12*(4), 403–419. doi:10.1002/hrdq.1005

Jones, R. J., Woods, S. A., & Zhou, Y. (2019). The effects of coachee personality and goal orientation on performance improvement following coaching: A controlled field experiment. *Applied Psychology: An International Review.* https://iaap-journals.onlinelibrary.wiley.com/doi/abs/10.1111/apps.12218

Kozlowski, S. W., Gully, S. M., Brown, K. G., Salas, E., Smith, E. M., & Nason, E. R. (2001). Effects of training goals and goal orientation traits on multidimensional training outcomes and performance adaptability. *Organizational Behavior and Human Decision Processes, 85*(1), 1–31. doi: 10.1006/obhd.2000.2930

Libri, V., & Kemp, T. (2006). Assessing the efficacy of a cognitive behavioural executive coaching programme. *International Coaching Psychology Review, 1*(2), 9–18.

Middleton, M. J., & Midgley, C. (1997). Avoiding the demonstration of lack of ability: An underexplored aspect of goal theory. *Journal of Educational Psychology, 89*(4), 710. doi:10.1037/0022-0663.89.4.710

Neff, K. D., Hsieh, Y. P., & Dejitterat, K. (2005). Self-compassion, achievement goals, and coping with academic failure. *Self and identity, 4*(3), 263–287. doi: org/10.1080/13576500444000317

Palmer, S., & Szymanska, K. (2019). Cognitive behavioural coaching: An integrative approach. In S. Palmer & A. Whybrow (Eds.), *Handbook of coaching psychology: A guide for practitioners.* Oxon, UK: Routledge.

Schwarz, N. (1990). Feelings as information: Information and motivational functions of affective states. In E. T. Higgins & R. M. Sorrentino (Eds.), *Handbook of motivation and cognition: Foundation of social behaviour* (Vol. 2, pp. 527–561). New York: Guilford.

Scriffignano, R. S. (2011). Coaching within organisations: Examining the influence of goal orientation on leaders' professional development. *Coaching: An International Journal of Theory, Research and Practice, 4*(1), 20–31. doi:10.1080/17521882.2010.550898

Tooth, J. A., Nielsen, S., & Armstrong, H. (2013). Coaching effectiveness survey instruments: Taking stock of measuring the immeasurable. *Coaching: An International Journal of Theory, Research and Practice, 6*(2), 137–151. doi:10.1080/1752 1882.2013.802365

Trapnell, P. D., & Campbell, J. D. (1999). Private self-consciousness and the five-factor model of personality: Distinguishing rumination from reflection. *Journal of Personality and Social Psychology, 76*(2), 284. doi:10.1037%2F0022-3514.76.2.284

VandeWalle, D., & Cummings, L. L. (1997). A test of the influence of goal orientation on the feedback-seeking process. *Journal of Applied Psychology, 82*(3), 390–400. doi:10.1037/0021–9010.82.3.390

Wang, Y., Wu, C. H., Parker, S. K., & Griffin, M. A. (2018). Developing goal orientations conducive to learning and performance: An intervention study. *Journal of Occupational and Organizational Psychology, 91*(4), 875–895. doi:10.1111/joop.12227

Chapter 6

Coachee self-efficacy

Self-efficacy is the extent of our belief that we can achieve something or successfully behave or perform in a particular way (Woods & West, 2015). Research on self-efficacy has focused on how individuals' self-judgments of efficacy affect either their acquisition of knowledge and skills or execution of action (Gist & Mitchell, 1992). Findings indicate that individuals higher in self-efficacy have strong beliefs in their task-related capabilities and set more challenging goals than those with lower self-efficacy (Bandura, 1982). Individuals are also more likely to feel committed to their goals if they believe that they can achieve the goals (Woods & West, 2015). Self-efficacy has emerged as a powerful predictor of motivation, engagement, and performance in the realm of learning and development (Choi, Price, & Vinokur, 2003). High perceived self-efficacy as a learner is associated with the investment of effort and superior learning. A lack of self-efficacy has been linked to failure to fully realize individual career potential (Hackett & Betz, 1981).

In the coaching literature, coachee self-efficacy has been investigated as both a predictor of coaching outcomes and an outcome of coaching in its own right. The quality of evidence related to self-efficacy can be rated as relatively high, as the evidence is fairly robust and consistent across studies. However, there is only a moderate level of confidence in relation to the directness of outcome as the majority of outcomes are self-reported at the coachee level rather than from third-party or objective sources. Specifically, coachee self-efficacy has been found to be an important antecedent of affective coaching outcomes as reflected in perceived coaching effectiveness (de Haan, Duckworth, Birch, & Jones, 2013; de Haan, Grant, Burger, & Erikkson, 2016) and improved coachee self-awareness and responsibility (Gegner, 1997). Additionally, coachee self-efficacy has been found to be an antecedent of skill-based outcomes as reflected in improved self-reported job performance (Bozer, Sarros, & Santora, 2013) and transformational leadership (Mackie, 2015). Coachee self-efficacy has also been conceptualized as an affective coaching outcome, meaning that following coaching, coachees experience a higher degree of self-belief (e.g. Baron & Morin, 2009, 2010; Baron, Morin, & Morin, 2011; Dingman, 2004; Finn,

Mason, & Bradley, 2007; Grant, 2014; Grant et al., 2017; Ladegard & Gjerde, 2014; Libri & Kemp, 2006; Moen & Allgood, 2009; Moen & Federici, 2012; Moen & Skaalvik, 2009; Tooth, Nielsen, & Armstrong, 2013).

An example of this is an MSc in Coaching and Behavioural Change dissertation student I supervised, who conducted an interesting piece of research to investigate whether self-coaching is a viable alternative to traditional one-to-one coaching to increase coachee self-efficacy. To test this, Demetriou (2018) conducted a quasi-experiment where 18 participants took part in a self-coaching training programme (the intervention group) and 25 participants were in the control group and therefore received no training. The two-day self-coaching training programme included an introduction to the concept and purpose of self-coaching, the role of powerful questions to enhance awareness, a number of coaching models including the GROW model, and the role of feedback and reflection to monitor progress towards goal achievement. Following the two-day self-coaching workshop, participants were instructed to set between one and three goals that they would work on over the following four weeks. Demetriou (2018) found that there was a significant increase in self-efficacy following the self-coaching programme for the intervention group but not for the control group. This meant that following the self-coaching programme, participants felt an enhanced sense of their own ability to achieve their goals and be successful. These findings support the idea that self-efficacy is malleable and can be increased (Bandura, 1982), and furthermore, coaching is particularly well placed as an intervention to create the right conditions to increase self-efficacy. For example, an aim of coaching is to build coachees' self-awareness and sense of responsibility for change to encourage learning, goal achievement, and, ultimately, performance improvement (Whitmore, 2017). An underlying assumption of this premise is that all individuals have the ability to achieve their goals (Gallwey, 2002). By questioning faulty assumptions, re-examining the reality based on the evidence and promoting insight into personal strengths, coachees' self-efficacy in relation to their goals is indirectly targeted, with the research findings that position post-coaching self-efficacy as an outcome of coaching, supporting this premise (e.g. Baron & Morin, 2010; Ladegard & Gjerde, 2014; Moen & Allgood, 2009).

In addition to being explored as an outcome from coaching, it is also interesting to understand the impact of coachee self-efficacy on coaching outcomes. Dr. Holly Andrews, my colleague, and I investigated the influence of coachee self-efficacy in a controlled field experiment that examined whether one-to-one coaching could significantly enhance the ability of students to successfully secure an internship as part of their Business Studies degree (Andrews & Jones, 2020). A total of 172 participants were coached and compared to a control group of 185 participants who did not receive coaching; however, they were still pursuing an internship. Contrary to some of the earlier findings in relation to coachee self-efficacy, we predicted that while all coachees would benefit from coaching, it would be coachees low in self-efficacy who would benefit the most. We proposed that specific characteristics of the coaching intervention would compensate for and to some degree directly address the consequence of low self-efficacy. First, in the context of the research setting, coachees with low self-efficacy may doubt their ability to successfully secure an internship and be hired by a recruiting organization in the face of fierce competition from other applicants. Through the use of questioning techniques to raise awareness, the coachee is encouraged to ensure that their self-judgments are based on evidence rather than perceptions of competence. A consequence of this is likely to be that those who doubt their ability to secure an internship due to low self-efficacy will experience an increase in their beliefs on their likelihood to be successfully selected as they objectively review their strengths, experiences, and achievements. Second, coachees with low self-efficacy may find it challenging to successfully promote themselves during the selection process, such as when completing an application form or during the interview. By focusing on identifying strengths and how to effectively communicate these during the selection process, including practising or role-playing these skills, coaching will enable those low in self-efficacy to develop the skills required for self-promotion than those high in self-efficacy may find comes more naturally. Finally, coachees with low self-efficacy may also set themselves less challenging goals in terms of the number of applications they make for internships and therefore invest fewer cognitive resources in the selection process. By working with the coach to set selection-related goals, the coach will encourage the coachee to challenge themselves to increase their chances of selection success, therefore encouraging the coachee to set more challenging goals than they may do on their own. Therefore, we suggest that the processes utilized in one-to-one coaching to achieve desired outcomes, interact with self-efficacy to increase motivation, engagement, effort, and allocation of resources to the selection processes. While individuals who are high in self-efficacy will also benefit from these same processes, it is those who are low in self-efficacy who will benefit the most, as these individuals have the greatest developmental needs in these areas. Our findings indicated that while both participants who are high and low in self-efficacy were significantly more likely to secure an internship when coached (versus not coached), the impact of coaching was greatest for those low in self-efficacy and selection success significantly improved in line with the number of coaching sessions for the low self-efficacy group only.

Recommendations for practice

The findings around coachee self-efficacy have positive implications in that they suggest that regardless of whether coachee self-efficacy is high or low at the start of coaching, both groups are likely to benefit. Furthermore, the evidence indicates that self-efficacy is likely to be enhanced as part of the coaching process; therefore, after coaching, coachees are likely to experience greater levels of confidence in their general ability. In terms of specific recommendations for practice, the first step is to understand your coachee's level of self-efficacy. This may be evidenced in the way they describe their own abilities; however, it can also be assessed using a questionnaire such as the one provided in the link in the further resources at the end of this chapter. When coaching an individual who has low self-efficacy, it will be important to directly target this low self-efficacy during the coaching conversation. For example, by enabling the coachee to examine the evidence around their low beliefs in their own ability and realign these to ones which are performance-enhancing rather than performance-inhibiting. For example, a coachee may question their ability to successfully achieve a promotion at work. This self-doubt may then indirectly influence the types of goals that they set themselves; for example, they may be more likely to set less challenging goals as they perceive that there is little point pursuing goals linked to a promotion that they do not believe that they can achieve. They may also experience lower levels of motivation and persistence to pursue these goals. A coach working with a case such as this could explore the reasons for the low self-efficacy in this respect. By working directly on the self-belief first, there will be indirect benefits for the coachee in relation to the types of goals they may set and the pursuit of these goals once self-efficacy is increased. If a coachee is struggling to maintain action towards goal achievement activities, one reason may be that deep down they do not believe in their own ability to achieve these goals. Consequently, it is always essential to explore self-belief as part of the coaching process.

These recommendations regarding the use of coaching techniques to enhance self-efficacy apply equally to the leader as a coach. The advantage for the leader as a coach is that as the leader has frequent day-to-day contact with the coachee, in addition to the actions detailed above, they are also able to provide opportunities that will enable the development of self-efficacy and provide feedback to enhance self-efficacy. By providing opportunities in which the coachee can test out new behaviours at work, take on new challenges and extend their skills, the leader as a coach is able to create conditions within the day-to-day work environment which will enable the coachee to experience situations in which they challenge themselves and experience success. These experiences can then be discussed as part of developmental one-to-one's. Furthermore, the leader as a coach is able to directly observe the behaviour of the coachee and therefore is aptly placed to provide the coachee with a positive feedback on their performance which will further enhance coachee self-efficacy.

RESEARCH IN ACTION: A COACH'S EXPERIENCE

This particular case involves a public sector manager who had recently been transferred to a new post as part of a leadership restructure. The chief executive, who had been in the post about six months, had commissioned a leadership programme which included coaching for the management team. I was engaged as the coach on this programme and the coaching consisted of monthly sessions over six months. The coachee's previous function was in one area, and he had been given a very different area of activity to engage with in his new post, which included IT. The coachee wasn't very happy with the way that the chief executive had cut out the cake and allocated part of it to him. His mindset at the start of the coaching relationship was very much along the lines of: "well, I'm not very good at this... it's going to be a disaster... I'm going to let down my colleagues..." The coachee was in his late 50s and during the initial coaching session, he made clear his intention to start to think about retirement. His attitude was "I've really only got a year to go, if I can coast my way through the year, I get to 60, then I can call it a day". During the initial coaching session, he talked about this unhappiness with the new role and his lack of confidence in understanding the technical aspects of the functions he had been charged with leading. Although there were individuals who were leaders of those specific activities, he felt that he needed to have a detailed understanding of those functions to be able to perform his role effectively. It was his belief that he needed this technical understanding so that he could ask people questions, to hold them to account, and to offer advice, guidance, and support. This belief was based on his leadership experience over the last 30 years where he had been a technical expert and gradually progressed up in that area of technical knowledge. Consequently, he had successfully mentored and developed others, providing expert solutions based on his experience. Now his confidence or his self-efficacy in his capabilities to perform this new role was in question, as he was reliant on his leadership capability and not on his technical expertise, on which he had previously relied upon. This lack of self-efficacy in his ability to effectively perform his new role limited the goals that he was setting himself in this new role – his goal was just to 'coast his way through' his final year of work before retirement.

During the initial coaching sessions, after identifying the underlying issue of a lack of self-efficacy in relation to his new role, one of the approaches I tried was to use affirmation. Therefore, I aimed to help build his self-confidence by reflecting positive statements that he had made about himself during our conversations concerning the variety of issues that he brought to the coaching sessions. I was looking for ways to build his confidence by giving feedback to him such as: "actually you are a good leader". However, where this led us interestingly, and the lesson for me was, the more affirmations that I gave and the more I was encouraging him to see himself in a more confident, capable light, the more the burden of that problem shifted from him to me. I felt that I was carrying the burden, not him. For example, when I was encouraging him, there was a shift in the relationship. I noticed that he started to ask more frequently: "what do you think I could do?" He was looking to me for the solution so that I was then working hard to try and help him. The harder I worked, the more the burden felt as though it was shifting on to me and it wasn't his problem anymore. It was as though he felt that as I was his coach, it was my responsibility to help him to be a better leader. When I reflected on the first couple of coaching sessions during supervision, I realized that actually we were heading in the wrong direction. It was very easy for him to say "what do you think I should do in this situation" and the solutions were potentially ones that I was being invited to give. By changing the dynamic during our sessions, he was encouraging me to motivate him. I realized that we needed to shift this source of motivation so that instead of looking for others to motivate him and provide him with solutions, we needed to work together to identify intrinsically what would motivate him and enable him to identify his own solutions. Ultimately, the affirmation approach never would have addressed his self-confidence issue because he would have always needed someone else to help him solve the issues. The praise and affirmation I provided to bolster his self-confidence would have needed to have been replaced by praise and affirmation from elsewhere when the coaching had ended.

Following this reflection, I made the decision to change from this affirmation approach to a mix of cognitive-behavioural and motivational interviewing. I was very much moving away from: "It sounds as though that is working out really well.... You're doing a really good job... what could you learn from that.... what could you apply to new contexts..." type of questions, to an approach where we explored his responsibility for coming up with his own solutions and how he could take this forward using a motivational interviewing based approach. The focus becomes concerned with developing his intrinsic motivation. In particular, working with him to understand his values, what was important to him, and how a focus on fulfilling these values could help to motivate him. This focus meant that he could shift his attention away from his perceived gaps in expertise towards a focus on fulfilling these motivational values.

(Continued)

We identified during our coaching conversation that one of the things that he placed importance on was what other people thought of him and he wanted to make sure that when he stepped out of the organization, people were not going to say "gosh, glad to get rid of that old git, he didn't do anything for the last year that he was here, he was just serving out his time" and instead for people to say "well, do you know he kept going to the end, he's a real inspiration" or "wow, he really committed himself to this role and I have really gained a lot from what he was able to do here". In his last year before retirement, deep down, he wanted to leave a legacy. His fear was that because of the change of role, he would not be able to do this, which was adversely affecting his experience at work. We then started to explore what this legacy would look like and identified that this would consist of helping to develop his team. Through our conversation, he identified the opportunity he had to help his team to grow in their leadership capability and he began to see what he could offer. He identified that while he wasn't going to be a tech expert, he didn't need to as he could rely on his team to do this. Instead, what he could do was to help his team to develop their leadership capability, particularly using a coaching style. He realized that he could build his 'technical' leadership and people development skills, with a solid foundation based on what he already knew from over 30 years of successful people management experience.

The outcome of the coaching process when we had finished the piece of work together was that he had committed that he was going to carry on rather than to retire. In the end, he could see what he could offer to the team. He realized that even though he moved into a very different role, he could use his leadership expertise and focus on helping others to develop. The reframing of the nature of leadership helped him to recognize his strengths and to grow in confidence in his ability to be able to take on this particular role. This ultimately meant that he also reframed the value that he put on himself. He had previously seen himself as a technical expert, attributing his technical expertise as the reason for his career success to-date. By identifying his underlying values and motivations (to leave a legacy at work by developing others), he was able to understand the strengths that he could bring to fulfilling these values and consequently realized that he had more to offer. He could draw on his wisdom and experience of being a leader rather than his wisdom and knowledge of being a technical expert. One of the consequences of this process was that he experienced a boost in his self-efficacy which had far-reaching positive effects.

For details of the coaches who were interviewed for the 'research in action' vignettes, see page 191.

Resources

Online self-efficacy questionnaire: https://www.excelatlife.com/questionnaires/self-efficacy.htm

This chapter in summary

- Self-efficacy is the extent of our belief that we can achieve something or successfully behave or perform in a particular way
- Coachees who are both high and low in self-efficacy are likely to experience positive outcomes from coaching; however, coaching can be particularly beneficial to those low in self-efficacy as it can enable the coachee to directly examine and realign beliefs that lead to low self-efficacy
- Coachees who are low in self-efficacy directly target self-efficacy by examining the evidence underpinning this self-belief and realigning performance-inhibiting thoughts into performance-enhancing thoughts
- The leader as a coach can develop employee self-efficacy by providing opportunities to practise new skills and providing positive feedback on performance.

References

Andrews, H., & Jones, R. J. (2020). Can one-to-one coaching improve selection success and who benefits most? The role of candidate generalized self-efficacy. *Unpublished manuscript.*

Bandura, A. (1982). Self-efficacy mechanism in human agency. *American Psychologist, 37*(2), 122–147. doi:10.1037/0003–066X.37.2.122

Baron, L., & Morin, L. (2009). The coach-coachee relationship in executive coaching: A field study. *Human Resource Development Quarterly, 20*(1), 85–106. doi:10.1002/hrdq.20009

Baron, L., & Morin, L. (2010). The impact of executive coaching on self-efficacy related to management soft-skills. *Leadership & Organization Development Journal, 31*(1), 18–38. doi:10.1108/01437731011010362

Baron, L., Morin, L., & Morin, D. (2011). Executive coaching: The effect of working alliance discrepancy on the development of coachees' self-efficacy. *Journal of Management Development, 30*(9), 847–864. doi:10.1108/02621711111164330

Bozer, G., Sarros, J. C., & Santora, J. C. (2013). The role of coachee characteristics in executive coaching for effective sustainability. *Journal of Management Development, 32*(3), 277–294. doi:10.1108/02621711311318319

Choi, J. N., Price, R. H., & Vinokur, A. D. (2003). Self-efficacy changes in groups: Effects of diversity, leadership, and group climate. *Journal of Organizational Behaviour, 24*(4), 357–372. doi:10.1002/job.195

de Haan, E., Duckworth, A., Birch, D., & Jones, C. (2013). Executive coaching outcome research: The predictive value of common factors such as relationship, personality match and self-efficacy. *Consulting Psychology Journal: Practice and Research, 65*(1), 40–57. doi:10.1037/a0031635

de Haan, E., Grant, A. M., Burger, Y., & Eriksson, P. O. (2016). A large-scale study of executive and workplace coaching: The relative contributions of relationship, personality match, and self-efficacy. *Consulting Psychology Journal: Practice and Research, 68*(3), 189–207. doi:10.1037/cpb0000058

Demetriou, J. (2018). *The power of self-coaching: A quasi-experimental study on the impact of self-coaching.* Unpublished master's thesis. Henley Business School. Oxfordshire, UK.

Dingman, M. E. (2004). *The effects of executive coaching on job-related attitudes.* Doctoral Dissertation. Regent University. Virginia Beach, Virginia.

Finn, F. A., Mason, C. M., & Bradley, L. M. (2007). *Doing well with executive coaching: Psychological and behavioral impacts.* Paper presented at the Academy of Management Annual Meeting Proceedings. Philadelphia, Pennsylvania.

Gallwey, W. T. (2002). *The inner game of work: Overcoming mental obstacles for maximum performance.* London, UK: Texere.

Gegner, C. (1997). *Coaching: Theory and practice.* Unpublished master's thesis. University of California. San Francisco.

Gist, M. E., & Mitchell, T. R. (1992). Self-efficacy: A theoretical analysis of its determinants and malleability. *Academy of Management review, 17*(2), 183–211.

Grant, A. M. (2014). The efficacy of executive coaching in times of organisational change. *Journal of Change Management, 14*(2), 258–280. doi:10.1080/14697017.2013.805159

Grant, A. M., Studholme, I., Verma, R., Kirkwood, L., Paton, B., & O'Connor, S. (2017). The impact of leadership coaching in an Australian healthcare setting. *Journal of Health Organization and Management, 31*(2), 237–252. doi:10.1108/JHOM-09-2016-0187

Hackett, G., & Betz, N. E. (1981). A self-efficacy approach to the career development of women. *Journal of Vocational Behavior, 18*(3), 326–339. doi:10.1016/0001-8791(81)90019-1

Ladegard, G., & Gjerde, S. (2014). Leadership coaching, leader role-efficacy, and trust in subordinates: A mixed methods study assessing leadership coaching as a leadership development tool. *The Leadership Quarterly, 25*(4), 631–646. doi:10.1016/j.leaqua.2014.02.002

Libri, V., & Kemp, T. (2006). Assessing the efficacy of a cognitive behavioural executive coaching programme. *International Coaching Psychology Review, 1*(2), 9–18.

Mackie, D. (2015). The effects of coachee readiness and core self-evaluations on leadership coaching outcomes: A controlled trial. *Coaching: An International Journal of Theory, Research and Practice, 8*(2), 120–136. doi:10.1080/17521882.2015.1019532

Moen, F., & Allgood, E. (2009). Coaching and the effect on self-efficacy. *Organization Development Journal, 27*(4), 69–82.

Moen, F., & Federici, R. A. (2012). The effect from external executive coaching. *Coaching: An International Journal of Theory, Research and Practice, 5*(2), 113–131. doi:10.1080/17521882.2012.708355

Moen, F., & Skaalvik, E. (2009). The effect from executive coaching on performance psychology. *International Journal of Evidence Based Coaching and Mentoring, 7*(2), 32–49.

Tooth, J. A., Nielsen, S., & Armstrong, H. (2013). Coaching effectiveness survey instruments: Taking stock of measuring the immeasurable. *Coaching: An International Journal of Theory, Research and Practice, 6*(2), 137–151. doi:10.1080/17521882.2013.802365

Whitmore, J. (2017). *Coaching for performance.* London, UK: Nicholas Brealey.

Woods, S. A., & West, M. (2015). *The psychology of work and organizations.* Hampshire, UK: Cengage Learning EMEA.

Chapter 7

Coachee skills

Coachee skills could be considered a new angle from which to understand coaching outcomes, which is as yet relatively under-researched. At the time of writing, Dr. Paul Stokes, Tunde Erdos, and I were developing a research project that will directly examine whether we are able to develop specific skills in coachees, prior to the start of their coaching intervention. Based on Paul's previous research (Stokes, 2018), we are predicting that coachees who are already skilled in a number of key areas will experience positive outcomes from coaching at a faster rate and also be more likely to sustain engagement in the coaching process. This is based on the premise that as coaching is a process led by the coachee, skilled coachees will respond to and engage with particular coaching interventions more positively than others because of the relevant skills they possess. In our research project, we plan to deliver specific interventions prior to coaching to develop these skills to prepare the coachee for coaching. As this is an under-researched area, we need to treat the implications of coachee skills tentatively until further findings validate these predications; however, as with many other aspects of the coaching evidence-base, we can look to the wider literature to translate these findings into the coaching context. In terms of coachee skills, I will explore two specific skills in this chapter: reflexivity and the use of creative language.

Reflexivity

Reflexivity describes the ability of the coachee to be willing and able to examine their own thinking and behaviour, analyse patterns and issues that arise from this examination, and to be willing and able to put in place strategies for changing their thinking and behaviour. Reflection and reflexivity have their roots in the work of Dewey's (1933) approach to reflective practice and more recently in the work of Schon (1983, 1991). Like coaching itself, these approaches emphasize the importance of self-awareness and taking action on reflection. Reflective practice emphasizes the agency of the individual in making sense of their own experience and the recognition of some process skill on the part of the coachee in accepting and being able to utilize the help of the coach to take action.

As mentioned in Section one, enabling behavioural change through raising awareness and reflection is a defining feature of coaching. How reflection enables behavioural change in coaching is dealt with in detail in Chapter 9; however, in this section, I would like to draw attention to the role the coachee plays in learning from reflection. Reflexivity is a skill that can be developed, and individuals vary a great deal in their levels of self-awareness (Bolton, 2018). Therefore, the degree to which the coachee can learn from the reflective components of the coaching experience is likely to vary depending on the level of skill in reflexivity. Experiential learning theory assumes that individuals can construct a rich understanding of their own experiences and then generalize the lessons of those experiences to improve their performance (Kolb, 1984). Yet, leadership development research is replete with examples where individuals struggle to learn from experience or even learn the wrong lessons (Vince, 1998). One of the limitations of Kolb's experiential learning cycle is the assumption that individuals are open to experience and not defended against it. People's behaviour emerges out of deeply held patterns and unconscious processes, which both encourage and discourage learning from experience. Therefore, to learn from our experiences, we must find ways of working with our underlying or unconscious processes, in particular, our defence mechanisms. One of the reasons why individuals vary in their ability to reflect on experience is likely to be because some individuals have stronger defences to protect themselves against these experiences than others.

When reflecting in coaching, the coachee is generally using a narrative: a spoken account that describes or explains an event, bringing together different elements to make a whole, and therefore making sense out of these events (Bolton, 2018). However, this is not automatically a reflective process. For example, if the coachee merely recounts an unplotted (non-developmental) list of events (I did this, I did that and then I did...), then the account would develop no meaning and consequently would not enable learning. For learning to take place, we must focus a critical lens on our experience, asking critical questions. The role of the coach is to provide this critical lens to facilitate the learning through the reflective narrative; however, some coachees will automatically provide a critically reflective narrative during the coaching session, consequently enabling deeper learning and insight to occur at a faster pace, whereas other coachees may start with a much more descriptive account of events, requiring a greater degree of probing questions and interventions from the coach to enable the narrative to move from one that is purely descriptive to one that is reflective and consequently facilitative to learning.

In addition to coachee skill in providing a reflective rather than descriptive narrative, coachees are also likely to differ in the degree to which they are defended against potentially uncomfortable, deeply held feelings such as humiliation, remorse, doubt, and shame. If events in our lives lead us to experience these emotions, to protect ourselves, we reframe our thinking around these experiences or avoid thinking about them in detail. Steiner (2011) argues that humiliation in particular, of all the human emotions, seems to have something especially unbearable about it, which consequently demands urgent relief. Steiner suggests that the importance of feelings of humiliation is shown in the number of words associated with it in the English language, and that there are subtle distinctions along the spectrum when humiliation is experienced, with discomfort generally lessening as we move from humiliation through shame to embarrassment. However 'even those who suffer from shyness, blushing, and modesty, seem to seek relief with great urgency' (Steiner, 2011, p. 27). I am sure that most readers will easily be able to recall an embarrassing experience at some point in your life – these experiences stick with us. If we turn the mirror on ourselves and the reality of these experiences are revealed through self-reflection, the level of vulnerability to potential humiliation and shame may be unbearable or too uncomfortable to tolerate. This may involve confronting beliefs that are deeply rooted and painful to expose and so they remain well hidden within the individual's unconsciousness. This explains why the events that we perhaps need to reflect on the most can also be those in which the reflection is most challenging. The ability to allow oneself to be exposed to uncomfortable or painful reflections will vary from coachee to coachee. Some coachees will be more open, willing, and able to engage in this level of self-reflection, whereas others will find it more difficult. In the same way, the degree to which the coachee's narrative may be reflective versus descriptive, the depth of reflective content will vary significantly. Some coachees will require relatively minor input from the coach to generate further insight, whereas other coachees who are more defended against their reflections will take longer to achieve the same level of insight. These differences in the coachees skill in reflective capability will inevitably impact on the outcomes coaching is likely to generate and the speed in which these outcomes are likely to be achieved.

RESEARCH IN ACTION: A COACH'S EXPERIENCE

One of the techniques that I often use with coachees is chair work. With this technique, you imagine yourself talking to somebody else; however, you actually talk to this other person (an empty chair) and then you sit in the empty chair and you become that other person, hearing yourself. Then you move into the observer position, looking at the two people, hearing what was said, hearing how it has landed, you reflect on what that tells you about the approach that you were planning on taking. It's potentially hugely transformative experience.

(Continued)

An example of this was with a coachee who was a director in a big organization and he was going to have a half a day meeting with his new boss who was based in the states. At this meeting, he would have the opportunity to talk with his boss about how he saw himself in the role and he would be able to ask his boss what he wanted. This was his opportunity to make it work. One complicating factor was that my coachee, let's call him Bill, had worked for the boss before in the same organization and it hadn't gone particularly well; there were difficulties in the communication between the two of them. The boss had not selected Bill, and Bill had been foisted upon him so it was quite complicated. I suggested to my coachee that we try a piece of chair work. "You can say what you think you might say to your boss and we can see how you receive that and see how you might respond to it." He was up for this approach. So we embarked on this exercise, and I just asked him "what do you want to say to your boss" and he talked for a while about how he wanted to do whatever his boss needed and the way that he was talking was actually quite powerful. Then he changed chairs and he was his boss. I said, "well you've just heard everything that Bill has to say to you, how do you feel about it and what do you want to say back?" Bill went a little bit quiet, and he did make a response but I had the sense that his heart wasn't in it with the response that he was making. Then I said, "so now would you like to go to the observer position where you can see yourself and your boss talking and you can just see what you make of that". So he went and he stood for quite a while. He stood and he looked at these two chairs, and after a while, he said, "no that doesn't work. That doesn't work does it?" So I said, "well do you just want to get back into your chair and try again. What would you say to your boss now based on what you've just observed?" He went back and his presentation of himself had changed completely. It was actually very exciting to observe the change, and there was no way you could have predicted it. He was saying what he really felt, that he felt unsure about his job, that he wasn't sure about how to do it, and that he needed guidance from his boss. It was a much more genuine approach. The thing that was really interesting, that he commented on after the exercise, was the way that he reflected and that's because he understood about reflection. He was really open for reflecting at quite a deep level about what was going on, and he could use that reflection to then implement what he had got from the exercise very quickly because he went straight into doing the exercise again. He told me after that what he saw when he was in the observer role was just incredible, it was so useful to him. I would say that his reflective ability was key to that insight.

A contrasting example was a coachee I had worked with a long time before, years before this encounter. He contacted me again and said that he wanted to come back and do a bit more work with me. He arrived really distressed because he was being forced to retire when he didn't want to. He was obviously experiencing this as a massive rejection by his boss, who he felt extremely betrayed by. My coachee had lots and lots of good reasons why he shouldn't be required to retire which he put in front of me. He said he had tried talking to his boss and had tried explaining to him why he can make an exception. So far this approach had not worked; however, my coachee said that he had one final chance to persuade his boss to change his mind. He had a trip with his boss and on this trip, he was going to be able to have his boss's ear for a period of time and then he would really have the opportunity to present his case. Through our discussion, it became apparent that he had already presented his case on numerous occasions with no success. So I said to him, would you just like to take the opportunity to sit in your boss's chair and perhaps get an insight into the pressures that he's under and the things that he is feeling and get an understanding as to why he might be resistant? The coachee agreed.

However, he wasn't able to take his boss's perspective at all. He wasn't comfortable putting himself in his boss's position, he couldn't sit with it. He talked all of the time. He talked a lot when he was in his own chair, putting his case, restating his arguments. When he shifted to his boss's chair, he just produced all the arguments that he had already stated, nothing new arose. He just wasn't reflecting at all. Although I did invite him to take the observer position, which he did, the whole exercise was a complete failure. I don't want to say that he doesn't have the reflective capability, because he may well have, but at that point in his life, he didn't want to exercise reflective capability, because he was simply too hurt. He didn't actually complete the task in the way that it was intended, he just reiterated what he had already said: it was almost like a role play times three.

We can talk very glibly in coaching about the importance of reflecting and the importance of reflective practice; however, it is not straightforward, and I think that's one of the reasons why people say coaching just doesn't work for me. In this case, we don't know if my coachee was just too close to the pain to be able to be reflective or he might have just been a very non-reflective person. Reflection is really, really hard and often when we read about reflection, that isn't acknowledged. Some people might never get there. I don't think that is because they can't; perhaps, for different reasons, they don't want to.

For details of the coaches who were interviewed for the 'research in action' vignettes, see page 191.

Recommendations for practice

A practical implication in relation to coachee reflectivity is that it may be helpful to encourage coachees to consider their ability to reflect prior to the start of the coaching intervention and potentially engage in some 'pre-work' activities to develop this skill. For example, there are a number of specific methods that can be used to enable reflection. The most common of these is reflective writing. The activity of writing with the intention of getting a new perspective can facilitate reflective thinking. Reflective writing methods include a diary, writing an unsent letter to your past or future self or a significant other or story-telling. In addition to written methods of reflection, alternatives include creating an audio or video diary. The key to engaging in reflection is to find the method that works best for the individual. Coaches could raise awareness with the coachee on the importance of reflection for behavioural change in coaching and encourage coachees to complete a series of reflective exercises prior to the start of coaching and also potentially as 'homework' between the coaching session. In addition, by raising the coachees' awareness of the elements of reflection and why it is important, coaches can empower coachees to take responsibility for developing this skill further. For example, there are a number of characteristics of critical reflection that apply to all methods or techniques of reflecting to ensure that the experience enables learning to take place:

- First, reflection is about changing perspective. Therefore, our method of reflection should allow us to either analyse our experiences either in detail or allow us to consider the bigger picture.
- Second, we might find it helpful to reflect on a significant, one-off incident or challenge, a recurrent situation, or an issue or theme where patterns in our responses can be observed.
- Finally, reflection should focus on our own role rather than hypothesizing on the motives of others.

These suggestions apply equally to the leader as a coach. While, as a leader, it is unlikely that you will work at the same deep level as an independent coach, the ability to encourage learning from reflection within your employees is just as important. Therefore, raising awareness of reflection, how to reflect, and providing time within the workday to engage in reflective practice are important actions you can take as a leader to facilitate reflective skill development. Reflection is a skill that, with practice, can be developed and strengthened like any other skill. There are also many great books written on the subject of reflection and how to be reflective, I have provided some recommendations for those who would like to read more on this subject in the further resources section at the end of this chapter. Of course, reading more on the subject is another great method of strengthening the skill of reflecting!

Use of creative language

As a talking intervention, coaching relies on the ability of the coach and coachee to communicate with one another; therefore, language becomes a tool within the coaching process. How we use language and in particular the use of creative language is frequently discussed in the literature and in coach training programmes, from the perspective of the coach – i.e. how can the coach use creative language to enable behavioural change? However, what about the coachee? Coaching is a two-way process; therefore, the coachee's openness and ability to use creative language should also be considered as an important factor that may influence the effectiveness of the coaching process.

One established way in which creative language as a skill is used in coaching is through clean language (Grove & Panzer, 1989). Clean language is a technique that helps coachees discover and elicit symbols and metaphors without any content introduced to them by the coach (Madsen, 2016). The argument provided by proponents of clean language in coaching is that coachees naturally describe their issues in metaphor and the more that coaches use clean language (i.e. use the exact words and even non-verbal expressions used by the coachee), the more our coachees are able to use and develop their own metaphors to explore their world (Thomson, 2013). The use of clean language in coaching, therefore, links closely to the use of metaphor: the process of understanding and experiencing one kind of thing in terms of another. It is suggested that playing with a metaphor can illuminate our thinking as we approach the topic indirectly, we focus upon the metaphorical object, which can be far less personally emotive than what it stands for (Bolton, 2018). The metaphors we use can highlight uncritically assumed views, values, and principles. Thompson (2013) suggests that when a coachee is helped to explore their metaphors, they often go on to develop other metaphors that provide the solution to their problem or challenge. Therefore, the metaphor is not only symbolic of the problem, but it also contains pointers or clues to the solution.

However, much of what has been written about the use of language in coaching, fails to consider differences in the coachees use of language. Clearly, there are individual differences in our ability to use language to communicate. Some individuals are highly eloquent, easily grasping rich, descriptive language to paint a clear picture of the experience they wish to describe. Others consistently struggle to put into words what they are thinking and feeling inside, becoming frustrated as their message becomes lost in translation. This point has implications for working with clean language. If a coachee uses very limited, stilted, and unclear language during the coaching conversation, unable to effectively find the words they seek to convey the message to the coach, working with the coachee's own words, using clean language may have a limited effect on generating additional insight and awareness on the issue in hand. In addition to ability to use language to communicate, coachees will also vary in how comfortable they feel working with metaphors. Some coachees will automatically provide a wide range of metaphors to illustrate their reflections, whereas others will use these less frequently. For example, in a study of eight executives who had received coaching, Emson (2016) concluded that individuals have significantly different propensities to use metaphor both in their unconscious internal communication and consciously in their reflection. Coachees will also vary in their openness to the manipulation of these metaphors by the coach. Some coachees may feel resistant to the coach using the metaphors they have provided, whereas others will feel quite comfortable to work and build on these metaphors. All of these factors combined are likely to influence not only the types of interventions that the coach may go on to select to use during the coaching intervention but also the types of outcomes and speed in which these outcomes are experienced. A coachee who uses rich, eloquent language to clearly paint a picture for the coach, who is comfortable working with metaphors, providing a number of their own metaphors during the conversation and is open to working with and expanding these metaphors is likely to experience greater levels of insight during these coaching conversations at a greater pace.

Recommendations for practice

In terms of recommendations for coaches wishing to maximize the impact of their coaching, I propose that coaches will need to be flexible in considering which coaching intervention will work best for which coachee. For example, coachees who struggle to find the right words to communicate during coaching may benefit from other interventions such as using reflective writing, constellation work, or drawing. As with many of the other areas discussed in this chapter, raising awareness prior to coaching may also be helpful. For example, by providing clear guidance on what to expect during coaching in terms of the nature of the conversation and other interventions that will be used may help coachees to prepare for the session by considering the type of language they might use to communicate to the coach. Although not an approach generally adopted in coaching, when working with a coachee who struggles to articulate their thoughts on the spot during coaching, the coach could consider sharing some prompts for the coachee to consider in advance of the coaching session.

For the leader as coach, you are likely to be in the fortunate position that you know your employees well and therefore will already be aware of those who have a natural aptitude in their use of language and metaphor and those who may struggle a little in these areas. This will enable you to consider the different approaches that you might use to the best effect with individual members of your team.

The key message here is that the strength of coaching is the ability to tailor the intervention to the individual coachee; therefore, my argument is that not all coachees will benefit equally from all interventions. Instead, consider the strengths and preferences of your coachee and work with those to find the most effective intervention for them. Clean language may be a powerful tool; however, it does not mean that it will be equally powerful for all coachees.

Resources

Bolton, G. (2018). *Reflective practice: Writing and professional development*. London, UK: SAGE.

> This text explains why reflection is essential, where to start and how to develop your reflection skills, covers the theory behind reflective practice to give the context as to why it is important. Covers different methods to gain different perspectives such as the use of metaphor, reflective writing and team reflection. A good general book that covers reflective practice in detail.

Kahneman, D., & Egan, P. (2011). *Thinking, fast and slow*. New York: Farrar, Straus and Giroux.

> This text provides an alternative way to think about reflection. The author classifies two different ways of thinking (fast and slow) and provides a compelling argument as to why we need more slow thinking in our lives.

This chapter in summary

- Coachees will vary in their ability to engage in reflection which will consequently impact on the outcome of coaching.
  - Coachees can be encouraged to develop their reflective skills prior to the start of coaching (and ongoing between sessions) by engaging in practices such as reflective writing
  - Coaches can raise coachee awareness of the elements or process of reflection to enhance the depth of coachee reflective practice
- Coachees will vary in their ability to express their thoughts, emotions, and experiences during their coaching conversation and their ability and willingness to work with metaphor
  - Tailor your approach based on the needs of your coachee. For coachees who struggle to articulate themselves, consider using tools and techniques less reliant on language
  - Coachees who struggle to articulate themselves clearly may benefit from having some prompts regarding the anticipated focus of the coaching session in advance. This will allow them to formulate their thoughts into a format they can communicate to someone else prior to the coaching meeting.

References

Bolton, G. (2018). *Reflective practice: Writing and professional development*. London, UK: SAGE.

Dewey, J. (1933). *How we think: A restatement of the relation of reflective thinking to the educative process*. Boston, MA: D.C. Heath.

Emson, N. (2016). Exploring metaphor use and its insight into sense making with executive coaching clients. *International Journal of Evidence-Based Coaching and Mentoring, 10*, 59–75.

Grove, D. J., & Panzer, B. I. (1989). *Resolving traumatic memories: Metaphors and symbols in psychotherapy*. New York: Irvington.

Kolb, D. A. (1984). *Experiential learning: Experience as the source of learning and development*. Upper Saddle River, NJ: Prentice-Hall.

Madsen, M. W. (2016). Cognitive metaphor theory and the metaphysics of immediacy. *Cognitive Science, 40*(4), 881–908.

Schon, D. A. (1983). *Reflective practitioner: How professionals think in action*. New York: Basic Books.

Schon, D. A. (1991). *The reflective turn: Case studies in and on educational practice*. New York: Teacher's College Press.

Steiner, J. (2011). *Seeing and being seen: Emerging from a psychic retreat*. Oxon, UK: Routledge.

Stokes, P. (2018). The skilled coachee. In B. Garvey, P. Stokes, & D. Megginson (Eds.), *Coaching and mentoring: Theory and practice*. London, UK: SAGE Publications.

Thomson, B. (2013). *Non-directive coaching: Attitudes, approaches and applications*. Northwich, UK: Critical Publishing.

Vince, R. (1998). Behind and beyond Kolb's Learning Cycle. *Journal of Management Education, 3*, 304–319.

Section Three

The coaching process

Given the number of books that have been published that focus on the content of this chapter – the coaching process – and the fact that generally, coach education concentrates on understanding different tools, techniques, and approaches in coaching, I am going to start this section with a potentially controversial claim: there is minimal evidence to suggest that there is any difference in the impact of these coaching approaches, tools, and techniques on the outcomes from coaching. Let us first look at the minimal evidence that has been conducted in this respect.

Grant and colleagues (Braunstein & Grant, 2016; Grant, 2012; Grant & Gerrard, 2020; Grant & O'Connor, 2010) have sought to compare the relative effectiveness of solution-focused coaching questions compared to problem-focused coaching questions in a series of experimental studies. While these studies do not purport to replicate actual coaching conditions (they are all conducted in the space of a one-hour session in which participants answer a series of either solution-focused or problem-focused questions in relation to a personal problem they would like to address), they do offer some initial evidence that solution-focused questions (compared to problem-focused questions) tend to have greater effects on outcomes such as increasing positive affect or mood, increasing self-efficacy, and perceived goal progression and decreasing negative affect or mood. However, it should be noted that these studies are all conducted on student samples, and data is collected at both time one (the pre-measure) and time two (the post-intervention measure) in the space of one hour. These conditions mean that the intervention used in these studies have little comparability to a real-life coaching intervention.

Sun et al. (2013) sought to compare the impact of coaching approaches on the relationship between coach and coachee. In this study, 39 support staff working within mental health organizations in Australia attended a three-day training programme on coaching skills and were allocated to either skills or transformational coaching condition. The authors describe skills coaching as directed at improving a coachees' skill or competence, whereas transformational coaching is directed at helping coachees to shift to a higher level of functioning by changing habitual responses to issues (Hawkins & Smith, 2010). The final day of training varied depending on the condition participants were allocated to either focusing on skills or on transformational coaching. The participants then received 12 coaching sessions (one a month for 12 months), provided by an internal coach who coached the participants using either a skills or transformational coaching approach. Sun et al. (2013) hypothesized that participants in the transformational coaching approach would experience a stronger coaching relationship, including high levels of rapport, to enable the discussion of thoughts, feelings, and values. Whereas for participants in the skills coaching, the coaching relationship may be less important as issues discussed tend to be more skills performance-oriented (i.e. specific work-related behaviours) and less focused on personal development or change. Sun et al. (2013) proposed that coachees who participate in skills coaching may also be expected to invest less of 'themselves' in their coaching than those who participated in transformational coaching (Crowe, Oades, Deane, Ciarrochi, & Williams, 2011; Hawkins & Smith, 2010). Sun et al. (2013) found that transformational coaching resulted in a stronger coaching relationship from the perspective of both coaches and coachees, in that, after three or more sessions, rating of the coaching relationship had improved in transformational coaching but not in skills coaching. This is an interesting study that provides an exploration of the role of the coaching relationship in two different types of coaching; however, unfortunately, the authors do not report any detail on coaching outcomes, and therefore, it is not known whether these different approaches and the difference in the coaching relationship had any impact on the achievement of outcomes following coaching.

When we look at these studies in relation to the quality of evidence, the conclusion is not very favourable. For example, neither the series of studies by Grant and colleagues nor the study by Sun et al. (2013) has a clear theoretical underpinning to explain why they anticipate the effects that they predict. In relation to the consistency of evidence, Sun et al.'s (2013) study is the first study investigating this topic; therefore, we are unable to draw any conclusions regarding the consistency of evidence. Grant and colleagues have found relatively consistent results; however, this is not particularly surprising given that the studies reported are in essence a series of replication studies, with very little differences between either the intervention, sample, or measurements across the studies. In relation to the directness of intervention, the directness is very low for the Grant studies as they have isolated one aspect of coaching (the questions) and explored these in a highly controlled experimental setting over the course of one hour only – this intervention, therefore, bears little resemblance to coaching as has been defined in this text and elsewhere. The directness of intervention is also problematic with the Sun et al.'s (2013) study, as while the coaching (either skills or transformational) is more recognizable as 'coaching', the focus of the coaching for all participants was as part of a wider programme to learn coaching skills themselves; therefore, the context for this coaching intervention is relatively unique. Finally, with regard to the directness of outcome, no outcomes from coaching were measured in the Sun et al.'s (2013) study, instead the purpose was to assess whether there were differences in the depth of the relationship between coach and coachee dependant on the coaching approach. Therefore, we are unable to draw any conclusions regarding the subsequent impact of these differences on outcomes following coaching. With the Grant studies, all of the outcomes assessed were self-reported from the coachees' perspective, which means that we would conclude that these are low quality; ideally, third-party ratings or objective outcomes would also have been assessed. Consequently, we would have to conclude that, to date, very little research has been conducted to investigate whether the coaching approach makes a difference to the outcomes from coaching, and furthermore, the research that has been conducted is low in quality and therefore conclusions drawn from these studies must be tentative.

If we accept that the evidence related to coaching processes is limited, it may be helpful to review the evidence from other disciplines. Frequent comparisons have been drawn from the research evidence in the field of counselling and psychotherapy to coaching. As both counselling and psychotherapy hold many similarities to coaching, particularly in terms of the focus on the one-to-one relationship between the client and the practitioner and the role the practitioner takes as more of a listener than an advisor, these comparisons can provide valuable insights into what might make coaching effective. As practitioners working in the field of coaching, we can benefit from the many decades of research that have been dedicated to exploring what works in counselling and psychotherapy, such as the exploration of the impact of the process, approach, or technique on client outcomes in counselling and psychotherapy.

In his text summarizing the research findings related to the practice of counselling and psychotherapy, which was commissioned by the British Association for Counselling and Psychotherapy, Cooper (2008) highlights that 'there is an overwhelming body of evidence to suggest that there is little difference in how efficacious different psychological therapies are (even though it is evident that the therapists are doing quite different things)' (p. 50). Linked to this point, it has been suggested by Asay and Lambert (1999) that the therapists' approach or model and technique account for just around 15% of the variance in client improvement following psychotherapy. Instead, the largest contributing factor is thought to be client variables, including events occurring in the client's life outside of therapy, which are thought to account for around 40% of the variance in client improvement. Next is the therapeutic relationship which is thought to account for around 30% of the variance and finally the client's expectations or hope around improvement following psychotherapy (otherwise known as the placebo effect) is thought to account for around 15% of variance in improvement.

It is important to be conscious that while we can learn from the counselling and psychotherapy evidence, it is unlikely that all findings will directly translate to coaching, due in part to the differences in the reasons why individuals seek coaching compared to the reasons why individuals seek counselling and psychotherapy. Despite the differences between counselling, psychotherapy, and coaching, it is likely, based on the evidence, that the coaching process is not one of the biggest contributing factors to positive outcomes following coaching.

If, therefore, we are arguing that the coaching process is likely to make little difference to the outcomes from coaching, what is the focus of the chapters in this section? While I propose that coaching approaches, tools, and techniques all have a similar impact on coaching outcomes, this is because they all serve a similar purpose. It is this purpose that is the focus of these chapters. In my view, all coaching approaches, tools, and techniques facilitate the application of three core processes. It is these three core processes that impact how effective coaching is, and, therefore, a coach can ensure they engage with these three core processes during their coaching to make their coaching as effective as possible. These core processes are the use of goal-setting, enabling learning through reflection, and planning for action. It is these core processes that influence the impact of coaching regardless of which specific tool or technique you use in coaching, as long as they are facilitating the application of these processes. It is these processes that will make a difference, not the tool or technique or framework for structuring the format of the questions, or even the type of questions that are asked. As outlined in the previous section on the coachee, your coachee will have preferences that might influence how likely they are to engage positively with these tools and techniques, and this may have an influence on the impact of coaching, this is why it is so important to understand your coachee and tailor your approach appropriately. However, this is as far, in my view, as the difference in this impact goes.

The chapters in this section are focused on these three processes: goal-setting (Chapter 8), enabling learning through reflection (Chapter 9), and planning for action (Chapter 10). In each chapter, I will explain what we know about how this process is likely to influence the effectiveness of coaching based on the evidence and then provide some specific recommendations for your own practice.

References

Asay, T. P., & Lambert, M. J. (1999). The empirical case for the common factors in therapy: Quantitative findings. In M. A. Hubble, B. L. Duncan, & S. D. Miller (Eds.), *The heart and soul of change: What works in therapy,* (pp. 23–55). Washington, DC: American Psychological Association.

Braunstein, K., & Grant, A. M. (2016). Approaching solutions or avoiding problems? The differential effects of approach and avoidance goals with solution-focused and problem-focused coaching questions. *Coaching: An International Journal of Theory, Research and Practice, 9*(2), 93–109.

Cooper, M. (2008). *Essential research findings in counselling and psychotherapy: The facts are friendly.* London, UK: SAGE Publications.

Crowe, T. P., Oades, L. G., Deane, F. P., Ciarrochi, J., & Williams, V. (2011). Parallel processes in clinical supervision: Implications for coaching mental health practitioners. *International Journal of Evidence-Based Coaching and Mentoring, 9*(2), 56–66.

Grant, A. M. (2012). Making positive change: A randomized study comparing solution-focused vs. problem-focused coaching questions. *Journal of Systemic Therapies, 31*(2), 21–35.

Grant, A. M., & Gerrard, B. (2020). Comparing problem-focused, solution-focused and combined problem-focused/solution-focused coaching approach: Solution-focused coaching questions mitigate the negative impact of dysfunctional attitudes. *Coaching: An International Journal of Theory, Research and Practice, 13*(1), 61–77

Grant, A. M., & O'Connor, S. A. (2010). The differential effects of solution-focused and problem focused coaching questions: A pilot study with implications for practice. *Industrial and Commercial Training, 42*(2), 102–111.

Hawkins, P., & Smith, N. (2010). Transformational coaching. In E. Cox, T. Bachkirova, & D. Clutterbuck (Eds.), *The complete handbook of coaching,* (pp. 231–244). London, UK: Sage.

Sun, B. J., Deane, F., Crowe, T., Andresen, R., Oades, L. G., & Ciarrochi, J. (2013). A preliminary exploration of the working allliance and 'real relationship' in two coaching approaches with mental health workers. *International Coaching Psychology Review, 8*(2), 6–17.

Chapter 8

Goal-setting

It is interesting that as coaches seem to get more experienced, are closer towards becoming what one might consider to be a 'master' coach, they often tend to become a little distant from the importance of goal-setting in coaching. True, that anyone learning about coaching almost certainly starts by learning about the GROW model as outlined originally by Whitmore (2017), with the 'G' in this model forming the goal-setting element. This framework shows us how to frame a coaching conversation, with the discussion of the coachee's goal forming the start point of this discussion. Perhaps then, there is the perception among some, that as goal-setting is used so centrally in this 'beginners' approach to coaching, that once you move beyond being a 'beginner' coach, you don't need to worry so much about goal-setting. However, I am going to present the case in this chapter that as coaches, we should very much worry about goal-setting, regardless of how experienced or advanced we are as coaches. The reason for this is that there are not many aspects of behavioural change that compare to goal-setting in terms of the wealth of evidence that demonstrate how effective it is at generating changes in performance. We know from decades of well-designed, well-executed research, that goal-setting motivates individuals and makes a difference in how they perform. Furthermore, we know a significant amount about the different conditions in goal-setting that influence this motivation and performance change. More than 1,000 empirical studies of the effects of goal-setting consistently show that specific, challenging goals lead to improved performance (Mitchell & Daniels, 2003). However, interestingly, despite the wealth of research on goal-setting generally and the centrality of goals in most coaching approaches, there is virtually no research that directly explores the role of goal-setting in coaching.

In my experience, while many coaches might start with goal-setting as a 'beginner' coach, they actually know very little about creating the right conditions to maximize the impact of this goal-setting. Frustratingly, as I have noted, more experienced coaches often then tend to move on from using goals, perhaps considering them too much of a basic approach to be of concern. In this chapter, I will hopefully convince the reader why it is important to always use goal-setting in coaching (whether that is using the GROW model or any other tool, technique, or approach in coaching). Furthermore, to use goal-setting right, it is far from a beginner or basic technique as there are a number of important conditions or factors that will influence the impact of how effective goal-setting is. Let's start by defining what we mean by goal-setting in the context of coaching.

What is goal-setting?

Setting goals is such a common aspect of our everyday life that it almost seems ridiculous to write this section titled 'what is goal-setting' – surely this is common sense? One aspect of research that gives me a sense of perverse satisfaction is when we conduct research and confirm a finding that people say 'well, duh! that's obvious, it's common sense, what's surprising about that!'[1] The truth is that although something might be common sense or obvious now, that doesn't always mean that this has been the case and goal-setting is one of these areas. Until about 40 years ago, the idea of setting goals did not really exist as a 'thing'. It wasn't until researchers started to investigate the impact of goal-setting on motivation and demonstrated how important setting goals was to performance that the practice infiltrated into our everyday lives and became something which we might consider to be 'obvious'. Even though it is well-known that we need to set goals to achieve goals, many people still don't know enough about how to set the right type of goals and what else we can do to influence the impact of the goals we set, on enabling behavioural change. I explored this a little in Chapter 5 in the context of goal orientation. In that chapter, I detailed how we are naturally oriented towards setting different types of goals and goals that are oriented or focused on achieving mastery are more effective than goals that are oriented towards avoiding failure. However, there is much more that we can understand how to effectively use goal-setting in coaching.

Let us start with a definition. Goals are an explicit standard by which individuals can judge their progress and performance. The key researchers in the field of goal-setting are Locke and Latham. Locke and Latham (2002) describe how specific and challenging goals lead to the highest results and that goals affect performance through specific mechanisms: by directing attention and effort; increasing enthusiasm and persistence and activating the discovery of task-relevant knowledge. Studies consistently demonstrate that goals have a positive impact on performance. For example, Morisano, Hirsh, Peterson, Pihl, and Shore (2010) sought to explore if participation in a formalized, intensive, online, personal goal-setting programme might serve as an effective intervention for struggling university students. A total of 85 students who met the criteria of experiencing academic difficulty and volunteered to participate in the research were randomly allocated to either a goal-setting group or the control group. In the goal-setting group, an online programme led participants through eight steps that facilitated the setting of specific personal goals with detailed strategies for achievement. The control group participated in three different web-based tasks that were deemed to be comparable. First, they completed a series of positive psychology questionnaires (no feedback on the results of these questionnaires was provided to participants). Second, they wrote about some positive past experiences, and finally they completed a career interest inventory and were sent the results after the research was completed. Compared with the control group, students who completed the goal-setting exercise experienced three benefits in the post-intervention semester: increased grades, the higher probability of maintaining a full course load, and reductions in self-reported negative affect or emotion. A benefit of such a large volume of research in respect of goal-setting is that a body of evidence has accumulated to help us to understand why goal-setting has such a positive impact on performance. Next I will explore each of the mechanisms that explain how and why goal-setting positively impacts performance and illustrate how we can engage these mechanisms in coaching.

Goals direct attention and effort

Individuals with specific and challenging goals seem more able to direct their attention and effort towards goal-relevant activities and away from goal-irrelevant activities. We are limited in our capacity to pay attention, with multiple demands being placed on our attention at any single point in time. By selectively paying attention to goal-supporting information (i.e. anything that will help us in the pursuit of achieving our goal), we will remain undistracted by irrelevant stimuli, consequently inhibiting the processing of information related to competing aims. By selectively paying attention, we can guide our goal-directed activities, organize incoming stimuli to maintain a calm state of mind, delay gratification, and tolerate change (Luszczynska, Diehl, Gutiérrez-Dona, Kuusinen, & Schwarzer, 2004). Luszczynska et al. (2004) argue that when individuals are in the phase of goal pursuit, they usually face difficulties in maintaining their action. Focusing their attention on the task at hand and keeping a favourable emotional balance might help to maintain behaviour towards achieving the goal. Individuals need to concentrate even when barriers arise and interferences to attend to other tasks emerge. For example, if a manager sets the goal to reframe mistakes within the team as learning opportunities and to discuss these during the weekly team meetings, the setting of this goal will mean that the manager is directing his or her attention towards first spotting relevant learning opportunities to reframe, second, ensuring that when mistakes within the team do arise, their own attention is oriented towards understanding what can be learned from this mistake rather than just reacting to or rectifying the mistake, and finally, the manager's attention will be oriented towards creating opportunities and processes to support the learning from these mistakes. Without articulating the specific goal related to reframing mistakes as learning opportunities, the manager may form a general intention to use mistakes as learning opportunities; however, in the 'heat of the moment', his or her attention is likely to get diverted away from maximizing the learning opportunity and towards dealing with the mistake, as the goal is not specific enough to activate his or her attention.

By working with the coachee to set a specific goal during a coaching session, establishing a time frame for achieving the goal, discussing the actions he or she might be able to carry out to work towards achieving the goal, barriers that might get in the way of goal achievement and what he or she might be able to do to overcome these, the coachee's attention is highly focused towards the steps needed to achieve the goal. This focus of attention will have a positive impact on the level of effort available to allocate to goal-directed activities, enabling the coachee to remain undistracted by goal irrelevant activities. The coach can support the coachee in appropriately directing their attention by exploring various scenarios during the coaching session. For example, returning to the example provided above regarding the manager's desire to reframe mistakes as learning opportunities for his or her team, the coach could discuss with the coachee in various ways in which the coachee might ensure that they appropriately record relevant information following the mistake to ensure that the relevant detail for the example is captured. This should take into consideration the fact that the coachee will most likely still need to respond to the mistake in their role as a manager, and therefore, it may be challenging to ensure the relevant details are appropriately captured at the moment. Without the focus of attention, it would be very easy for the coachee to lose sight of the goal while being challenged to deal with the mistake and consequently miss opportunities to engage in goal-relevant behaviours.

The coach can further facilitate the engagement of attention towards goal-relevant behaviours by encouraging the coachee to report back in the next coaching session with progress on goal completion. This ensures that the coachee remains focused on working towards the goal even after the coaching session has finished and the coachee has returned to the workplace. This reporting back function in coaching is also important in the context of goal-setting theory as Locke and Latham (2002) suggest that individuals need to be provided with summary feedback on progress towards goal achievement. For example, if individuals do not know how they are performing in relation to the goal, it is difficult for them to adjust the level or direction of effort to match what the goal requires. In coaching, the coachee often provides their own feedback regarding how they feel they are performing in relation to the goal. Therefore, an important function of coaching is, at the goal-setting stage, to explore how the coachee will generate feedback on their performance in relation to the goal, including how they know whether they are making progress. For some goals, gaining this feedback might be relatively straightforward, for example, if the goal is to refrain from checking work emails at home, the coachee could log how many days between coaching sessions they achieve this goal. This provides a clear feedback on how they are progressing in relation to achieving this goal. On the other hand, returning to our earlier example of reframing mistakes into learning opportunities, assessing progress, and therefore capturing feedback in relation to this goal might be slightly more challenging. An important function of coaching would be to explore different ways in which this feedback could be captured. With this specific example, the coachee could keep a record of when they have managed to discuss the learning opportunities from mistakes in team meetings and the feedback or response from the team on these discussions. They might also want to make a note of any mistakes that they recognize in hindsight that they didn't manage to reframe as learning opportunities and reflect on why this might have been. The simple act of discussing how feedback will be gathered during the coaching session will also reinforce the influence of goal-setting on attention regulation by focusing the coachee's attention not only on strategies for goal achievement but also on strategies for collecting feedback to monitor goal progress. The coachee might decide that in addition to the feedback they can provide as a self-assessment of their progress towards their goal, they might also discuss their goals with others and identify additional sources of feedback information. This strategy might further enhance the likelihood of goal achievement as research has shown that publically agreeing to strive for a goal can enhance the commitment to the goal than agreeing to it only in private (Hollenbeck, Williams, & Klein, 1989).

The process of specific and challenging goals directing attention and effort is equally as relevant to the leader as a coach. In one-to-ones with employees, the leader as a coach is able to support their employees in setting specific goals, establishing timeframes, exploring potential barriers, as well as agreeing how progress towards goal achievement can be measured. The leader as a coach is also able to support the employee in obtaining feedback on goal progress more directly due to the opportunities that may arise in observing goal-related behaviours at work. The leader as a coach could discuss and agree with their employee the format in which the employee would find external feedback on goal progress most useful.

RESEARCH IN ACTION: A COACH'S EXPERIENCE

Around 20 years ago, I was coaching an executive in Silicon Valley who headed up the R&D division of a high-tech company. He was a typical executive, very smart, with a PhD in engineering; however, he had received feedback that he was not a great listener and had, therefore, sought coaching to improve his listening skills.

We agreed that often nearly anyone can be a great listener as long as they have listening at the forefront of their mind, the key is to consistently pay attention to the need to be a good listener. Therefore, in our coaching sessions, we explored ways in which he could bring his desire to be a good listener to the forefront of his mind during the times in between our coaching sessions.

I suggested a very simple technique where he could give himself a score, on a 1–10 scale, on how he perceived he had 'performed' in relation to his listening for that day. He could write this score down on a pad of paper next to his bed every night. So while this would be a self-score of how he felt he had 'performed' in relation to his listening for the day and therefore would not be a completely objective assessment, it would help to keep the task of improving his listening skills at the forefront of his mind. I also suggested that before each of our coaching sessions, he could fax me (remember this was 20 years ago!) his sheet of paper with his daily listening scores. This meant that during our next coaching session, we could discuss his scores.

Interestingly, in our follow-up coaching sessions, my coachee observed that while he knew that he was just giving himself a score and that this score was just for the two of us to discuss, he noticed that this task was forcing him to reflect on his listening much more regularly and that alone was probably the most effective technique of all of the things that we had discussed that he could do to improve his listening skills. This process of simply being aware of his listening and giving himself a score provided a way to measure his 'performance' and track his progress.

This is a clear example of how setting a very specific goal (to improve listening skills) and deciding how to measure this (by self-scoring listening on a scale of 1–10 each day) can focus the attention towards behaviours that moved him closer to achieving this goal. Actually writing down his score each day also helped by providing him with data that could be used as feedback on how he was progressing towards his goal. He could clearly see whether his scores were going up or down.

What was also important in relation to understanding the impact of this technique is that being in charge of R&D, he was also in charge of product development. Therefore, if he was to get the best out his team of scientists, researchers, and technologists, they needed to feel as though their ideas were being listened to. He needed his team to be at their best to be able to contribute and if they were feeling shut down and cut off, he wouldn't get the best out of them. My coachee understood how improving his listening skills would link to his other goals regarding the innovative and creative ability of his team as a whole.

(*Continued*)

Towards the end of our coaching engagement, we did an official measurement where we conducted a multi-source feedback survey on listening, and this indicated that he had improved according to everyone worked for him. Therefore, for this particular coachee, this simple goal of tracking and monitoring his listening behaviour proved to be extremely effective.

For details of the coaches who were interviewed for the 'research in action' vignettes, see page 191.

Goals increase enthusiasm and persistence

Locke and Latham (2002) state that specific and challenging goals increase enthusiasm, with more important goals leading to the production of greater energy than less important goals. Pritchard, Harrell, DiazGranados, and Guzman (2008) write that individuals have a certain amount of energy which they call 'the energy pool'. The energy pool varies across people and time, and we decide how to allocate energy from our energy pool to satisfy our needs. If energy is applied to actions, then results are produced. For example, if we apply our energy to typing (an action), then a report is produced (the result). We have a finite amount of energy that we can allocate and expend how we wish. By setting specific and challenging goals, we can help to maintain the enthusiasm to allocate our energy pool towards actions that will move us closer to the results that we desire rather than to competing demands that will not take us closer to achieving our goals. When we have more enthusiasm, we are able to exert greater levels of energy towards goal-directed behaviours and we are also better able to effectively deal with setbacks and manage any negative emotions that may arise during the pursuit of our goal. If our enthusiasm and subsequent energy towards pursuing our goal are low, we will inevitably allocate less of our time and resources towards goal-directed activities.

Goals also increase persistence, making individuals less susceptible to the undermining effects of negative emotions such as anxiety, disappointment, and frustration. Persistence refers to whether a person maintains or changes the duration and the path of an action directed at attaining a goal. Being persistent means that people invest a high amount of resources such as time and energy in their endeavour to pursue a goal, despite the potential problems or barriers that may occur in the process of goal pursuit (Seo, Barret, & Bartunek, 2004). However, for goals to increase enthusiasm and persistence, the goals need to be important to the coachee so that the coachee feels committed to the goals. If we are not committed to our goal, if we don't understand why it is important to us, we will not be able to tap into the internal resources required to persist towards achieving this goal in the face of adversity and challenges. We are unlikely to be able to find the resilience we need to pick ourselves up and continue after being knocked back if we are unclear as to why we are doing it in the first place or how achieving the goal fulfils a greater purpose. This also applies if the goal is not something that we really care about, such as if we have been set the goal by someone else. An important point to note from the goal-setting research is that often this research is conducted in experimental, laboratory settings, and consequently, the goals are often artificially created as part of the research experiment. Alternatively, research within the field often explores goals that have been set for employees by their managers. Interestingly, even under these conditions, where it could be assumed that goal commitment could be lower than when goals are set by the individual, goal commitment still appears to be an important predictor of performance. For example, Seijts and Latham (2011) assigned 128 undergraduate students to either a high (challenging) or low (less challenging) learning goal condition. Students then participated in a business simulation game and were asked to focus on discovering or learning strategies that would help them to increase their market share in the simulation. In the low goal condition, participants were instructed to identify two or more strategies compared to six or more for the high goal condition. Seijts and Latham (2011) found that participants who reported high commitment to the high learning goal outperformed participants who reported low commitment to the high learning goal. Commitment made less difference on the performance of participants in the low learning goal condition. Within a real-life setting, Porter and Latham (2013) surveyed 174 managers and 870 employees working in a range of industries (including financial, technology, and manufacturing) in the south-eastern United States. Employees answered questions on the type of goals set for them by their managers (whether they were focused on learning, performance, or were vague/abstract) and how committed they were to goals set for them by their manager. The managers provided information on their department's performance. The findings indicated a significant positive relationship between employee goal commitment and departmental performance, therefore when employees' commitment to goals was high, departmental performance was also high.

These results clearly indicate the importance of feeling committed to one's goal to activate the power of goal-setting in relation to achieving our goals. Therefore, the next important point to consider is how best to ensure that goal commitment is high. One way of doing this is to ensure that our goals are aligned with what really matters to us in our lives. Unfortunately, all too often, we storm through our lives on auto-pilot, without mindfully considering what is really important to us and what we want from our lives. Rarely do we take time to reflect on and identify what it is that we want from our lives and whether the way that we are currently operating is creating the conditions in which we can achieve this. To address this, the first step is to identify goals that we can be committed to. One of the ways in which we can do this is by focusing on our values and understanding how to set goals that are aligned with our values. Boniwell (2008) describes values as the things that are important to us. They are deeply held beliefs that we usually internalize during our upbringing or decide on as we grow older. Values are qualities linked to action but are not something that can be obtained or finished (Chase et al., 2013). In order for us to be committed to our goals and therefore for goal-setting to be effective, we must ensure that the goals we set are aligned with our values. If we can achieve this, then these goals will be important to us, we will feel enthusiasm and energy when we consider working towards achieving these goals, and we will have greater internal resources to persist at achieving our goals when faced with setbacks. An example of the importance of aligning goals with values is provided by Chase et al. (2013) who sought to explore the contribution of a values exploration exercise makes added to goal-setting on academic performance. Participants were 132 undergraduate students and were assigned to one of three conditions: goal-setting, goal-setting plus values, or waitlist control. Participants completed a 30–45-minute online programme focused on either goal-setting or goal-setting plus values exploration. The results showed that when combined with goal-setting, training participants in a definition of values, the distinction between values and goals, and having participants explore and write about their personally important educational values, significantly increased their academic performance as measured by grade, relative to a waitlist. Interestingly, goal-setting alone had no positive impact on academic performance. This may be because the goal-setting was not accompanied with action planning. Action planning is an important next step in maximizing goal striving behaviour and is explored in detail in Chapter 10. It would be interesting to examine what the impact of goal-setting, plus values plus action planning would have on performance.

Given the important role of values in goal-setting, the first step to enable us to set goals which we are committed to is first to understand what our values are. As coaches, we can support our coachees through a process of exploring, identifying, and articulating their values. For some coachees, they may arrive at coaching fully aware of their values, able to articulate them easily, for others, it may take longer to reflect on and explore during the coaching conversation to identify what those values are as the first step in the coaching process. The exploration of values in coaching, particularly during the early sessions, is relatively commonplace (Spaten & Green, 2019), and is particularly important in the acceptance and commitment therapy approach to coaching, with value clarification forming one of the first activities in coaching and values being referred to frequently throughout the coaching process (Anstiss & Blonna, 2014).

A useful tool that may facilitate the identification of values is the typology of values provided by Shwartz (1994). These values are outlined in Table 8.1, and Shwartz (1994) suggests that these values are relatively consistent across

Table 8.1 Motivational types of values (adapted from Schwartz, 1994)

Definition	Exemplary value
Power: Social status and prestige, control or dominance over people and resources	Social Power Authority Wealth
Achievement: Personal success through demonstrating competence according to social standards	Successful Capable Ambitious
Hedonism: Pleasure and sensuous gratification for oneself	Pleasure Enjoying life
Stimulation: Excitement, novelty, and challenge in life	Daring Varied life Exciting life
Self-direction: Independent thought and action – choosing, creating, exploring	Creativity Curious Freedom
Universalism: Understanding, appreciation, tolerance, and protection for the welfare of all people and for nature	Broad-minded Social justice Equality Protecting the environment
Benevolence: Preservation and enhancement of the welfare of people with whom one is frequently in contact with	Helpful Honest Forgiving
Tradition: Respect, commitment, and acceptance of the customs and ideas that traditional culture or religion provide	Humble Devout Accepting my portion in life
Conformity: Restraint of actions, inclinations, and impulses likely to upset or harm others and violate social expectations or norms	Politeness Obedient Honouring parents and elders
Security: Safety, harmony, and stability of society of relationship and of self	National security Social order Clean

cultures. You may find it useful to discuss these values with your coachee, using them as prompts for them to reflect on, to identify their own values. For example, you may ask:

• Which values resonate with you?
• Which values are most important to you and why do you think this is the case?

- Can you think back to some experience in your life so far that has led you to develop this as a core value?
- How would you rank the values that you identify as important to you?

Once we have identified and articulated our values, to create goals that we are committed to and therefore are energizing, the next step is to utilize these values as the basis of formulating a series of goals that will guide our behaviour and actions. By mindfully linking our goals to our values and considering our behaviour in relation to these goals and values, we are able to encourage persistence towards achieving our goals. Goals are energizing as by thinking about our goal and importantly why we want to achieve that goal – why it is important to us – we are more likely to feel energized and motivated into action, working on that goal, rather than doing nothing. The goal has to be linked to the bigger picture so that we can see how it is worth continuing to persist.

To be able to create inspiring goals that we can feel committed to, we need to recognize that there are different levels of goals and that we have to attend to each level. Whitmore (2017) suggests that we can present our goals as a pyramid (see Figure 8.1). At the very top, we have our dream goal. This is our desired future or vision, and this reflects our purpose, meaning, or values. Our dream goal is what we are ultimately working towards. It's what keeps us inspired, and this links most closely to our values. Next we have our end goal. This is the concrete manifestation of the dream goal, values, or vision and provides a clear target for us to work towards. Our end goal is followed by performance goals. These are tangible as well as precise or specific and are within our control. They always serve the end goal and the dream goal. Finally, we have our process goals. These are the steps that we can take to reach our performance goal.

Let us take an example to illustrate. Let us say that a coachee identifies from the typology of values that self-direction is a very important value that they aspire to achieve in all areas of their life and in particular to have the ability to be creative and have freedom in their role at work. The ability to be self-directed, work creatively, and have freedom to pursue work

Figure 8.1 Goal-setting pyramid (adapted from Whitmore, 2017, p. 105).

objectives that stimulate them may form the dream goal. Following on from this, the end goal may be the identification of a job role that would enable the coachee to achieve this or alternatively it might be identifying that they would like to become self-employed – this is the concrete manifestation of the dream goal. Next comes the performance goals which are a series of goals, all specific goals that are within the coachee's control. If the end goal is to become self-employed, the performance goals will link directly to this. For example, they may decide that to become self-employed, they first need to conduct research into the legal side of setting up their own business; they might need to upskill in certain areas such as marketing; and they might need to start building their network of contacts and so on. Finally, the process goals are the steps needed to fulfil these performance goals and each performance goal will likely have a number of linked process goals. For example, with the performance goal of building their network, the coachee may have a series of process goals which will enable this to be achieved, for example, attending a relevant conference; building an online presence; reaching out to others who are working in the same industry, for example. It is also important to note that all of these goals, at all levels, should be as specific as possible to enable them to be most effective. Therefore, the performance goal of 'building my network' needs to be made specific and measurable, and this is particularly important in the context of gaining feedback in relation to performance towards achieving the goal as discussed earlier. Therefore, how will the coachee know when they have sufficiently built their network? How long are they going to dedicate to this task? It is important to explore this with your coachee as it is very easy for some goals to stretch on indefinitely, making it very difficult to assess how they are progressing towards achieving their goal. Setting specific goals can also help to instigate and guide behaviour. For example, the process goal to attend a conference linked to the performance goal of building a network is specific; however, attending a conference can easily do nothing in relation to building one's network if no networking takes place! Therefore, the process goal of attending a conference needs to be made even more specific, for example, 'I will ensure that I approach and introduce myself to at least one speaker during the conference'. By ensuring that goals are this specific, they can accurately guide behaviour. By working through the values exercise and also the goal-setting pyramid, the individual can also remain highly aware of how each action (such as ensuring that they introduce themselves to a speaker at a conference) feeds into their dream goal and life values (to be self-directive, work creatively, and have freedom).

So far we have explored how aligning goals with values increases goal commitment which, in turn, increases enthusiasm and persistence in goal striving behaviour. An interesting vein of research that should also be considered in the context of enthusiasm and persistence in goal striving is what happens after a 'goal-failure'? Sharif and Shu (2019) argue that to achieve our long-term goals, we must set short-term goals (as I have detailed above in relation to the goal pyramid). However, within a given day, people have multiple demands on their time and energy resources and, therefore, have to prioritize some tasks over others, leading to short-term goal failures. Unfortunately, these short-term goal failures can derail people in reaching their larger goals. Failure can be particularly detrimental to goal-striving when it is accompanied by shame, as shame occurs with an appraisal of global (i.e. 'whole self') failure and lack of personal control (Lewis, 2000). Shame can motivate an avoidance-response (Tangney, 1995) meaning that individuals who experience shame in relation to a perceived failure may then be motivated to avoid further failures (and associated feelings of shame) and consequently abandon their future goals. To overcome the detrimental emotional effects of perceived failures in the pursuit of goals, individuals regulate their emotions, a process that can occur either consciously or unconsciously and automatically or controlled. Emotion regulation is the process by which individuals influence the emotions they have, when they have them, and how these emotions are experienced or expressed (Gross, 1998). There are a number of different types of emotion regulation strategies and these can be classified as either antecedent-focused or response-focused regulation (Boss & Sims, 2008).

Antecedent-focused regulation is emotion regulation that occurs before an emotion has become completely active. Boss and Sims (2008) describe four types of antecedent-focused regulation:

- Situation selection – choosing situations based on the emotions they might elicit (i.e. avoiding certain situations such as not attending a meeting where you know a colleague who annoys you will be in attendance)
- Situation modification - altering the situation (i.e. calling a break during a meeting that has become emotional)
- Attentional deployment – focusing on a different aspect of the situation (i.e. flying makes me very anxious so whenever I fly, one way that I regulate this emotion is by ensuring that I have a number of 'treats' such as my favourite types of food and a good book that I can focus my attention on during the flight. Another example is that I have horses and an important but boring part of looking after horses is clearing their poop from the field each day. I used to view this as a waste of my time (when I could be riding) and get frustrated with how long it took; however, I now focus on the number of steps that I get in when doing this and I feel much more positive about it as it helps me hit my steps target each day (which helps me to achieve my other goal, to stay fit and healthy)
- Cognitive change – deciding which of many possible meanings will be assigned to the situation. Cognitive change addresses how one thinks about the situation. Because this is an antecedent-focused regulation

strategy, this involves the individual planning on how they will think about the situation before it has taken place. For example, I had to attend a plagiarism interview with a student which I was feeling anxious about as I anticipated that it would be an unpleasant experience. I decided to view this interview as a learning experience as this was something I had never done before, yet was part of becoming a well-rounded academic. Thinking about the interview in this way helped me to feel less anxious both before and during the interview.

Response-focused regulation strategies, on the other hand, take place after an emotion is underway. Boss and Sims (2008) detail two types of response-focused strategies:

- Reappraisal – similar to cognitive change, reappraisal involves looking back at a potentially emotion-eliciting situation and defining it in non-emotional terms. For example, you might think back to a difficult conversation that you had with a colleague and rather than focusing on the emotions that this conversation elicited, you consider the actions you took during the conversation to manage it and what you consequently learned from this situation
- Suppression – inhibiting or hiding emotion expressive behaviour. For example, the process of having to 'bite your tongue' at the moment rather than instinctively reacting to an emotional situation.

We use these emotion regulation strategies on a day-to-day basis, either consciously or unconsciously, to ensure that we effectively manage our emotions to function in our daily lives. Understanding emotion regulation can be particularly useful in the context of goal failure. As outlined earlier, goal-setting stimulates behaviour and subsequent performance as individuals experience energy and enthusiasm towards engaging in behaviours that will take them closer to achieving their goal. When individuals experience failure in relation to short-term goals (which they inevitably will), it is likely to be difficult to maintain the same levels of energy and enthusiasm towards goal-striving behaviours if negative emotions such as shame, frustration, anger or disappointment in relation to the goal failure are being experienced. As coaches, we can work with our coachees to identify and understand the emotions they are experiencing and find appropriate regulation strategies to enable them to effectively maintain goal striving behaviours. For example, Turner and Husman (2008) conducted interviews with eight students who reported experiencing shame in relation to completing a challenging course as part of their degree. Turner and Husman (2008) found that participants who were able to mitigate these feelings of shame in relation to goal failure were those who were highly committed to future goals as compared to those who were not highly committed or were unclear about future goals.

Furthermore, they found that motivation to continue to pursue their goals was facilitated when participants reflected on the importance of future goals which helped to renew their commitment to achieving this goal. In terms of the emotion regulation strategies outlined above, this is an example of reappraisal, as the participants were able to distance themselves from the detrimental feelings of shame associated with the perceived goal failure and instead focus on the energizing prospect of working towards their long-term goal. This research further enforces the importance of ensuring that short-term goals are aligned with underlying values to ensure that they remain motivating, even in the face of short-term or sub-goal failure. Coaches are ideally placed to facilitate a process of reappraisal by encouraging the coachee to reflect on their longer-term goals and the importance of these to refocus their attention following a sub-goal failure. The role of reflection in coaching is the topic of the next chapter.

Another example of a strategy to help encourage persistence in goal-striving is provided by Sharif and Shu (2019) who explored whether the framing of the goal itself can influence peoples' ability to persist after a failure. In particular, Sahrif and Shu examine the effect of framing goals with an 'emergency reserve' on persistence following goal failure. Emergency reserves are slack around a goal that can be used if needed but at a small psychological cost. For example, a reserve can be an extra 20 emergency pounds in a budget, two emergency late arrival excuses from work or an emergency day skipping exercise (Sharif & Shu, 2019). To test this, Sharif and Shu (2019) recruited 273 participants (a mixture of students and university staff) to participate in a five-week step tracking exercise. During the first week of the study, participants logged the number of steps taken each day (using a pedometer app on their smartphone), this formed a baseline measure. Participants were then allocated to one of four experimental conditions: easy goal (to complete their step goal five days a week); hard goal (to complete their step goal seven days a week); reserve weekly (the same as the hard goal condition but with two optional emergency skips they could apply each week); or reserve monthly (the same as the hard goal condition but with eight optional emergency skips they could apply across the four weeks). Participants then logged their steps each day over four weeks and were provided with data to indicate how they were performing against their goal. The results indicated that individuals with goals framed with emergency reserves were more likely to persist after a subgoal violation than those with goals framed without emergency reserves. This persistence was thought to occur as these participants experienced an increased sense of progress, even after failure and thus commitment to the larger end goal. This study provides an example of an antecedent-focused regulation strategy in the form of cognitive change. The individual is changing the way that they think about their goal and potential failure to achieve their goal before any potential negative emotion around goal failure has become active, deciding to think about a 'failure' as using an emergency reserve rather than a failure. In addition to providing an example to illustrate how the cognitive change antecedent-focused emotion regulation strategy can be applied, these findings also have important implications that should be considered when working with coachees to set goals around the level of challenge that is most effective. While Locke and Latham's (2002) findings around goal-setting theory indicate that a goal should be challenging to improve performance, Sharif and Shu's (2019) research suggests that if the goal is too challenging and, therefore, leads to a series of frequent sub-goal failures, the goal may reduce persistence and negatively impact goal commitment over the long term. Perhaps an alternative is to set a challenging goal, however, explore with the coachee the idea of using the concept of emergency reserves to help the coachee to protect themselves from the negative impact of goal failure.

The process of exploring values and using these values as the basis of goal-setting, working through different levels of goal-setting as guided by the goal-setting pyramid and understanding emotion regulation strategies to mitigate the negative impact of goal failure on goal striving, can apply equally to the leader as coach. However, for the leader as a coach, exploring the core values with their employees may potentially be more challenging if those core values do not align with the core values of the organization or the team. However, even if this is the case, a conversation around values in relation to the employee's role within the organization may still prove to be highly beneficial at forming the basis of a goal-setting exercise, in particular around identifying potential areas of professional development for career progression within the organization. With regard to regulating emotion following goal failure to maintain persistence, the leader as a coach can encourage openness within the team to discuss and explore failures. This can include providing the opportunity for team members to share strategies they have employed to keep motivated and continue to persist towards goals. This can be an effective method of not only providing an opportunity for team members to learn effective strategies from one another but also to help reduce negative emotions around failure generally, by encouraging the team to be more open in discussing when failure has happened. I return to the importance of creating an environment that facilitates learning from failure in Section four.

Goals activate the discovery of task relevant knowledge

In addition to directing the individuals' attention towards completing actions that will move them closer to achieving their goal and increasing the enthusiasm and consequently amount of persistence towards continuing to complete these actions, Lock and Latham (2002) explain how goal-setting also affects performance by indirectly leading to the arousal, discovery, and use of task-relevant knowledge and strategies. For example, when confronted with goals, individuals use existing relevant knowledge and skills to assist in goal attainment. Locke (2000) argues that the subconscious refers to all the knowledge or mental content that is in consciousness but not, at a given time, in focal awareness. The knowledge that we hold in our subconscious could be considered 'in storage', waiting to be accessed on demand. Therefore, once the goal is held in the individual's attention, they will subconsciously search for knowledge that will help them to decide how best to pursue the goal. This mechanism of goal-setting is less widely researched than the mechanisms discussed so far in this chapter. This is likely because it involves the subconscious process of activating existing knowledge which is difficult to measure in research.

Coaches and the leader as a coach can support this mechanism further by providing the forum for the coachee to make sense and explore the knowledge and skills they already have to filter through to what is most relevant to achieving the goal in-hand. Locke and Latham (2002) state that individuals draw from a repertoire of skills that they have used previously in related contexts and apply them to the present situation. However, not everyone is apt at applying skills or knowledge from one situation to a new situation or challenge. Coaches and the leader as a coach can assist this process by encouraging the coachee to reflect on how they have handled similar problems in the past and to draw out the relevant information from their repertoire of knowledge and skills to encourage them to apply these to the new issue. For example, imagine that a coachee has been asked to deliver a project to organize a conference and therefore sets a goal related to the successful delivery of this project. The coachee may have no previous experience of organizing a conference or even organizing a similar event in the past. However, through asking open questions, the coach can encourage the coachee to consider whether other experiences and therefore the linked knowledge and skills gained in these experiences may be helpful. Perhaps the coachee has more general experience of project management. For example, they may have previously delivered a project to manage a site move. On the face of it, this project has little similarity to the first project, however, some of the knowledge and skills gained will likely be transferable. For example, knowledge about how to break the project down into smaller tasks to manage the project timeline, managing a project budget, and coordinating the communication between project team members will all be useful strands of knowledge and skills that the coachee holds. The coach can facilitate the coachees' exploration of how they can apply these existing strands of knowledge and skills to the new challenge.

Smith, Locke, and Barry (1990) also suggest that if the task for which a goal is assigned is new, and, therefore, the individual may need to acquire new knowledge and skills to help them to achieve the goal, then the individual will engage in deliberate planning to develop strategies that will enable them to attain their goals. Once again, the coach and the leader as a coach can assist with this process by providing the reflective space for coachees to plan these strategies. Returning to our earlier example, the coachee may identify that in relation to their goal of delivering the conference project, the coachee may recognize that they lack the relevant knowledge they need on the criteria for a successful conference. The coachee may, therefore, plan the various actions they need to engage with, to obtain this knowledge. For example, gathering some data from past conference delegates on what made for a good and bad conference experience and gathering information online about the criteria for a successful conference.

While the use of goal-setting will to some extent automatically activate the discovery of task-relevant knowledge, this is further facilitated in coaching by enabling reflection. Reflection is the process of learning from our own experiences and, therefore, links clearly to this mechanism of goal-setting. Activating the discovery of task-relevant knowledge means considering what we already know and how we can use this to help us to achieve our goal. As explored in the examples above, how to apply existing knowledge may not always be obvious or straightforward, which is why reflection can facilitate this process further. The role of reflection in coaching is the subject of the next chapter.

This chapter in summary

- Goals are an explicit standard by which individuals can judge their progress and performance
- Specific and challenging goals lead to the highest performance
- Goals direct attention and effort towards goal-relevant activities and away from goal-irrelevant activities
  - Coaches can facilitate this attention and effort by supporting coachees to set specific goals, establish time frames for goal completion, and explore potential barriers to goal achievement
  - Discussing how to measure progress towards goal achievement provides a format for coachees to obtain feedback on goal progress
- If we are committed to our goals, they increase enthusiasm and persistence
  - Aligning goals with values increases commitment, goals should feed into a higher purpose
  - Persistence following 'goal failure' can be enhanced via emotion regulation strategies
- Goals activate the discovery of task-relevant knowledge. Coaches can further facilitate this discovery by encouraging reflective thinking

Note

1   In fact, there are many common practices and accepted beliefs that are not supported by the evidence but continue to prevail regardless of this. One of my fa-
vourites is the impact of feedback on performance. The evidence is very mixed,
showing that while sometimes feedback can enhance performance, sometimes
it has no impact, and sometimes it can even have a negative impact (Kluger &
DeNisi, 1996). Researchers don't seem to know why this difference exists. Despite this, feedback has been accepted as a common practice in organizations
based on the assumption that we need this feedback from others to perform
better. Another soap box of mine is the use of type personality profiles (as opposed to trait profiles which I explored in Chapter 4) such as MBTI but that's for
another time perhaps.....

References

Anstiss, T., & Blonna, R. (2014). Acceptance and commitment coaching. In J.
Passmore (Ed.), *Mastery in caching: A complete psychological toolkit for advance
coaching,* (pp. 253–276). London, UK: Kogan Page Publishing.

Boniwell, I. (2008). *Positive psychology in a nutshell: A balanced introduction to the
science of optimal functioning.* London, UK: Personal Well-Being Centre.

Boss, A. D., & Sims, H. P., Jr. (2008). Everyone fails! Using emotion regulation and
self-leadership for recovery. *Journal of Managerial Psychology, 23*(2), 135–150.
doi:10.1108/02683940810850781

Chase, J. A., Houmanfar, R., Hayes, S. C., Ward, T. A., Vilardaga, J. P., & Follette,
V. (2013). Values are not just goals: Online ACT-based values training adds to
goal setting in improving undergraduate college student performance. *Journal of
Contextual Behavioral Science, 2*(3–4), 79–84. doi:10.1016/j.jcbs.2013.08.002

Gross, J. J. (1998). The emerging field of emotion regulation: an integrative review.
Review of General Psychology, 2, 271–299.

Hollenbeck, F. R., Williams, C. R., & Klein, H. J. (1989). An empirical examination
of the antecedents of commitment to ditEcult goals. *Journal of Applied Psychology, 74,* 18–23.

Kluger, A. N., & DeNisi, A. (1996). The effects of feedback intentions on performance: A historical review, a meta-analysis, and a preliminary feedback intention
theory. *Psychological Bulletin, 119*(2), 254–284. doi:10.1037/0033–2909.119.2.254

Lewis, M. (2000). Self-conscious emotions: Embarrassment, pride, shame, and guilt.
In M. Lewis & J. M. Haviland-Jones (Eds.), *Handbook of emotions,* (pp. 623–636).
New York: Guilford Press.

Locke, E. (2000). Motivation, cognition, and action: An analysis of studies of task goals
and knowledge. *Applied Psychology, 49*(3), 408–429. doi:10.1111/1464–0597.00023

Locke, E. A., & Latham, G. P. (2002). Building a practically useful theory of goal
setting and task motivation: a 35 year odyssey. *American Psychologist, 57,* 705–717.
doi:10.1037//0003–066X.57.9.705

Luszczynska, A., Diehl, M., Gutiérrez-Dona, B., Kuusinen, P., & Schwarzer, R.
(2004). Measuring one component of dispositional self-regulation: Attention
control in goal pursuit. *Personality and Individual Differences, 37*(3), 555–566.
doi:10.1016/j.paid.2003.09.026

Morisano, D., Hirsh, J. B., Peterson, J. B., Pihl, R. O., & Shore, B. M. (2010). Setting, elaborating, and reflecting on personal goals improves academic performance. *Journal of Applied Psychology, 95*(2), 255–264. doi:10.1037/ a0018478

Mitchell, T. R., & Daniels, D. (2003). Motivation. In W. C. Borman, D. R. Ilgen, & R. J. Klimoski (Eds.), *Handbook of psychology: Industrial and organizational psychology,* (Vol. 12, pp. 225–254). Hoboken, NJ: Wiley.

Porter, R. L., & Latham, G. P. (2013). The effect of employee learning goals and goal commitment on departmental performance. *Journal of Leadership & Organizational Studies, 20*(1), 62–68. doi:10.1177/1548051812467208

Pritchard, R. D., Harrell, M. M., DiazGranados, D., & Guzman, M. J. (2008). The productivity measurement and enhancement system: a meta-analysis. *Journal of Applied Psychology, 93*(3), 540. doi:10.1037/0021–9010.93.3.540

Seijts, G. H., & Latham, G. P. (2011). The effect of commitment to a learning goal, self-efficacy, and the interaction between learning goal difficulty and commitment on performance in a business simulation. *Human Performance, 24*(3), 189–204. doi:10.1080/08959285.2011.580807

Schwartz, S. H. (1994). Beyond individualism/collectivism: New cultural dimensions of values. In U. Kim, H. C. Triandis, Ç. Kâğitçibaşi, S. C. Choi, & G. Yoon (Eds.), *Cross-cultural research and methodology series, Vol. 18. Individualism and collectivism: Theory, method, and applications,* (pp. 85–119). Thousand Oaks, CA: Sage Publications, Inc.

Seo, M. G., Barret, F., L., & Bartunek, J. M. (2004). The role of affective experience in work motivation. *Academy of Management Review, 29*, 423–439.

Sharif, M. A., & Shu, S. B. (2019). Nudging persistence after failure through emergency reserves. *Organizational Behavior and Human Decision Processes.* doi:10.1016/j.obhdp.2019.01.004

Smith, K. G., Locke, E., & Barry, D. (1990). Goal setting, planning, and organizational performance: An experimental simulation. *Organizational Behavior & Human Decision Processes, 46*, 118–134. doi:10.1016/0749–5978(90)90025-5

Spaten, O. M., & Green, S. (2019). Delivering value in coaching through exploring meaning, purpose, values, and strengths. In J. Passmore, B. O. Underhill, & M. Goldsmith (Eds.), *Mastering executive coaching,* (pp. 90–109). Oxon, UK: Routledge.

Tangney, J. P. (1995). Recent advances in the empirical study of shame and guilt. *American Behavioral Scientist, 38*, 1132–1145.

Turner, J. E., & Husman, J. (2008). Emotional and cognitive self-regulation following academic shame. *Journal of Advanced Academics, 20*, 138–173.

Whitmore, J. (2017). *Coaching for performance: The principles and practice of coaching and leadership.* London, UK: Nicholas Brealey Publishing.

Chapter 9

Learning through reflection

Reflection is the structured, focused, and conscious process that we go through to develop our understanding. Reflection can be described as listening to ourselves (Stevens & Cooper, 2009). As outlined in Section one of this book, one of the fundamental principles in coaching is that coaching enables behavioural change through raising awareness and reflection. Linked to this is the fundamental principle that a trusting relationship between the coach and the coachee is essential. The process of reflection involves raising awareness of why we might feel, think, and behave in a particular way so that we are able to make conscious decisions as to whether to continue in the same way or change our thoughts and behaviour. However, reflecting on and thinking about the reasons why we feel, think, and behave in particular ways can be extremely confronting. For example, it can be hard to admit to ourselves why our behaviours are so deeply ingrained or when we have behaved in a way that perhaps doesn't align with our core values. Sometimes this can involve looking back at past events and considering how those have influenced the person we are today. These past events can continue to influence our thoughts, feelings, and behaviours without us even realizing it. Reflective thought brings our awareness to these influences.

The challenge is that part of the reason why these influences on our thoughts, feelings, and behaviours are unconscious is that this protects us from being hurt by them. Acknowledging these influences means removing our protective barriers. This can result in intolerable feelings of humiliation or shame that may be associated with perceived or actual limitations with our character or skill set. These influences sit in our unconscious for a reason, our unconscious protects us, it 'works hard, efficiently and tirelessly on your behalf' (Fine, 2007, p. 128). If we were to spend our lives being acutely aware of every flaw in our character, every mistake, error, attempt when we have tried and failed, inadvertently offended someone (or intentionally offended someone!), every faux pas, each embarrassing gaffe or blunder, we would be emotional wrecks. Incapable of functioning in everyday life as we become racked with reminders of our incompetence. Unable to put ourselves out there to try new things or meet new people as we are reminded constantly, based on our experience, of our likelihood of failure. However, most of the time, our unconscious mind protects us from excessively ruminating over these events. The process of reflection can be challenging as we need to open the door to let these unconscious thoughts into our conscious mind. We need to consider these shortcomings to learn from them. By raising awareness of why we might think and behave in a particular way, we are able to make conscious decisions as to whether to continue in the same way or change our thoughts and behaviour. A lack of awareness can mean that we may avoid developing our limitations, and therefore there is no opportunity for these weaknesses to become strengths. Some individuals naturally reflect more effectively than others as I discussed in Chapter 7. For some, the process of reflection will be so challenging, the risk of exposing themselves to vulnerability so high that they may be unwilling or unable to bear it. However, without engaging in reflection, we are unlikely to ever understand who we are, where we are going, and how to get there.

Although reflective practice is fundamental to learning from our experience and forms the underlying process of how we learn and change our behaviour, it is often ignored as a concept in coaching texts. I propose that most of what coaches do is enabling this reflective process, even when it is not labelled as such. As with goal-setting, I suggest that it is important to understand how these processes in coaching relate to the wider theory so that we can ensure that our practice is as effective as possible. By understanding how we learn from our experience through reflection and how this can be effectively integrated into coaching, we can ensure that we are engaging in the consistently effective practice in this respect. In the next section, I elaborate on the question 'what is reflection?' and integrate a theory of reflective learning with the coaching process. In the final section, I expand on the importance of the trusting relationship in coaching to facilitate learning from reflection.

What is reflection?

'Reflection is the process whereby we reconstruct and make meaning of our experience' (Stevens & Cooper, 2009). Extensive research has demonstrated the benefits of reflection on learning. A large proportion of this research has explored the impact of reflective journaling. For example, Brown, McCracken, and Kane (2011) argue that reflective learning journals (RLJ) encourage learners to engage with content received in a formal training context by examining their experiences in applying the learned material. In this study, Brown et al. were interested in exploring whether RLJs can enhance the transfer of learning from training back to the workplace. To test this, Brown et al. (2011) utilized a qualitative methodology where 75 employees of a large Canadian utility company participated in an 11-day Leadership Development Programme and then completed a RLJ. At the beginning of the programme, the RLJ was discussed with participants, and the role of the RLJ in transfer and evaluation was outlined. Participants were encouraged to keep a daily learning diary to record key observations surrounding each module on the programme. Roughly three months post-training, participants were asked to create and submit their individual RLJ reporting on three questions:

- What I learned in this module (learning/retention)
- How I have applied or plan to apply the learning to my work (transfer)?
- What barriers have I experienced in applying the learning (barriers)

The RLJs were analysed using grounded theory. The key findings were that the RLJs enhanced the participants' ability to engage in reflection by bringing reflection skills into their everyday working life (i.e. they become conscious about what they were doing); there was a positive reaction to reflection spaces (i.e. creating the time and space to reflect; the very act of reflective practice, simply writing about their activities, appeared to be a useful exercise in improving confidence in relation to utilizing material covered in the programme); the reflective process appeared to facilitate enabling things to 'click' together; and help them to understand the 'root causes' of previous problems. Overall, the authors conclude that critical reflection should be integrated into training programmes as it gives learners the space and tools to make sense and articulate how they transferred the material as well as what hampered or facilitated such transfer. In particular, participants were able to think in-depth about their strengths and weakness through self-critique and, therefore, make sense of their daily lives. In terms of motivation and goal-setting, through writing in their RLJs, participants engaged in a process of making promises to themselves about how they could reappraise past practice and apply the material more effectively in the future.

To explore the impact of reflective journaling with individuals who had already been using journaling (rather than using journaling as a requirement for the research), Cooper and Stevens (2006) provide a case study exploring the journal-keeping methods of four higher education professionals who were already using journaling in their professional lives. In this study, Cooper and Stevens respond to calls that suggest that journal keeping is not sustained outside of the classroom by researching four cases where the individuals keep journals of their own accord (i.e. they are not doing it because they have to). Findings indicate that these professionals use their journals in four ways: to create conversations with themselves about their work and their lives; to organize their work experience and demands; to adapt unique and individual journal-keeping practices to match their current needs; and to review and reflect on overall, long-term career goals and organizational directions. Through the journal, these individuals cope with the complex external demands of work life, enabling them to inhabit multiple roles, maintain balance, and to see the larger picture in their lives and organizations. They believe that taking the time to journal leads to a more organized and meaningful professional life.

Research has also evidenced the impact of reflection on outcomes beyond professional practice. Durgahee (2002) investigated whether journaling could lead to relief from mental health problems. In this study, the aim of journaling was to encourage patients to think for themselves and restore their confidence in their abilities. Participants were seven patients diagnosed with either anxiety or depression. Patients were encouraged to keep a journal with the purpose of providing an avenue to express their views and thoughts. However, the patients were free to write as frequently as they liked and were not given guidance on what to write or the format of writing. The researcher then interviewed the patients on their experience of keeping the journal. Findings indicated three themes: (1) 'What do I do now?' (2) 'Fact and fiction: this one isn't me' and (3) 'Ignore the funny words'. What do I do now described how patients used the journal when they felt anxious or depressed. The journal acted as 'someone' the patient could have a conversation with about their illness. For the theme 'Fact and fiction: this one isn't me,' the author describes how fictional narratives in the disrupted world of mental health are resolutions of real problems. Therefore, fiction is a resource for understanding the non-fictional world. Patients discover the meaning of what they are saying, debate issues, and enter discussions through a process of deciphering which one is their real self and what is imagined. This is how the patients arrived at isolating, 'This one isn't me'. Writing in the journal helps this process of telling a tale and putting the case forward. Finally, the theme 'Ignore the funny words' describes how the journals expose the depth of concern that patients have about the way they are treated. They begin to perceive themselves as a bundle of attributes generated by carers. This is of concern to patients and they choose to express them but 'asked them to be ignored'. The reality is that these attributes cause concern, lead to changes in self-perception, and, in the longer-term, perhaps depersonalization.

Also extending the findings on the impact of reflection, Klein and Boals (2001) investigated whether reflective or expressive writing could have a positive impact on working memory by reducing the draw on cognitive resources required to cope with stressful events. In study one, 71 participants were asked to either write about a stressful event, in this case, their deepest thoughts and feelings about coming to college (all were college students), or the control group was asked to write about a non-stressful event (time management). Participants completed a working memory test at time one. Then over two weeks, they completed three writing sessions (each lasting 20 minutes). Following this, they completed a second working memory test. The results showed that seven weeks after the writing sessions, participants assigned to write about their deepest thoughts and feelings about coming to college exhibited working memory improvements compared with the control group who wrote about time management. The gains in working memory scores were highest for participants who reported high levels of disclosure of personal information and emotions in their writing. In study two, 35 students were randomly assigned to write about time management, 36 to write about a negative event, and 35 to write about a positive event. As with experiment one, working memory was assessed at time one, followed by three separate writing events. Seven to eight weeks after the final writing exercise working memory was measured again. This time, participants also completed a questionnaire to measure intrusive thoughts. The results showed that expressive writing produced significant improvements in working memory, however only for those who wrote about a negative experience and not a positive experience. Participants in the negative experience writing group showed the greatest decline in intrusive and avoidant thinking about the negative event, which suggests that it is the reduction in intrusive thoughts following expressive writing that is freeing up cognitive resources and consequently impacting positively on working memory.

These studies suggest that there is a range of benefits to reflective practice, in particular in terms of helping individuals to sort through and make sense of their situation, apply existing knowledge to new challenges, and consequently improve their professional practice. Reflection also provides a forum for individuals to express themselves and to deal with challenging thoughts and emotions. Furthermore, this expression of thoughts and emotions through reflection appears to benefit cognitive functions by freeing up mental resources by proving an outlet for intrusive thoughts – the reflection provides the 'release' to allow individuals to move on.

It is important to note that these studies have all focused on the practice of reflective writing, a format of reflection quite different to that experienced in coaching. Moving beyond the impact of reflective writing, an important study in this context explored individual choice around the reflective practice. Holden and Griggs (2011) conducted an action research project with participants studying for an MA in Human Resource Management, in which students were provided with a choice on which type of reflective practice they wished to engage in to support their learning. The majority of students opted for what may be perceived as 'safe' techniques, such as the unsent letter and storytelling (all written reflection) rather than potentially riskier choices of an audio or video diary (verbalized reflection). The authors' findings also indicate that the more structured techniques encouraged deeper reflection than when reflection was free form. With weaker students (i.e. those with less developed reflective skills), the unsent letter, diary, and storytelling were particularly descriptive (rather than reflective). They also found benefits with methods of social and interactive reflection, including reflective dialogue with a colleague who acted as a critical friend and an interactive reflective dialogue which culminated in a group reflective presentation through a story-board. These reflective practices encouraged a more creative reflective process and produced some insightful reflections. The social context of reflection did appear to overcome some of the criticisms of individual reflection by ensuring that content was critically reflective rather than purely descriptive. Reflective learning by its very nature requires a 'critical' perspective; assumptions need to be questioned and alternative perspectives considered. In Chapter 7, I explored individual differences in coachees' levels of reflexivity. This study picks up on this point. Critical reflection is a skill that will not be equally developed in all individuals. Coupled with the fact that reflection can be emotionally challenging, even when actively engaging in reflective practice, some may tend to opt for 'easier' methods of reflection, such as reflective writing, where the reflective content may be more descriptive than truly reflective. This type of superficial 'reflection' is unlikely to bring the benefits of learning and behaviour change discussed so far. This is supported by the finding from Holden and Griggs (2011) that social forms of reflection appeared to encourage a more critically reflective stance. The dialogue with another prompted the challenge that encouraged the individual to reflect on a deeper level. Chivers (2003) expands on this point by arguing that generally in life we tend to do more of what we like to do, become better at it, like being better at it and therefore do more of it. Unless there is some counter pressure of necessity or obligation, the opposite is also true. So could it be that individual reflection is conducted less frequently and therefore conducted less well because it does not offer any 'feel-good' aspects for some people? If this is the case, simply drawing attention to the need for reflection will not be effective. This explains why first, individuals engaging in reflective writing may not take that reflection to a deeper level that may prove to be sufficiently challenging and second, the practice of reflective writing may not be sustained in the longer-term.

When considered together, these findings suggest the benefits of reflection; however, they also highlight that the practice of reflective writing may not be particularly beneficial for all, as not everyone will have the requisite skills to naturally engage in *critically* reflective writing. However, engaging in a reflective discussion with another, such as a coach, who can provide the supportive challenge needed to ensure that the discussion is critically reflective, rather than purely descriptive, is likely to maximize the impact of reflection on learning and behaviour change. Additionally, while these studies illustrate some of the many benefits of engaging in reflection and they suggest the importance of engaging in reflection through dialogue with a partner, they do not explain *how* we learn from reflection.

How does reflection enable behaviour change?

There are a number of theories that propose to explain reflective learning; however, my favourite is Kolb's (1984) experiential learning theory. Kolb's theory assumes that learning is best facilitated by a process that draws out the learners' beliefs and ideas about a topic so that they can be examined, tested, and integrated with new, more refined ideas. Learning is also seen as a holistic process as it involves the integrated functioning of the total person: thinking, feeling, perceiving, and behaving. The way we process the possibilities of each new experience determines the range of choices and decisions we see. Kolb (1984) portrays the experiential learning process as an idealized learning cycle where the learner should 'touch all the bases' of experiencing, reflecting, thinking, and acting to maximize learning through experience. Kolb's model outlines four stages of learning activity, each leading to the next in a cyclical fashion. First, the individual has a concrete experience (i.e. something happens to me). Next, the individual reflects on the experience (i.e. what happened to me). Third, the individual creates meaning from the experience (i.e. what do I take from that?), and finally the individual tests their learning (i.e. how can I apply this?). The theory is based on the integration of a number of assumptions. Kolb (1984) proposes that all learning is re-learning. Learning is best facilitated by a process that draws out the learners' beliefs and ideas about a topic so that they can be examined, tested, and integrated with new, more refined ideas. Learning requires the resolution of conflicts, differences, and disagreement. In the process of learning, one is called upon to move back and forth between opposing perspectives. Finally, learning is the process of creating knowledge. Experiential learning theory proposes a constructivist theory of learning whereby social knowledge is created and recreated in the personal knowledge of the learner. This stands in contrast to the "transmission" model on which the majority of current educational practice is based, where pre-existing fixed ideas are transmitted to the learner (Fenwick, 2003).

Kolb's experiential learning theory provides a useful framework to understand how reflection enables learning; however, a limitation of experiential learning theory is that it assumes that individuals can construct a rich understanding of their own experiences and then generalize the lessons of those experiences to improve their performance. Yet, training and development research provides many examples where individuals struggle to learn from experience or even learn the wrong lessons. One of the limitations of Kolb's experiential learning cycle is the assumption that individuals are open to experience and not defended against it. People's behaviour emerges out of deeply held patterns and unconscious processes that both encourage and discourage learning from experience. Therefore, to learn from our experiences, we must find ways of working with our underlying or unconscious processes, in particular our defence mechanisms (Vince, 1998). We have already examined this, to some extent, in this section in the context of why reflection can be confronting and the tendency for research participants to opt for 'easier' forms of reflective practice, that in reality are more descriptive than reflective. These criticisms help to explain why the experiential learning process can be used to understand how the coaching process can enable learning. Experiential learning provides an explanation of how individuals learn from experience; however, not all individuals are effective at naturally transitioning through the stages in the theory of their own accord. In these cases, coaching is a useful tool that proactively encourages individuals to maximize their learning from experience. In the next section, I will provide some examples of how different coaching tools, techniques, and approaches can be used to facilitate this reflective process and support coachees to 'touch all the bases' of the experiential learning cycle.

Integration of learning through reflection and coaching approaches

Let's start with perhaps one of the simplest coaching approaches. Using Whitmore's (2017) GROW model as a framework for the coaching sessions, the stage of exploring the reality (the R in GROW) involves asking the coachee probing questions to encourage the coachee to reflect on their experiences and create meaning from those experiences in relation to the goal. For example, questions such as 'How do you know this?' 'What do you mean by?' and 'What are you assuming?' will ensure that the coachee moves beyond simply describing their situation and move to a level of deeper critical reflection to raise awareness and truly understand the factors influencing their current behaviour and subsequent situation. In addition to supporting coachees to move through the reflection stage of the experiential learning cycle, coaching using the GROW framework, also encourages coachees to consider how they can apply this learning in the stage of exploring options (the O in GROW). For example, the coachee may reflect on why he or she believes a presentation was not delivered as effectively as intended, discuss what could have been done differently and how this could have affected the outcome. Furthermore, coachees are encouraged to commit to active testing through the form of action planning (for example, selecting which solution to put into practice). By implementing action plans, coachees engage in the final stage of the cycle by exploring how they can apply their learning. The importance of effective action planning will be explored in greater detail in Chapter 10. Coaching also provides a tool to help individuals to deal with the challenge posed by Vince (1998) whereby unconscious processes may discourage learning from experience. The role of the coach is to challenge the coachee when he or she resorts to habitual behaviours that are not beneficial in the process of achieving the goal. By challenging and exploring these habitual behaviours, the underlying or unconscious processes that may be stopping the individual from learning from experience may come to light and can then be addressed. For example, Rogers (2016) proposes how when the coachee wants to make major changes in their life, it is inevitable that the coach will need to combine support with a challenge. If as a coach, most of what we do is agree with the coachee, we are unlikely to be encouraging them to consider their perspective in any other way than they are already doing so. In these cases, while coaching is likely to provide a forum for the coachee to 'offload', the coachee is unlikely to learn much from this offloading. The challenge comes in encouraging the coachee to consider an alternative perspective to their situation. This can be challenging as it may reveal information that the coachee does not necessarily feel comfortable with.

When we reflect, we tend to do so in a range of specific ways. One way of reflecting is to change our perspective: either zooming in to explore the focal experience in greater detail or zooming out to look at the bigger picture or examining the experience from an alternative perspective (by putting ourselves in another's 'shoes'). Positive psychology approaches to coaching tend to draw on this type of reflection to encourage behavioural change. A characteristic of positive psychology interventions is that they encourage the coachee to focus on the positive aspects of life. For example, both the three good things technique (where the coachee is asked to recall three good things that happened during a day) and using strengths in new ways (coachees are asked to consider their top strengths and apply one of their key strengths to resolve a challenging situation) (Kauffman, Boniwell, & Silberman, 2014) facilitate reflection by requiring the coachee to zoom in and focus reflection on specific elements of experience (either positive aspects of their day in the three good things technique or a more detailed understanding of their strengths). Whereas an exercise such as best possible future self (where coachees are asked to imagine a future where life has turned out how they wanted) involves zooming out to reflect on desires for the future and how these might manifest as part of the bigger picture.

An example of an approach that encourages reflection by examining the experience from an alternative perspective (by putting ourselves in another's 'shoes') as well as zooming out from the issue is the systemic constellations approach in coaching. Farr and Shepheard (2019) state that the aim through constellations in coaching is to reveal what has been previously hidden or obscured by considering the situation from a wider system perspective. One specific technique used in this approach is the physical map. The coachee is first invited to map the elements of the system in relation to each other. With a specific focal issue in mind, the coachee takes physical objects to represent each of the individuals, groups, and other components important in consideration of the issue (often purposely made constellation pieces are used for this exercise) and place them out on the table in relation to each other to form the constellation. When placing markers, coachees are encouraged to consider the distance between the elements and the system boundary and the direction of focus. The coach and coachee can then discuss what they see and interact with the map to get a sense of the relationship between the elements (therefore reflecting by zooming out of the experience) and how it is to occupy certain places in the system (therefore reflecting by placing ourselves in another's 'shoes'). Another example of reflection by encouraging a change of perspective in this way is the cognitive behavioural coaching technique of befriending yourself (Palmer & Szymanska, 2019). This technique encourages coachees to examine negative thoughts by asking them to consider if a friend made a similar mistake, would they be as critical or harsh as they are towards themselves? This approach encourages the coachee to reflect on how they are thinking about themselves by putting themselves in their friend's shoes. How would I feel as the friend if these things were said to me? Gestalt coaching also frequently encourages reflection by exploring a situation from someone else's perspective. For example, Allan and Whybrow (2019) propose that a gestalt approach to coaching can facilitate awareness through encouraging the coachee to hold a conversation with the part of themselves critical to the focal issue or the absent other from whom these beliefs, assumptions, and values were learned. The process of holding a conversation (where the coachee responds to both sides of the conversation) encourages the coachee to consider how the 'other' would respond (either an imagined specific part of themselves or someone else). The process of responding in the conversation facilitates reflective thought, enabling the coachee to identify underlying patterns of perception that may be influencing their current behaviour.

Another way that we can reflect is by returning to an experience. Often coachees will wish to discuss a one-off incident or issue; however, it can also be helpful to encourage reflection by exploring whether there is a recurrent situation that we can learn from, where we might identify themes or patterns in our actions and behaviours. One technique that encourages us to move beyond the isolated issue to explore patterns is the cognitive behavioural coaching technique of looking for the evidence (Palmer & Szymanska, 2019). This technique assumes that we can make faulty assessments of ourselves based on flawed assumptions. Therefore, if the coachee believes that their performance was poor, they are encouraged to gather evidence to inform their belief rather than making assumptions that may be inaccurate. This technique encourages reflection by requiring the coaching to think back to similar scenarios and considering what actually happened to look for the evidence. So for example, if the coachee believes that they will mess up an upcoming presentation, during coaching, the coachee could be asked to consider other similar scenarios they have been involved in and reflect on how these went, therefore looking for patterns in their actions and behaviours that can be used to base their beliefs on and apply to the situation in-hand.

Perhaps the group of coaching approaches that most openly engage in raising awareness and facilitating reflection at its deepest level are psychodynamic approaches in coaching. For example, these approaches prompt the coachee to reflect on their issue from a different perspective, as the coach introduces information that may provide this new perspective. One such technique is using one's own feelings as data (Roberts & Brunning, 2019). This is based on the assumption that any feelings experienced by the coach are likely to be a mirror of those felt by the coachee and therefore by sharing with the coachee during the coaching conversation the feelings that the coach is experiencing, the coachee may gain useful information of what is going on under the surface. These shared observations will encourage the coachee to reflect on the issue from a new perspective (do these emotions ring true for me and if so why am I experiencing these emotions?). Another important principle in psychodynamic coaching is that the coach provides containment. Roberts and Brunning (2019) suggest that for potentially challenging unconscious thoughts and feelings to come to the surface, the coachee needs to feel safe. The coaching setting has a number of features that provide this safety or containment, consequently keeping the coachee's anxieties at a tolerable level so that they are able to relax habitual defences and therefore become more available to learning. I touched on this issue at the start of the chapter when exploring why reflection may sometimes be challenging. I proposed that a fundamental principle of coaching is that a trusting relationship between the coach and the coachee is essential. In a similar way to the concept of containment in psychodynamic coaching, I propose that the trusting relationship facilitates reflection. I expand on the reasons for this, including how coaches can facilitate the development of a trusting relationship later in this chapter.

Generally, all of these coaching tools and techniques are working towards the same goal – to raise awareness by probing deeper, changing perspective, and ultimately encouraging reflection. The difference is the way that they go about this. Some tools and techniques will work better than others depending on your preference as a coach and the coachee's preferential way of learning, as discussed in the chapters in Section two when I explored the coachee factors that influence the effectiveness of coaching. The challenge as a coach is to know when is the appropriate time to use which tool to raise awareness through reflection.

What is the evidence that learning through reflection works in coaching?

There have been few direct tests of the role of reflection in coaching; therefore, most of the reasoning explored so far has been drawn from other evidence-bases. Part of the challenge with researching reflection in coaching is that unlike the research on the impact of reflective writing, it is difficult to isolate the reflective component of coaching to test it. In coaching, enabling learning through reflection is generally combined with other process such as goal-setting. Consequently, it is challenging to isolate these processes in research to fully test the impact and establish the boundary conditions of this impact. However, De Haan and colleagues (Day, De Haan, Sills,

Bertie, & Blass, 2008; De Haan, Bertie, Day, & Sills, 2010) have conducted research in this area. For example, Day et al. (2008) interviewed 28 experienced coaches about the critical moments they have experienced in coaching. A moment often becomes 'critical' when we see in retrospect that it 'proved to be' significant. Day et al. (2008) found that when they compared the critical moments which contain reflection with those that did not have any reflection, there was a marked difference in the outcome of the critical moment. Where no reflection was present, the critical moment often resulted in a distancing in the coaching relationship or a breakdown of the relationship. On the other hand, where the critical moment created a point of reflection, the result was a deepening in the coaching relationship and positive change for the coachee. Building on this, De Haan et al. (2010) conducted interviews with selected individuals who had described a critical moment and some who had indicated they had not experienced one. A total of 59 critical moments were analysed from 47 participants. De Haan et al. (2010) found that coachees primarily hoped to find personal realizations such as a deeper understanding of themselves through coaching and often related positive outcomes following coaching to an increase in insight and realization.

In our experimental study to explore the influence of coachee personality on outcomes from coaching discussed in detail in Chapter 5 on coachee goal orientation (Jones, Woods, & Zhou, 2019), we explained the interactions we observed between coachee avoid goal orientation (where individuals are focused on avoiding incompetence in comparison with others) and performance change following coaching, by the coaching process of facilitating learning through reflection. In this study, we found that individuals high in avoid goal orientation (they set goals that are focused on avoiding incompetence in comparison with others) demonstrated greater performance gains following coaching than individuals low in avoid goal orientation. For coachees high in avoid goal orientation, we argued that the intrapersonal focus of learning through reflection in coaching allows individuals high on avoid goal orientation to effectively explore and extend their goals beyond avoidance of failure and consequently enable the greater application of self-regulatory resources to goal achievement behaviours. Our prediction is supported by the evidence from the coaching literature that indicates that coaching can lead to increased self-efficacy (Grant, 2014). Furthermore, research by Neff, Hsieh, and Dejitterat (2005) found that self-compassion was negatively associated with avoid goal orientations; therefore, individuals high in avoid goal orientation tended to demonstrate less self-compassion. Individuals who struggle to demonstrate self-compassion may be inclined to ruminate (i.e. focus on perceived threats, losses, or injustices to the self) rather than reflect (i.e. focus on challenging self-limiting beliefs and noticing previously overlooked strengths). Therefore, those individuals who are high in avoid goal orientation appear to particularly benefit from working with a coach, as the coach can facilitate learning from reflection and directly address the negative consequence of low self-compassion by exploring the consequence of negative self-talk (Palmer & Szymanska, 2019).

I found further support for these arguments in the experimental study on the impact of coaching on selection success also discussed in detail in Chapter 6 on coachee self-efficacy (Andrews & Jones, 2020). In this study, we were interested in the influence of coachee self-efficacy (an individual's belief in their ability to successfully execute behaviours) on outcomes from coaching. We found that coachee's low in self-efficacy (who doubt their ability to successfully execute behaviours) benefitted the most from coaching and were, therefore, more likely to be successfully selected for a job. We believe that the role of reflection in the coaching process is key to explaining this finding. For example, self-efficacy beliefs influence the self-regulation of thought processes (Chen, Gully, Whiteman, & Kilcullen, 2000; Raub & Liao, 2012). Regardless of objective skill levels, perceived self-efficacy influences the beliefs held by an individual about what they are capable of in different circumstances (Bandura, 1997). Low self-efficacy can result in self-doubt, even in highly skilled individuals (Chen et al., 2000). In difficult circumstances, these individuals may focus on their shortcomings, the difficulty of the task before them and the negative consequences of not succeeding. This negative thinking diverts attention away from the task (Chen et al., 2000), which further undermines performance (Bandura, 1997). For example, coachees with low self-efficacy are more likely to find it challenging to successfully promote themselves during the selection process, such as when completing an application form or during the interview. They may dwell on their deficiencies and therefore find it difficult to identify and articulate their strengths in the same way that may come more easily to an individual high in self-efficacy. However, the core component of enabling behavioural change through raising awareness and reflection in coaching (Connor & Pokara, 2012; Hawkins & Smith, 2013) appears to interact with self-efficacy, so that coaching can help individuals low in self-efficacy to compensate for the negative impact of their low regulation of thought processes. Engaging in reflection may lead to excessive emotionality in individuals with low self-efficacy (Gully & Chen, 2010), which can lead to a preoccupation with negative thoughts and emotions. A coach can reduce this effect, using various tools and techniques such as challenging self-limiting beliefs (Palmer & Szymanska, 2019), consequently ensuring that the coachee maintains a focus on gaining insight that enables learning. By using reflective questioning to raise the individuals' awareness of their strengths and how to effectively communicate these during the selection process, coaching will enable those who are low in self-efficacy to develop the skills required for self-promotion, which comes more naturally for those who are high in self-efficacy.

While there is still a shortage of direct tests of the impact of reflection in coaching on outcomes, there is sufficient evidence on the role of reflection in learning more widely which means that we can be relatively confident that reflection is very important in understanding how coaching works. Further support for this is the evidence that indicates that self-awareness or insight is a cognitive outcome of coaching. If we understand that reflection is an essential component of effective coaching, then a necessary outcome of this is that the coachee will become more self-aware (which will subsequently impact on behaviour change). There is a more substantial body of research that investigates whether self-awareness or insight is an outcome of coaching. For example, the positive impact of coaching on self-awareness was identified in a qualitative study by Wales (2003). Wales (2003) conducted a case study where a manager and 15 employees within a major UK bank were asked to complete an open-ended, self-report questionnaire following coaching to explore their views and experiences of coaching. The data indicated that an outcome from coaching was enhanced reflective skills. Wales (2003) argues that the ability to examine experiences, reflect on situations, formulate hypotheses, and develop new approaches enables individuals to improve and develop their management style.

Further support for the impact of coaching on self-awareness has been found in a number of quantitative studies. For example, Yu, Collins, Cavanagh, White, and Fairbrother (2008) conducted a within-group, pre-post-test research project that tested the impact of a coaching programme aimed at enhancing the work behaviours and well-being of 17 managers in a large Australian teaching hospital. The coaching was conducted over a period of six months and was described as solution-focused, cognitive-behavioural coaching. The coaching intervention comprised of a mixture of individual coaching (an average of six sessions per participant), group coaching, coaching seminars, workplace group projects, and individual personal development plans. Yu et al. (2008) found that coaching significantly increased self-insight however there was no significant change in self-reflection. There are a few important points to note with this study in relation to the quality of the research and therefore the reliability of the findings. First, Yu et al. (2008) did not use a control group, and therefore we cannot be sure that any changes observed in the coaching group would not have happened anyway. Second, the sample is very small (only 17 participants). In almost all behavioural science research, the size of the effect that we expect to observe is very small. The effect size is the extent to which an intervention (in this case, coaching) has on the outcomes we can measure (in this case, self-reflection). A large effect would describe a dramatic change in the outcome that would be easily observed. On the other hand, a small effect is less noticeable or easily detected. However, even small effects are meaningful and should not be discounted as unimportant. The key to research is whether the effect observed is statistically significant. This means that we can be confident that the change (regardless of how big or small) happened due to the intervention and not due to chance. It is rare that we find an intervention that has a large effect on behaviour change, this is likely because of the multitude of factors that contribute to the way we behave. However, if we are able to identify that an intervention consistently has a positive, albeit small, impact on behaviour change then we can be satisfied in the effectiveness of the intervention. The challenge is, in quantitative research such as the study by Yu et al. (2008), a small effect becomes harder to detect in statistical analysis the smaller the sample size. Therefore, we cannot be sure that Yu et al. (2008) utilized a larger sample than 17 participants, and they may have also found that coaching had a positive impact on self-reflection as well as on self-insight.

Other examples of research findings supporting the positive impact of coaching on self-insight, however with the limitation of no control group for comparison, are provided by Grant and colleagues. Grant (2014) ex-amined the impact of four coaching sessions conducted over a 10–12 week period with 49 participants and found that there was a significant increase in self-insight. Similarly, Grant et al. (2017) found a significant increase in self-insight in 31 participants who undertook six, one-hour coaching sessions where the coaching was conducted by professional leadership coaches. Grant et al. (2017) also collected qualitative data which provided support for the quantitative results. For example, participants reported that they were able to take better or different perspectives and the coaching challenged their thinking providing an important impetus for change. Grant (2014) argues that the increase in self-insight following coaching makes sense in that the process of being coached requires that coachees engage in a reflective process, reflecting both in relation to their day-to-day activities related to the goal striving process and during the actual coaching sessions themselves.

A more robust research design was adopted by Bozer, Sarros, and Santora (2014) who compared the impact of cognitive-behavioural, solution-focused coaching with a control group that received no coaching, on a range of outcomes including self-awareness. Participants in the experimental con-dition ($n = 72$) received between 10 and 12 weekly coaching sessions spread across four months. All participants were based in Israel, and the coaching was provided by 68 coaches working across four external coaching firms. Data were collected from these participants before and after coaching and compared to a control group ($n = 29$) who received no coaching. Interest-ingly, Bozer et al. (2014) did not find a significant increase in self-awareness when comparing the pre- and post-data for the coaching group to the con-trol group. However, their analysis did reveal a significant interaction effect for self-awareness and the coaches' academic background in psychology, in that participants whose coach had an academic background in psychol-ogy, demonstrated greater increased in self-awareness following coaching than participants whose coach did not have an academic background in psychology. Bozer et al. (2014) explained this finding by proposing that the academic background of coaches may define their coaching approach and consequently influence outcomes. They argue that psychologists are potentially best equipped to conduct coaching because of their particular training in psychological dynamics and adult development, their understanding of personality and performance assessment, and their skills in listening and counselling and in establishing, handling, and maintaining confidential and trusting relationships with coaches.

With regards to the quality of evidence, we can conclude that the overall rating is of moderate quality. The strengths of the research in this area are the explicit theoretical underpinning and the consistency of evidence, particularly from the qualitative studies. However, the directness of intervention is low as many studies report coaching coupled with additional interventions and the directness of outcome is moderate to low as the studies in this area generally rely on self-report data. While the evidence towards the impact of coaching on self-insight or self-awareness may be described as of just moderate quality, the results do indicate that an effect does appear to be present; however, this effect may be small or it may be complex in that it relies on the skills of the coach. These findings potentially provide support for the argument that a strong relationship between the coach and coachee is fundamental to facilitate reflection in coaching which is the topic of the next section.

What in coaching facilitates reflection?

When seeking to understand why reflecting in coaching may be more powerful than reflecting alone, it is first necessary to consider the nature of reflection and the conditions under which reflection can occur. Kahneman (2011) describes the state needed for reflection as slow thinking: a conscious, explicit, analytical process that tends to require a high level of effort. Thinking slow is much harder than thinking fast, which tends to happen unconsciously and automatically; however, it is the state needed to engage in a reflective thought. This means that we are unlikely to be able to think reflectively when we are faced with a highly demanding situation when we are under stress or feeling anxious or overstretched. It is, therefore, important to create the correct conditions where we can take the time to think slowly, to reflect, and raise awareness of the unconscious motives behind our thoughts and behaviours. The need for the right conditions to reflect helps to explain why individuals can find it difficult to reflect on their own. For example, often, time pressures can lead one to feel that they don't have the time to reflect and feeling time-pressured is one sure way of ensuring that deep reflective thought is just not going to happen.

If we also understand that engaging in reflective thought can be challenging in terms of highlighting aspects of the individual that are uncomfortable to bear, having the right conditions to ensure that the accompanying thoughts and emotions are tolerable becomes even more important. This is what coaching can provide. First, when a coachee is present in a coaching session, they are automatically in the right conditions as outlined by Kahneman (2011) to reflect. They have permission to slow down, and they are removed from the pressures of their daily life – if just for the hour or two of their coaching session. Second and perhaps most importantly, the coach can create the right conditions to ensure that the coachee feels able to tolerate any challenging or uncomfortable thoughts and feelings that may arise during deep reflection. These conditions are created via the coaching relationship.

The importance of a trusting relationship has been established in research in other domains similar to coaching. For example, in the context of mentoring, a similar, relational development intervention, research has established the importance of the relationship between mentor and protégé in producing effective outcomes from mentoring (e.g. Ensher & Murphy, 2010; Eby, 2007). Similarly, research into the relative efficacy of internal versus external employee assistance programmes (EAPs) has found that external EAPs appear to be more effective, a finding which is believed to be due to the fact that external EAP providers are viewed by employees as promoting feelings of confidentiality in comparison with internal providers (Csiernik, 1999). Furthermore, in relation to external versus internal outplacement counselling provision, external providers were viewed as being more credible, sophisticated, and with greater expertise when compared to internal providers (Kilcrease, 2013).

The relationship in coaching research has frequently been investigated from the perspective of understanding trust between the coach and the coachee. For example, Boyce, Jackson and Neal (2010) explored the coachees' level of trust in the coach and the coaches' perceptions of the coachees' honesty and candidness in the coaching conversations. Boyce et al. found that coachees' ratings of trust were a significant predictor of affective outcomes in the format of coachees' ratings of satisfaction and success of their coaching programme. However, coachee perceptions of trust were not a significant predictor at the skill-based outcome level for self-reported improvements in leadership performance following coaching. From the coaches' perspective, perceptions of the coachees' honesty and candidness were significant predictors of affective outcomes in the format of the coaches' perceptions of the success of the coaching intervention. Gan and Chong (2015) collected data from a sample of 172 coachees in Malaysia, who completed a survey reporting on the levels of rapport, commitment, and trust they felt with their coach and their perceived coaching effectiveness. Gan and Chong (2015) found that while rapport and commitment were significantly related to perceived coaching effectiveness, trust was not. However, these findings should be treated with caution giving the limitations associated with cross-sectional data such as this. In particular, a survey study such as this is reliant on the participants' memory of their perceptions of the variables measured (in this case rapport, commitment, and trust) which is likely to be influenced by a variety of factors including the length of time between receiving coaching and completing the questionnaire.

The role of trust in coaching has been researched more extensively utilizing qualitative methodologies, with many of these studies highlighting the importance of the coachees' perceptions of trust (Alvey & Barclay, 2007; Gyllensten & Palmer, 2007; Jowett, Kanakoglou, & Passmore, 2012; Rekalde, Landeta, & Albizu, 2015; Salomaa, 2015). Particularly, these studies highlighted the importance the coachees placed on trusting that the coach would maintain their confidentiality. Therefore, the evidence appears to highlight the importance of being confident in levels of confidentiality and credibility in terms of competence of the practitioner (i.e. coach, mentor or counsellor) are important aspects in facilitating a strong trusting relationship which will consequently lead to positive outcomes.

Another important body of research that coaches can draw on regarding the importance of the coaching relationship comes from the field of psychotherapy. Earlier, when exploring how reflection is used in psychotherapeutic approaches to coaching, I touched on the concept of containment (i.e. that the coach creates a safe space to allow the coachee to explore potentially challenging experiences without being overwhelmed by negative emotions). Brown and Stobart (2007) argue how, in the context of psychotherapy, when powerful emotions are being addressed, or are in the background, a secure container for those feelings is important if not essential. Brown and Stobart discuss containment in relation to boundaries in psychotherapy, including how the presence of a routine provides a safe and reliable setting in which to experience that which is not safe and reliable. At the start of this chapter, I highlighted that we are often defended against reflection to protect ourselves from feelings of shame or humiliation in relation to our perceived or actual shortcomings. As such, the concept of containment as discussed in the psychotherapy research is likely to be applicable to helping us to understand the role of the coaching relationship in securing positive outcomes from coaching. Day et al. (2008) found some evidence for this argument in their research conducting interviews with 28 experienced coaches about the critical moments they have experienced in coaching. They found that in moments where the coach was able to reflect on their emotional state and respond in a manner that 'contained' (Bion, 1965) the coachee's emotion, then the result tended to be a deepening of the relationship or evidence of change by the coachee. Day et al. (2008) highlight that shared reflection between the coach and the coachee on moments of emotional tension in the relationship is, therefore, very influential on whether this tension can be used to facilitate learning or become problematic for the work. This seems to confirm Bion's (1965) general idea that what clients try to achieve is to transform their emotional experience through thinking into new opportunities for action.

RESEARCH IN ACTION: A COACH'S PERSPECTIVE

When coaching starts, obviously one of the aspects of building trust is the detailed contracting and ensuring that the coachee has confidence in the confidentiality and the robustness of that. This is particularly important when one is dealing with and has access to the coachee's colleagues. The other thing that I think helps to create trust is the humility and vulnerability of the coach. Not so much in terms of role modelling it, but being able to relate at an adult-to-adult level. That sense of "we are equals here". Therefore being OK in oneself as the coach, with whatever will take place in the coaching. Being prepared for the unpredictable. Coming into coaching with that sense of letting go of any expectations. That's the way that I inhabit that space, that's my approach. I also believe in the value of normalizing people's challenges. So saying phrases like "don't think you're the only person with this issue. Your own response to it will be unique but it is a very common challenge". That sets one at ease, so the coachee may think, "Well I'm OK to share more about that as you have heard this a million times before. You're curious about me and my context and how I show up in that" so there is a normalization, while also holding the space for what occurs, not with any expectation of what road we might be going down. I think that another way I create trust is in being prepared to give feedback to my coachees about their impact on me. Demonstrating to coachees that the coaching conversation is entirely unique. It allows for a type of conversation that they wouldn't have anywhere else. This all links to the honesty in terms of relating to them on an adult-to-adult level, giving honest feedback or sharing what I notice that others might not say. Being prepared to take a bit of a risk. In terms of, if they don't like it, does it matter? Although I accept that for many coaches, this comes with experience, in the early days, it can be very hard to take this risk.

The ultimate aim of creating trust in coaching is to allow space for the coachee to be vulnerable, however, even with trust, it can be difficult for people to be vulnerable because of their ego defences. I think as coaches, we have to be careful at challenging the ego defences because they are there for a good reason and therefore we are not always going to get people to be vulnerable. I don't think it is our role as a coach to get people to be vulnerable, instead it is to create the space where the coachee can choose to be vulnerable, which is not the same thing at all.

For details of the coaches who were interviewed for the 'research in action' vignettes, see page 191.

Before moving on to explore how we can facilitate the development of a trusting relationship in coaching that will facilitate deep reflection, it is also important to touch on the role of challenge in coaching. In Section one of this book, I detailed that supportive challenge is one of the fundamental principles of coaching. The role of the coach goes beyond an empathic listener – a coach should encourage the coachee to think about their challenges differently and to do this, a supportive challenge is required. The term supportive is important as without the support, a challenge can be experienced as aggressive or confrontational. It is likely that this type of challenge will be received with resistance, with the recipient becoming defensive rather than open to considering questions that the challenge may bring. However, a supportive challenge within the context of a trusting relationship is more likely to achieve the desired objective of facilitating reflection by encouraging the coachee to consider an alternative perspective, challenging underlying assumptions or consider the bigger picture. Supportive challenge can come in many forms and how you provide supportive challenge will likely depend on your approach as a coach and the tools and techniques that you prefer to use. Rogers (2016) describes a number of different methods of providing a challenge in coaching. These are:

- Getting to the crux – forcing the client to name what is ultimately at stake
- Interrupting – when in the interest of the coachee, particularly when the coach suspects that the coachee is avoiding the real point of the issue
- Data at the moment – how is the coachee affecting you (the coach) now at this minute?
- Giving feedback – to comment on the immediate behaviour and impact of the coachee
- Provocation and humour – using an overt tone of teasing, joyfulness, lightness, and challenge
- Tough speaking and confrontation – to be a successful type of challenge, this must be motivated by the coaches desire to help
- When coachees make mistakes – agreeing that the coachee did something wrong

Other examples of supportive challenge linked to specific coaching approaches include a psychodynamic coach who uses their own feelings as data (the same as Rogers (2016) suggestion of using data at the moment) and share these feelings with the coachee, with the aim of raising awareness of what may be going on under the surface for the coachee. For example, if a coach were to comment to the coachee that the coach was experiencing feelings of fear at the moment, it is highly likely that the coachee will find it quite challenging to hear this. A cognitive-behavioural coach, on the other hand, can use supportive challenge by using a range of specific techniques, such as looking for the evidence, to identify thinking errors, such as mind-reading, blame or all-or-nothing thinking, rather than being complicit with the coachee by allowing the forum for these thinking errors to go unchecked. The most widely used and perhaps most simple tool to facilitate a supportive challenge in coaching is the use of Socratic questions (such as how do you know this? What do you mean by? What are you assuming?), which encourage the coachee to consider the issue from alternative perspectives.

Recommendations for practice

If we understand that a trusting relationship is fundamental in coaching to facilitate learning through reflection, then the next important point of consideration is how do we create a trusting relationship, and consequently we need to understand what factors influence whether a relationship is considered trusting or not. This is the point where the evidence-base is less useful. Like the psychotherapy research, while much research exists that illustrates that the relationship in coaching is important, we still do not know which 'bits' of the relationship are most important. For example, in relation to the body of psychotherapy and counselling research, Cooper (2008) highlights that the interrelated nature of factors that contribute to a strong therapeutic relationship means that it is difficult to identify discrete, distinguishable relational factors. Where discrete factors have been identified, the research indicates that they are highly correlated (Salvio, Beutler, Wood, & Engle, 1992), meaning that this evidence does not help us to distinguish whether one factor is contributing more to the therapeutic relationship than another. Other studies have indicated that from the clients' perspective, there is only one important relational factor which is that the therapist is experienced as being caring (Williams & Chambless, 1990). This is somewhat supported by the conclusion drawn by De Haan et al. (2010) who noted that coachees mention the coaching relationship infrequently when things are going well in coaching. This suggests that the coaching relationship could be considered a hygiene factor: a factor where the presence does not lead to satisfaction; however, the absence will lead to dissatisfaction. Therefore, when the relationship is good, coachees do not tend to notice the coaching relationship; however, when there is a weak or no coaching relationship, coachees will feel dissatisfied, have limited positive outcomes from coaching and consequently may lead to the early termination of coaching. The fact that coachee's struggle to notice the coaching relationship when it is going well is likely one of the contributing factors that make it difficult to measure the discrete relationship factors that contribute to positive outcomes from coaching, as the measurement of these factors is likely to rely on either the coach or a researchers' assessment of the factors and not include coachee's perspectives.

While the evidence-base has yet to conclusively highlight which specific factors facilitate trust in coaching, I theorize the factors that I consider to be the most important and explore these factors here. Earlier, in Section one, I highlighted five principles that underscore what it means to be an effective coach: openness, unconditional positive regard, non-judgmental attitude, growth mindset, and authenticity. I propose that these five principles are particularly important when considered in the context of developing a trusting relationship in coaching.

I propose that the five principles I outline as fundamental for effective coaches all underscore the same important aspect of providing containment and a safe environment to build a strong coaching relationship and consequently facilitate trust. These principles all influence the extent to which a coachee feels that the coach believes in them. For example, a coach who has a high level of openness is likely to be broad-minded and will, therefore, avoid passing judgements on others. A coach who has unconditional positive regard for their coachees will experience feelings of warmth and caring for another that is not conditional on the behaviour or actions of that individual. Again, this means that the coach will not pass judgement on the coachee and the coachee can be confident that whatever they discuss during coaching or their behaviour following coaching (such as failure to follow-up on agreed actions) will not impact on the feelings of warmth and caring the coach has for the coachee. The non-judgmental attitude of the coach clearly has an important role to play in the development of a trusting relationship. It is difficult, if not impossible to experience strong feelings of trust towards someone who you feel is judging you negatively. Finally, a growth mindset facilitates trust because it links to the issue of judgement. I am not passing judgment on you in relation to the limits of your ability. I believe in you. I believe that you can achieve whatever you set out to achieve. I believe that human potential is limitless when motivation and effort are present. The impact of holding a growth mindset is linked to the well-established psychological concept of self-fulfilling prophecy. Research into self-fulfilling prophecy has demonstrated the powerful influences other people's beliefs can have. The influence of self-fulfilling prophecy is so powerful that all clinical trials are now run as double-blind (i.e. neither the participant nor the researchers know whether a participant is being given a placebo drug or the experimental drug) as the researchers' knowledge that a participant was receiving the experimental drug (and the researchers' belief that this drug would positively impact participant outcomes) creates an actual change in participant outcomes (Fine, 2007). The impact of self-fulfilling prophecy has been investigated in a wide range of contexts including educational settings. For example, Rosenthal (2003) demonstrated that teachers' expectations in students' abilities lead to real and measurable enhancements in students' intelligence. The impact of the self-fulfilling prophecy is explained by the unconscious influence our expectations have on our behaviour. If I believe that you will succeed then I am more likely to invest more in supporting you. Consequently, if a coach holds a growth mindset, then they will sincerely expect all coachees to achieve their goals and fulfil their potential, creating the conditions for a positive self-fulfilling prophecy for all of their coachees. Finally, the authenticity of the coach is also fundamental to building a trusting relationship in coaching. This is based on the assumption that if an individual is not behaving authentically, for example, I don't really adopt a growth mindset but I am going to 'fake' it because I have read that it is important, others can tell. They might not be able to put their finger on what specifically isn't authentic; however, they will know that something isn't quite right, and this will lead to doubts about the credibility of the coach.

A helpful theoretical framework to consider in this context is from the leadership literature that proposes that the leader's character influences a follower's sense of vulnerability in a hierarchical relationship (e.g. Mayer, Davis, & Shoorman, 1995). Mayer et al. (1995) propose a model suggesting that when followers believe their leaders have integrity, capability, and benevolence, they will be more comfortable engaging in behaviours that put them at risk (e.g. sharing sensitive information). In the context of mentoring, Mayer et al. (1995) suggest that the psychological safety experienced by the protégé can be described as a willingness to engage in risk-taking actions and being vulnerable to the action of the mentor. We have already seen evidence of how this translates to coaching with the research detailing that confidence in confidentiality in coaching is a key aspect of a trusting relationship. Therefore, do I believe that my coach has integrity and will consequently keep what we discuss confidential? Benevolence can be linked to the concept of unconditional positive regard discussed earlier. Therefore, do I believe that my coach is a kind and well-meaning person? Finally, credibility is important in coaching. Do I believe that my coach has the capability to help me to achieve my goals? If I perceive that my coach is not authentic, it is unlikely that I am going to be confident in the other aspects required to facilitate trust. I may consequently doubt their benevolence and capability and most certainly their integrity.

So how does this translate to practice? First, be authentic! Bring yourself to coaching. This is most important in influencing the type of coaching you do. Don't try to use a coaching approach, tool, or technique that you don't fully believe in, as it will not come across authentically in coaching. The approaches that will work best for you as a coach are those that you believe in – regardless of what others might tell you about the technique. You can also engage in specific activities to demonstrate how you act with integrity in coaching and your capability as a coach. A great deal of this work can be done prior to the first coaching session and during the first session in the contracting stage. Before coaching starts, you can demonstrate capability in the chemistry or set-up phase of coaching by providing the coachee with information on your coaching expertise and background or references from other clients. To demonstrate integrity, an explicit discussion of confidentiality before the coaching starts, during the contracting stage, including what will or will not be disclosed to a sponsor must be completed. This is likely to be of even greater importance when coaching is provided by an internal coach. Demonstrating integrity by the way that the coach conducts themselves in terms of clearly serving the interests of the coachee and not themselves or the sponsor, for example in terms of recommending a flexible number of sessions rather than a fixed number of sessions may also help to achieve this.

Gettman, Edinger, and Wouters (2019) sought to examine coach behaviour involved in the contracting process. They define contracting as 'the collaborative determination of logistics, parameters, and framework of the coaching engagement, including the inclusion of others, and the goals, roles and responsibilities of each party' (p. 48). Gettman et al. (2019) propose that contracting can affect the coaching relationship in a number of ways. In particular, they suggest that contracting will impact coachee perceptions of the coaches' expertise. Therefore, strong contracting behaviours is one way of demonstrating knowledge and experience as a coach. Contracting is also likely to be related to mutual respect and, therefore, a trusting bond. Gettman et al. (2019) propose that the process of coming to a mutual agreement on goals, roles, and expectations should engender positive feelings of shared purpose, while the clear explication of parameters should increase trust in the coaches' motivations and intentions.

An important note in relation to contracting and trust in the context of the leader as a coach is that the leader as a coach should also consider the extent to which they 'contract' with their employees. While this 'contracting' while likely look quite different to the contracting completed by the independent coach, it is equally as important for the leader as a coach to explicitly discuss topics such as confidentiality, goals, roles, and responsibilities. Contracting between the leader as a coach and an employee can help to foster trust if the leader as a coach is explicit in the discussion of their approach. This is likely to be particularly important if the leader is changing their leadership approach and shifting towards a coaching approach to leadership. An abrupt change to a coaching style of leadership is likely to be perceived with at best surprise and worse suspicion if the leader does not discuss with the employee the change in approach. On the other hand, an explicit discussion of the new style of leadership models openness and transparency that in turn may help to foster openness and transparency in subsequent coaching style conversations between the leader and employee. Next, I expand on how the leader as a coach can enable behaviour change through reflection.

Leader as a coach and enabling reflection

In addition to adopting coaching techniques to enable learning through reflection, leaders as coaches are also able to create additional opportunities for employees to learn through reflection. For example, reflective practice can be further integrated into the working day to encourage employees to engage in reflective practice and further enhance this skill through repeated practice. For example, after-event reviews or post-shift debriefings can be a useful way to provide a structured format to encourage consistent reflection and learning from experience. An after-event review involves holding a meeting after a key event or completion of a project, or in the case of a post-shift debriefing, at the end of the working day, in which the purpose of the meeting is to review the major events, how these linked to the team objectives, what went well in facilitating the achievement of these objectives, and what didn't go so well. The review should involve the identification of specific next steps for future action based on these reflections. Not only is adopting an approach such as this likely to impact on the individual's ability to be reflective (by practicing reflection), research also indicates that shared reflection such as this has positive effects for the team. For example, Chen, Bamberger, Song, and Vashdi (2018) compared the impact of daily post-shift debriefings within a manufacturing plant of an electronics company in southern China, where 36 teams participated in structured daily post-shift debriefings and a control group of 37 teams did not (the total number of participants within these teams was 469). Chen et al. (2018) provided the intervention group with training on guided reflexivity and found that the post-shift debriefings and the teams' level of reflexivity had an important protective effect, in that it enhanced team members' sense of control and support at work and consequently improved well-being. Chen et al. (2018) suggest that team reflexivity enhances collaborative processes such as workload sharing, which helps the development of supportive relationships within the team. The structured debriefings also appear to create a sense of psychological safety so that reflexivity may have enhanced the team members' sense of trust in their teammates, therefore allowing them to seek and provide support to one another more freely. Leaders wishing to adopt an approach such as this to enhance team reflection should ensure that first, team members are trained in the process and purpose of team reflection and second, that the reflective meetings (whether these are daily post-shift debriefings or less regular after-event reviews) follow a structured approach to maximize the learning and other positive outcomes from reflection.

Leaders as coaches can also support individual employees in their own reflective practice by providing the physical time and space for employees to engage in reflection. In a study to understand the experience of daily reflective practice, an MSc dissertation student of mine asked ten operational managers working in a fast-moving consumer goods environment to reflect on one positive and one negative situation they experienced each day over three weeks (Blight, 2018). Prior to the start of the intervention, managers were provided with a half-day training workshop that covered the definition of reflection, setting development goals, barriers to reflection, and the structure of reflection. The participants' managers were also briefed on the research and given instructions to organize a face-to-face weekly meeting to facilitate a discussion of what the participants were learning, support participants by reducing any barriers to reflection, and provide feedback on any observable shifts in behaviour. Following the intervention, to gather views on the experience of engaging in daily reflective practice, the participants were interviewed and a focus group was conducted with the participants' managers. Findings indicated that factors that facilitated the daily reflections included the initial training programme, as this enabled participants to understand why it was important to reflect and how to reflect; the level of management support, particularly in relation to helping participants to identify examples for reflection and maintaining momentum and finally the structure to guide the reflection was highlighted as an important facilitator. Findings indicated that barriers to reflection included a lack of time to reflect, although participants also identified that the use of routine was effective at helping the daily reflection to become a habit; however, once this routine was broken, it was difficult to create the momentum again. Lack of line manager support was also identified as a barrier to reflection, with participants suggesting constant support from the line manager was important. While the findings indicated that in the early stages of the intervention, participants appreciated support from the manager in relation to identifying suitable examples to reflect on, during the later stages of the intervention, participants appreciated support in relation to discussing the reflections, gaining feedback on behaviour and linking the reflections to performance.

These findings suggest that leaders as coaches can take a number of specific steps to encourage their employees to reflect. For example, they can provide a structured process for reflection including training on why reflection is important and how to reflect; they can create a legitimate need for reflection to prioritize reflective practice and enable employees to take the time out of their work day to reflect without feeling guilty or that they are being self-indulgent; they can facilitate the formation of good reflective habits and routine by discussing with employees how and when they could fit regular reflection into their daily lives and facilitate the implementation of this where necessary (for example by creating the physical space or protecting this time for the employees); and finally by providing direct support in relation to encouraging reflective practice. This may involve discussing suitable examples to reflect on during the early stages of reflective practice. Once these skills are developed, support may involve providing positive feedback where leaders as coaches notice changes in behaviour, discussing the impact of the reflective practice during one-to-ones and exploring whether there are any other barriers to the reflection that the leader as a coach can support the employee in removing.

This chapter in summary

- Reflection is the structured, focused and conscious process to develop our understanding
- Coaches enable behaviour change by creating the conditions for coachee reflection
- Reflection can involve changing perspective (zooming in or out or examining the experience from an alternative perspective) or by identifying patterns
- Coaches facilitate coachee reflection by creating the right conditions. These are:
  - The time and space to reflect
  - Supportive challenge to enable critical reflection
  - The safe space to reflect through a strong relationship
- To create a strong relationship, coaches can:
  - Demonstrate capability (i.e. through contracting and pre-coaching communications)
  - Demonstrate integrity (i.e. that you have the coachee's best interests in mind)
  - Demonstrate benevolence (i.e. through adopting unconditional positive regard and a non-judgmental attitude)
- Leaders as coaches can build trust by modelling openness and transparency when discussing their leadership style
- Leaders as coaches can facilitate reflective practice in their team by providing the conditions and structure to support reflection and remove barriers to reflection

References

Andrews, H., & Jones, R. J. (2020). Can one-to-one coaching improve selection success and who benefits most? The role of candidate generalized self-efficacy. Unpublished manuscript.

Allan, J., & Whybrow, A. (2019). Gestalt coaching. In S. Palmer & A. Whybrow (Eds.), *Handbook of coaching psychology: A guide for practitioners.* London, UK: Routledge.

Alvey, S., & Barclay, K. (2007). The characteristics of dyadic trust in executive coaching. *Journal of Leadership Studies, 1*(1), 18–27. doi:10.1002/jls.20004

Bandura, A. (1997). *Self-efficacy: The exercise of control.* New York: W. H. Freeman and Company.

Bion, W. R. (1965). *Transformations.* London, UK: William Heinemann.

Blight, S. (2018). Press the pause button: Exploring the impact of a reflective practice intervention on the learning of managers. Unpublished master's thesis. Henley Business School. Oxfordshire, UK.

Boyce, L. A., Jackson, J. R., & Neal, L. J. (2010). Building successful leadership coaching relationships: Examining impact of matching criteria in a leadership coaching program. *Journal of Management Development, 29*(10), 914–931. doi:10.1108/02621711011084231

Bozer, G., Sarros, J. C., & Santora, J. C. (2014). Academic background and credibility in executive coaching effectiveness. *Personnel Review, 43*(6), 881–897. doi:10.1108/PR-10–2013–0171

Brown, T., McCracken, M., & O'Kane, P. (2011). Don't forget to write': how reflective learning journals can help to facilitate, assess and evaluate training transfer. *Human Resource Development International, 14*, 465–481.

Brown, R., & Stobart, K. (2007). *Understanding boundaries and containment in clinical practice.* London, UK: Routledge.

Chen, J., Bamberger, P. A., Song, Y., & Vashdi, D. R. (2018). The effects of team reflexivity on psychological well-being in manufacturing teams. *Journal of Applied Psychology, 103*(4), 443–462.

Chen, G., Gully, S. M., Whiteman, J. A., & Kilcullen, R. N. (2000). Examination of relationships among trait-like individual differences, state-like individual differences, and learning performance. *Journal of Applied Psychology, 85*(6), 835–847. doi:10.1037//0021–9010.85.6.835

Chivers, G. (2003). Utilising reflective practice interviews in professional development. *Journal of European Industrial Training, 27*, 5–15.

Connor, M., & Pokora, J. (2012). *Coaching & mentoring at work: Developing effective practice.* Berkshire, UK: Open University Press.

Cooper, M. (2008). *Essential research findings in counselling and psychotherapy: The facts are friendly.* London, UK: SAGE Publications.

Csiernik, R. (1999). Internal versus external employee assistance programs. *Employee Assistance Quarterly, 15*, 1–12, doi:10.1300/J022v15n02_01

Day, A., De Haan, E., Silis, C., Bertie, C., & Blass, E. (2008). Coaches' experience of critical moments in the coaching. *International Coaching Psychology Review, 3*(3), 207–218.

De Haan, E., Bertie, C., Day, A., & Silis, C. (2010). Clients' critical moments of coaching: Toward a "client model" of executive coaching. *Academy of Management Learning & Education, 9*(4), 607–621.

Durgahee, T. (2002). Dialogism in action: talking fact and fiction. *Journal of Psychiatric and Mental Health Nursing, 9*(4), 419–425.

Eby, L. T. (2007). Understanding relational problems in mentoring: a review and proposed investment model. In B. R. Ragins & K. E. Kram (Eds.), *The handbook of mentoring at work: Theory, research, and practice,* (pp. 323–344). London, UK: SAGE Publications.

Ensher, E. A., & Murphy, S. E. (2010). The mentoring relationship challenges scale: The impact of mentoring stage, type and gender. *Journal of Vocational Behavior, 79*, 253–266. doi:10.1016/j.jvb.2010.11.008

Farr, J., & Shepheard, M. (2019). Systemic constellations approach to coaching and coaching psychology practice. In S. Palmer & A. Whybrow (Eds.), *Handbook of coaching psychology: A guide for practitioners.* London, UK: Routledge.

Fenwick, T. (2003). Reclaiming and re-embodying experiential learning through complexity science. *Studies in the Education of Adults, 35*(2), 123–141.

Fine, C. (2007). *A mind of its own: How your brain distorts and deceives.* Cambridge, UK: Icon Books.

Gan, G. C. G., & Chong, C. W. (2015). Coaching relationship in executive coaching: A Malaysian study. *Journal of Management Development, 34*(4), 476–492. doi:10.1108/JMD-08–2013–0104

Gettman, H., Edinger, S., & Wouters, K. (2019). Assessing contracting and the coaching relationship: Necessary infrastructure? *International Journal of Evidence Based Coaching and Mentoring, 17*(1), 46–62. doi:10.24384/Onfx-0779

Grant, A. M. (2014). The efficacy of executive coaching in times of organisational change. *Journal of Change Management, 14*(2), 258–280. doi:10.1080/14697017.2013.805159

Grant, A. M., Studholme, I., Verma, R., Kirkwood, L., Paton, B., & O'Connor, S. (2017). The impact of leadership coaching in an Australian healthcare setting. *Journal of Health Organization and Management, 31*(2), 237–252. doi:10.1108/JHOM-09-2016-0187

Gully, S., & Chen, G. (2010). Individual differences, attribute-treatment interactions, and training outcomes. In S. W. J. Kozlowski & E. Salas (Eds.), *SIOP organizational frontiers series. Learning, training, and development in organizations,* (pp. 3–64). New York: Routledge/Taylor Francis Group.

Gyllensten, K., & Palmer, S. (2007). The coaching relationship: An interpretative phenomenological analysis. *International Coaching Psychology Review, 2*(2), 168–177.

Hawkins, P., & Smith, N. (2013). *Coaching, mentoring and organizational consultancy: Supervision, skills & development.* Berkshire, UK: Open University Press.

Holden, R., & Griggs, V. (2011). Not more learning logs! A research based perspective on teaching reflective learning within HR professional education. *Human Resource Development International, 14*, 483–491.

Jones, R. J., Woods, S. A., & Zhou, Y. (2019). The effects of coachee personality and goal orientation on performance improvement following coaching: A controlled field experiment. *Applied Psychology: An International Review.* doi: 1111/apps.12218

Jowett, S., Kanakoglou, K., & Passmore, J. (2012). The application of the 3+1Cs relationship model in executive coaching. *Consulting Psychology Journal: Practice and Research, 64*(3), 183–197. doi:10.1037/a0030316

Kahneman, D. (2011). *Thinking, fast and slow.* New York: Farrar, Straus and Giroux.

Kauffman, C., Boniwell, I., & Silberman, J. (2014). The positive psychology approach to coaching. In E. Cox., T. Bachkirova, & D. Clutterbuck (Eds.), *The complete handbook of coaching* (2nd ed.). London, UK: Sage Publications.

Kilcrease, K. M. (2013). Outplacement services for displaced employees: attitudes of human resource managers based on differences in internal and external delivery. *Journal of Employment Counselling, 50*, 2–13. doi:10.1002/j.2161-1920.2013.00020.x

Klein, K., & Boals, A. (2001). Expressive writing can increase working memory capacity. *Journal of experimental psychology: General, 130*(3), 520–533.

Kolb, D. A. (1984). *Experiential learning: Experience as the source of learning and development.* Upper Saddle River, NJ: Prentice-Hall.

Mayer, R. C., Davis, J. H., & Schoorman, F. D. (1995). An integrative model of organizational trust. *Academy of Management Review, 20*(3), 709–734. doi:10.5465/AMR.1995.9508080335

Neff, K. D., Hsieh, Y. P., & Dejitterat, K. (2005). Self-compassion, achievement goals, and coping with academic failure. *Self and identity, 4*(3), 263–287. doi:10.1080/13576500444000317

Palmer, S., & Szymanska, K. (2019). Cognitive-behavioural coaching: An integrative approach. In S. Palmer & A. Whybrow (Eds.), *Handbook of coaching psychology: A guide for practitioners*. London, UK: Routledge.

Raub, S., & Liao, H. (2012). Doing the right thing without being told: Joint effects of initiative climate and general self-efficacy on employee proactive customer service performance. *Journal of Applied Psychology, 97*, 651–667. doi:10.1037/a0026736

Rekalde, I., Landeta, J., & Albizu, E. (2015) Determining factors in the effectiveness of executive coaching as a management development tool. *Management Decision, 53*, 1677–1697. doi:10.1108/MD-12-2014-0666

Roberts, V. Z., & Brunning, H. (2019). Psychodynamic and systems-psychodynamic coaching. In S. Palmer & A. Whybrow (Eds.), *Handbook of coaching psychology: A guide for practitioners*. London, UK: Routledge.

Rogers, J. (2016). *Coaching skills: The definitive guide to being a coach*. Berkshire, UK: Open University Press.

Rosenthal, R. (2003). Covert communication in laboratories, classrooms and the truly real-world. *Current Directions in Psychological Science, 12*, 151–154.

Salomaa, R. (2015). Expatriate coaching: Factors impacting coaching success. *Journal of Global Mobility, 3*(3), 216–243. doi:10.1108/JGM-10-2014-0050

Salvio, M. A., Beutler, L. E., Wood, J. M., & Engle, D. (1992). The strength of the therapeutic alliance in three treatments for depression. *Psychotherapy Research, 2*(1), 31–36.

Stevens, D. D., & Cooper, J. E. (2009). *Journal keeping: How to use reflective writing for learning, teaching, professional insight, and positive change*. Sterling, VA: Stylus Publishing Ltd.

Vince, R. (1998). Behind and beyond Kolb's learning cycle. *Journal of Management Education, 22*(3), 304–319.

Wales, S. (2003). Why coaching? *Journal of Change Management, 3*(3), 275–282. doi:10.1080/714042542

Whitmore, J. (2017). *Coaching for performance: The principles and practice of coaching and leadership*. London, UK: Nicholas Brealey Publishing.

Williams, K. E., & Chambless, D. L. (1990). The relationship between therapist characteristics and outcome of in vivo exposure treatment for agoraphobia. *Behavior Therapy, 21*(1), 111–116.

Yu, N., Collins, C. G., Cavanagh, M., White, K., & Fairbrother, G. (2008). Positive coaching with frontline managers: Enhancing their effectiveness and understanding why. *International Coaching Psychology Review, 3*(2), 110–122.

Chapter 10

Planning for action

The final process that I propose is instrumental in creating behavioural change through coaching is again one that rarely appears in coaching texts, it is often neglected in terms of the amount of attention it garners, yet, on the whole, we do it extraordinarily poorly. That is planning for action. Like goals, planning for action or action plans are part of our everyday language. However, how often do we plan for action yet fail to achieve that plan? How often do we set out to achieve something yet our progress falls short? Consider plans to change eating habits, exercise more frequently, be more patient with others, improve work-life balance, and so on. If you are anything like me and the vast majority of the population, then it is likely that you frequently make plans yet just as frequently fail to fully achieve these. Why is this the case? As I have hopefully made clear so far in this book, humans are complex creatures. There are many, many factors that influence our behaviour. Forming good habits can be extremely difficult, yet forming bad habits surprisingly easy. Even if you work with the coachee to set effective goals and enable learning through reflection, it will not be enough for sustained behaviour change. How often do we know exactly what we need to do to change (such as exercise more frequently) yet still fail to change? Although sometimes the solution may remain hidden from us and require deep reflective thought to access it, often the solution is in plain sight, yet remains beyond our reach because of the challenges in changing behaviour. While reflection plays a big part in understanding why we have not managed to change our behaviour despite wanting to, there are also some very practical steps that can be taken to help enable behaviour change in the planning for the action stage. These steps are the focus of this chapter, and the importance of these steps should never be underestimated.

Before we move into discussing these steps, first let us understand the theory and research that describes why planning for action is so important in behaviour change. I 'discovered' the importance of planning for action in coaching when I was trying to explain some unexpected results in one of my research projects. In 2016, I published the meta-analysis on the effectiveness of coaching, I discuss this study in detail in Chapter 2. One of the most intriguing and important findings of this report was that when we aggregated all of the studies examining coaching effectiveness and compared which of the outcomes improved the most following coaching (affective, skills-based, or results), we found that the biggest effect was observed for results outcomes. This is important for two reasons. First, change at the results level is often a key organizational focus as this represents the translation of learning through to performance benefits. Therefore, evidence that coaching has a significantly positive impact on results indicates that businesses can expect positive performance and impact improvements from investment in coaching. Second, and most importantly in the context of this chapter, this finding is contrary to results from a meta-analysis of managerial training interventions which found the opposite to be true – the smallest effects were observed for results outcomes (Powell & Yalcin, 2010). These findings are explained with reference to potential issues in training transfer, leading to a smaller impact of training on results outcomes. The findings of Powell and Yalcin (2010) support the reoccurring message that despite significant investment in learning and development, much of the training conducted in organizations fails to transfer to the work setting (Glaveski, 2019). So what makes coaching different? Why did we observe the opposite to be true? Our findings indicate a high level of transfer, and, therefore, learning obtained from coaching had a large effect on results when the coachee returned to the workplace. I propose that the key to understanding this finding is the theoretical concept of psychological fidelity which, in turn, can help us to understand the importance of planning for action.

Coaching has high psychological fidelity

A challenge in instructional forms of learning and development (e.g. training) is the transfer of newly acquired skills to the workplace (Fitzgerald, 2001). Positive transfer of training is the degree to which trainees effectively apply the knowledge, skills, and attitudes gained in a training context to the job. For the transfer to have occurred, learned behaviour must be generalized to the job context and maintained over a period of time on the job (Baldwin & Ford, 1988).

One factor that has been investigated as an influence on training transfer is the degree to which the training was identical to the workplace. When considering the similarity between training and the work environment, the foci of early research has generally been either the physical training environment or the similarity in the nature of the tasks being completed. For example, research has supported a generalization gradient in which transfer is more likely with *near transfer tasks*, which are highly similar to the learning tasks (e.g. working on a small jet engine in training and a larger one in the field), and less likely as one moves to *far transfer*, in which the tasks and situations in the learning situation are quite different from the transfer setting (e.g. applying principles of electricity from training to troubleshooting complex mechanical problems under extreme time pressures; Royer, 1979). Van der Locht, van Dam, and Chiaburu (2013) suggest that similarity in stimuli is important since it increases the relevance of the training situation; moreover, when back at work, it will help trigger employees' effective responses, matching those developed in the training. Van der Locht et al. (2013) state that similarity in response is important because it guarantees that the skills that are practised in training are relevant and necessary for successful performance at work. These concepts draw on the identical elements theory (Thorndike & Woodworth, 1901), and the relevance to the training room has been confirmed in the research (i.e. Axtell, Maitlis, & Yearta, 1997; Holton, Bates, & Ruona, 2000; Lim & Morris, 2006; Yamnill & McLean, 2005).

The concept of identical elements is simple; however, when considered in the context of management training, identical elements become practically challenging to apply. Van der Locht et al. (2013) describe how owing to the complex nature of managers' work situations, full physical similarity might be difficult to obtain. A further reason why obtaining physical similarity in management training may be challenging is because management training often focuses on more variable, open skills, such as interpersonal skills or supervisory competencies. These skills are relevant for many different situations, and, therefore, it is not possible to specify a single correct way in which to act. However, scholars have asserted that in addition to physical similarities, similarity between training and the workplace can also take the form of psychological fidelity. With high psychological fidelity training, employees attach similar meanings to stimuli used in training and found in the organizational context. Furthermore, the training stimuli should elicit similar responses, emotions, and decision-making processes in real-life management situations (Baldwin & Ford, 1988; Salas, Tannenbaum, Kraiger, & Smith-Jentsch, 2012). Research has shown that when the stimuli and response that trainees are subjected to in training are too different from those in real work tasks, and the training can have only negligible or even a negative effect on trainee's job performance (Blume, Ford, Baldwin, & Huang, 2010; Taylor, Russ-Eft, & Chan, 2005). Research evidence has also supported the notion that the similarity or specificity of the learning environment compared to the work environment enhances transfer (Kozlowski & DeShon, 2004; Van der Locht et al., 2013).

Therefore, psychological fidelity explains how coaching impacts positively on behaviour change. The coaching conversation is a learning environment that has high psychological fidelity as the focus of the conversation is on workplace issues that are unique to the coachee; with each coaching session aimed at discussing and 'solving' a particular workplace issue. The coachee experiences clarity about how they can transfer the content of the coaching sessions to their work environment as they attach the same meaning to the stimuli discussed in coaching and the organizational context because these stimuli are the same. As opposed to training, where stimuli and examples have to be generalized across a group of learners, in coaching, the coachees' unique examples are the subject of the learning experience. Accordingly, coaching results in positive improvements in performance by focusing specifically on the coachee's work situation, thereby providing high psychological fidelity.

While high psychological fidelity makes it clear for the coachee *how* they can transfer learning from coaching back to the workplace, *what* enhances their ability to do this, to follow through with the change if we know that behaviour change is hard? This is where planning for action comes in and the related psychological concept of implementation intention. Research tells us that it is not enough to make a resolution to change (i.e. I will exercise more regularly) you must work out exactly how and when you will do it (i.e. I will go for a run for 30 minutes at 6.00 am, five days a week on Mondays to Fridays). You make a clear implementation intention.

Implementation intention and behaviour change

Intention is a representation of planned action and can be distinguished from a goal that reflects the object or aim of actions (Tubbs & Ekeberg, 1991); however, implementation intention is important in facilitating the achievement of goals. We know from Chapter 8, that a specific, challenging goal has a greater impact on performance than a vague goal. Implementation intentions can further enhance the impact of goal specificity on performance, as implementation intentions remove the ambiguity of how specific goals should be acted upon by specifying the behaviours required in any given situation that the individual may encounter ('... I will perform response y!') (Smit, 2015). Furthermore, by specifying the situation that will prompt behaviours linked to pursuing specific goals (i.e. 'When situation x arises...'), implementation intentions both provide reminder prompts to work on a goal, and remove the ambiguity of when specific goals should be acted on. Tubbs and Ekeberg (1991) describe that because implementation intentions involve the mental selection of a suitable future situation (i.e. a good opportunity), it is assumed that the mental representation of this situation becomes highly activated and, therefore, more easily accessible from the unconscious. This heightened accessibility makes it easier to detect when one is in a critical situation to facilitate behaviours linked to goal pursuit, even when one is busy with other things.

Tubbs and Ekeberg (1991) propose that a complex hierarchical intentional structure exists with various levels of abstraction with which people can identify their intentions and actions. Both intentions and actions can be identified on a continuum ranging from very abstract representations (e.g. being successful in life) to more specific representations (e.g. finishing the project by Friday). At any given moment, a person's attention is directed towards only a single level in the hierarchy; therefore, it is consciously attended to and guiding behaviour at a given moment. Given that a person's intentional structure is hierarchical, ranging from high-level objectives to low-level motor behaviours, some very low-level (but intended) actions are always unconscious. Tubbs and Ekeberg (1991) provide an example of the very conscious intention to buy a drink from the vending machine to illustrate this point. One does not actively think, "Put your hand into your pocket, pull out some change, count out the correct amount, grasp the proper coins, raise them to the coin slot..." and so on. Even though these low-level motor behaviours or actions could be attended to if required, they do not have to be attended to and, therefore, for efficiency's sake, generally aren't attended to. If we can do it unconsciously, then we will. Tubbs and Ekeberg (1991) highlight that no matter how low level a person's operative objective may be (e.g. "count your change"), there are always even lower-level actions that occur automatically. Therefore, responses to intentions and actions in general always contain some unconscious or automatic elements. Furthermore, as people always actively attend to some level in the hierarchy (albeit often a relatively high level), we can often complete unconscious actions that do not help us in fulfilling our higher-level goals as we are not actively attending to our lower-level actions.

This point is particularly salient when individuals have a choice over possible actions. For example, I may form the intention to get home by 5:30 pm to have dinner with my family; however, this may compete with the intention to finish the project I am working on before leaving work. Which action 'wins'? The issue of choice over action becomes even more complex when both actions are in the service of goals that are aligned with competing values. For example, I value my health and fitness and I also value enjoying the moment – how does the decision to have wine with my meal fit in with these competing values? While having wine may be fulfilling the value of enjoying the moment, having wine with my meal is less aligned with my value of improving my health and fitness. How can we help coachees to make these 'in the moment' decisions? The key is through consciously exploring and creating implementation intentions across a variety of scenarios. Understanding priorities and consciously deciding what to do. Attending to all levels of the hierarchy (i.e. considering all values and goals, high-level objectives to low-level actions), monitoring our behaviour consistently in all of these areas, and assessing the balance, therefore ensuring that we are not behaving automatically. Gollwitzer (1999) argues that when individuals make such decisions 'in the moment' rather than considering them ahead of time, effective goal pursuit is hampered. 'In the moment' decisions are restricted as individuals tend to primarily scrutinize the behaviours appropriate to the present situation in a rather limited way. Anticipative decisions, on the contrary, are less restricted because they allow for us to take a 'wide-angle' perspective of the situation and, therefore, incorporate a whole array of possible opportunities and behaviours. A person, therefore, can select the most effective behaviours and the most suitable opportunities in the context of the bigger picture. Returning to the example of having wine with my meal, by considering this choice ahead of time, I may decide to have wine with my meal when I eat out with friends but not when eating at home, consequently achieving a balance in allowing me to pursue behaviours that fulfil both values. The importance of planning decisions ahead of time is also important in relation to hypothetical scenarios to ensure that the individual is equipped with the information needed to make decisions 'in the moment' that are aligned with their values and goals. Gollwitzer (1999) argues that this is because good opportunities often present themselves only for a short time (e.g. when one wants to make one's point in a conversation; when medication has to be taken at a certain time of day). When goal pursuit is planned, goal-directed behaviours can be initiated immediately once a relevant situation is encountered, even if the opportunity had not been anticipated.

There are also clear benefits of implementation intentions in relation to the challenge of getting started in behaviours linked to pursuing one's goals, as demonstrated in research by Gollwitzer and Brandstatter (1997). University students were asked prior to Christmas break to name two projects they intended to achieve during the upcoming vacation, one difficult to implement and the other easy to implement. When participants were asked whether they had formed intentions on when and where to get started (i.e. implementation intentions), about two-thirds – for both types of goals – responded positively. Project completion was checked after the Christmas vacation. For difficult-to-implement projects, two-thirds of the participants who had formed implementation intentions had carried them out. Participants without implementation intentions, however, mostly failed to complete the projects. Only one-fourth of these participants were successful. For the projects that were easy to implement, the completion rate was very high (80%), regardless of whether participants had formed implementation intentions. Gollwitzer and Brandstatter (1997) argue that when a task is easy, and, therefore, it is easy to get started on, implementation intentions do not appear to produce an additional advantage. However, implementation intentions have a strong facilitating effect when action initiation is difficult, as is likely to be the case with the majority of actions discussed during coaching sessions.

The impact of implementation intentions has also been demonstrated across a variety of studies in relation to health promotion. For example, Orbell, Hodgkins, and Sheeran (1997) found that for women who had set themselves the goal of performing breast self-examination, 53% successfully did so over the study period. However, this increased to 100% of participants performing the breast self-examination when implementation intentions accompanied the goal. Sheeran and Orbell (1999) analysed whether implementation intentions facilitated the regular intake of a vitamin

supplement. They found that participants who formed implementation intentions around vitamin taking (i.e. when and where each day they would
take the vitamin) missed fewer pills than participants who formed the goal
to take the vitamin each day without the specific implementation intention.
Finally, Milne, Orbell, and Sheeran (2002) examined the impact of implementation intentions on the completion of regular vigorous exercise. They
found that the compliance rate to the exercise regime rose from 39% to 91%
when the regime was accompanied by implementation intentions.

Given that forming implementation intentions is fairly quick and simple, the research indicates that implementation intentions are a low stakes
method of enhancing the chances of successful behaviour change and consequent goal achievement. The process of writing down implementation
intentions is the process of creating the action plan. By creating formal
written action plans with our coachees, we are facilitating the process of
high psychological fidelity (by making it clear how learning from coaching
can transfer back to the workplace) and forming implementation intentions
around agreed changes including how to deal with competing decisions and
temptations in the face of behaviour change. These factors combined contribute to successful behaviour change following coaching. Therefore, one
of the most effective tools at a coach's disposal is the ability to work with the
coachee to comprehensively plan for action including exploration of factors
that may potentially derail these plans.

RESEARCH IN ACTION: A COACH'S EXPERIENCE

One thing that I would typically do in a coaching situation when the
coachee is contemplating a change, I would invite them to take out
their diary and plan this now. So let's say they want to exercise more. I
would ask 'When will you do that?' They might respond that they may
do this twice a week. I would then ask 'When exactly?' In which case
they might specify on a Tuesday and Thursday evening. So I would
invite them to take their diary, then and there and add this into their
diary. In my experience, my coachees will often tell me that by getting their actions into the diary, actually planning the action, not just
contemplating the action is what makes a big difference. This applies
whatever the action is. It could be planning a meeting with yourself,
planning to have a discussion with a certain individual, or planning
a retreat with your team. Whatever the case may be, planning the action is important. It helps to ensure that the actions that have been
discussed do take place, and then the change can take place. Because
if we are just discussing what we could do without planning when and

how we are doing it, then change is less likely to occur. This type of action planning takes place in almost all of my coaching sessions. If we have a conversation about a particular topic, then the action planning will take place right there. I don't wait until the end of the session to decide on actions. At the end of the session we might recap this, but going through the diary and planning might take place right in the middle of the session at the moment the subject has been addressed. Another practical point that helps me with this is to avoid running out of time, I take a lot of time in the coaching session. My coaching sessions, when I do them face-to-face, will last two and a half to three hours. This way we are not constantly rushing and running out of time. We can take our time and ensure that these important aspects do not fall through the cracks and that they are properly addressed. I like to keep the discussion quite fluid; however, it is my responsibility as the coach to ensure that we use the time properly and that we address during the coaching session what we wanted to address.

Are some coachees resistant to planning? If a coachee were to say that they haven't got their diary with them or they seem to push back from committing to actions, then that may be an indication that they are not really prepared yet to commit to the action. So that requires further conversation. So I might say 'Well, it looks like you are not fully ready to follow through with this. What is preventing you from setting these actions out now? What is in the way? What else do we need to talk about?' That would be an opportunity to talk some more and that would uncover potential barriers that hadn't been explored. It's a good test to see if they are ready to take action, to write that down in their diary. Because if they are not, then something is still missing.

For details of the coaches who were interviewed for the 'research in action' vignettes, see page 191.

Individual differences and planning for action

Of course, even the best-laid plans can still go awry, and both personal and environmental factors can have an effect on action plans. Environmental factors, such as time limits, task difficulty, and other people, will influence the intention–action relationship, as will personal factors such as skills, abilities, or personality. Earlier in this book, I proposed a variety of coachee individual differences that are important to consider in relation to the effectiveness of coaching. Specifically, in Chapter 3, I make the case for the importance of a high level of coaching motivation, and in Chapter 6, I argue how coachee self-efficacy will influence the ability of the coachee to successfully change their behaviour following coaching. For many years, I believed that the key to behaviour change was a desire to change and a belief in ability to change. Therefore, if motivation to change was high and belief in ability to change was high, change would eventually follow. While a motivation to change and belief in ability to change is essential, I have come to realize that this alone is not enough. A framework that has helped me to further understand individual differences in relation to change is provided by Gretchen Rubin and her four tendencies. The four tendencies is a personality framework that specifically describes how people respond to expectations – both the expectations they set themselves (inner expectations – such as setting New Year's resolutions) and expectations set by others (outer expectations – such as work deadlines). Rubin (2017) proposes that the majority of people fall into one of four categories, and these categories can help us to understand how we can facilitate our behaviour change. The categories are:

- Upholder – responds readily to both outer and inner expectations
- Questioner – questions all expectations; they meet an expectation only if they believe it's justified
- Obliger – respond readily to outer expectations but struggle to meet inner expectations
- Rebels – resist all expectations, outer and inner alike

One of the reasons why I was so convinced that the key to behaviour change lay with motivation to change was that I am an Upholder – I can respond readily to my own inner expectation to change as long as I want to! Rubin (2017) makes the important point in her book that we tend to assume that everyone thinks the same way as us; however, her framework highlights how individuals can differ widely on the narrow, yet important topic of meeting expectations. In the context of coaching and planning for action, understanding how coachees respond to inner expectations is important, as an action plan is all about formalizing those inner expectations regarding behaviour change. The key point to recognize here is that, even if all principles outlined in this book are followed, for example, the coachee's motivation to change is high, specific, and challenging goals that are aligned with values are formed, action plans are articulated with clear implementation intentions, and so on, for some coachees, this will not be enough to enable them to change. Particularly in the case of Obligers (who resist inner expectations), they are likely to struggle to follow through with actions that they set themselves. Interestingly, Rubin (2017) notes how this difficulty in meeting inner expectations is often viewed as a personality flaw, or worse, as shameful. The prevailing belief is that if we want something badly enough, if we have the willpower, then we will achieve it. The reality though demonstrates time and time again that this is not the case. Therefore, the key point is to help coachees to understand themselves better, including how they respond to inner expectations and what mechanisms need to be built into an action plan to ensure that they are able to meet these inner expectations. Rubin (2017) argues: 'to help people to change their habits or behaviour, we should help get them what they need to succeed, whether that's more clarity, more information, more accountability, or more choices' (p. 233). Discussing with your coachee their past experiences regarding meeting inner expectations will likely reveal important information that will help to ensure that any action plan created during coaching will include mechanisms that work for the individual coachee. Everyone is different and what works for one coachee may not work for another. For me, as an Upholder, the act of forming an implementation intention is enough to ensure that I will follow through with the action. However, this is unlikely to be an effective strategy for an Obliger who may need some external accountability to ensure that they follow through with their actions. Rubin (2017) also notes that Obligers must pick the right kind of accountability for them, as Obligers can vary dramatically in what makes them feel accountable. Rubin's (2017) book 'The four tendencies' includes a quiz so that readers can identify their tendency however the quiz is also available online and I have included a link in the further resources at the end of this chapter.

Research on the role of planning for action in coaching

Unfortunately, there is very little research that isolates the impact of planning for action in the context of exploring outcomes from coaching, with the exception of a couple of studies. For example, Hooijberg and Lane (2009) conducted a qualitative study with participants who had received coaching linked to multisource feedback. A total of 232 participants responded to their questionnaire, which was aimed at exploring what constitutes effective coaching in the context of facilitating learning and behaviour change from multisource feedback. Of particular relevance here was their finding that, when asked 'what helped you most in implementing your plan?' 14.1% of participants indicated that their 'actions taken' had helped them. These actions included creating and implementing action plans, setting goals and objectives, and being more focused. Hooijberg and Lane (2009) conclude by highlighting the importance of discussing action steps in the coaching process. Smith and Brummel (2013) also highlight the importance of action plans (referred to as development plans) in their study. Smith and Brummel (2013) interviewed 30 executives who had received executive coaching (the average time elapsed since the completion of coaching was 15 months). They found that less than 50% of participants reported creating a development plan as part of the coaching process although during the interviews, participants who indicated that they had not created a development plan often suggested that they had a mental model of how they would utilize the learning from coaching in current projects. Smith and Brummel (2013) also analysed their data quantitatively and found that participants who had created a development plan demonstrated greater change than participants without a development plan. However, these findings should be treated tentatively, given that the data was all retrospective and based on self-report change only. Despite these limitations, these findings highlight two important points: first, the coaches in this study were not automatically creating the time in the coaching session to work with the coachee to create plans. I propose that the creation of action plans is an essential element of coaching and should always be covered during the session. Second, when plans were created, they appear to have a positive impact on behaviour change following coaching, supporting the research findings regarding the impact of implementation intentions more generally.

Recommendations for practice

Encouraging implementation intentions and action planning is equally important for the leader as a coach and the independent coach in enabling behaviour change. I recommend that action planning will be maximally effective when the goals and objectives are aligned with values, and, therefore, it is important that we first work with the coachee to establish their values and subsequent dream goal as detailed in Chapter 8. Once this has been achieved, the process of forming implementation intentions is not particularly complicated and can be easily achieved by applying the following recommendations:

• Discuss with coachees the concept of implementation intention. Understanding how and why we behave the way that we do is one of the most powerful tools at our disposal. If we understand how implementation intention works, then we are able to utilize it to our advantage.
• Allow sufficient time in the coaching session to explore action planning – it shouldn't be an afterthought and is absolutely integral to creating behaviour change.
• Implementation intention needs to include (1) where, (2) when, and (3) how they will accomplish a goal. An action plan should include direction (the actual behavioural sequence), amplitude (the intensity of the action) and persistence (the duration of the action) (Campbell & Pritchard, 1976).
• Wherever possible, help the coachee to formulate multiple actions in an action plan, each with implementation intentions so that the coachee has options regarding how they can achieve their goal.
• Write it down! Consider where this should be stored to be most helpful (i.e. somewhere the coachee will see each day). A template action plan is provided at the end of this chapter.

- Hawkins and Smith (2013) argue that change will only occur if the change starts to happen during the coaching session. To facilitate this, they describe what they call a 'fast forward rehearsal' which involves enacting the initial step live in the room. They argue that in the pressurized conditions of the workplace, we are unlikely to experiment with new, untried, and potentially risky behaviours, instead our old behaviours will be triggered. Only when we are able to rehearse new behaviours in a safe environment, can we expect better outcomes from coaching. Therefore, Hawkins and Smith (2013) suggest that the action stage should happen live in the room, at least once, followed by reflection and an agreement on how to implement the change back at work.

- Consider using technology. For example, reminders on a smartphone or the PC can prompt the coachee to complete new behaviours until they become a habit. Following influencers on social media linked to the new habit (such as personal trainers or inspirational business people) can help to keep the new habit in the forefront of the coachee's mind as they encounter prompts in different ways and across many aspects of their life.

- Explore specific anticipated obstacles that might derail intentions and how the coachee intends to deal with these – form implementation intentions for obstacles as well as goal-related actions. For example, "if x happens then I will deal with it by y". This can include how to continue with the action plan during times of high stress or changes to routine – these are often the most challenging situations to stick with our good intentions.

- Consider competing goals – identify where competing goals might arise and how the coachee will assess which goal takes priority in which scenario – establish implementation intentions for dealing with competing goals.

- Decide how to monitor progress towards goal completion. Collecting data in relation to our behaviour helps us to uncover weak spots that derail us and gives us data to inform our decisions.

- Consider the coachee's tendencies. How can they help themselves to form better habits and stick to their implementation intentions? Explore when they have successfully adopted new behaviours in the past. What helped them achieve this change? How can they apply this learning to this situation?

- Discuss with the coachee whether they wish to share their plans with someone else to encourage them to stick with their action plan.

- Agree on the role the coachee would like you to play in helping them with their implementation intentions. Would it be useful for you to act as an accountability partner? When should the next coaching session be scheduled in the context of supporting the implementation intention?

- Plan for when to review the action plan. The action plan should be a living document, and, therefore, it will need to be revised and updated. While certain actions may have worked well at the start, they may become less effective as time progresses. Therefore, it may be necessary for the coachee to find new actions that will revitalize their progress towards achieving their goal.
- Do not underestimate the importance of reflection in relation to implementation intentions. Reflection can increase the coachee's self-awareness regarding when they have successfully changed behaviour, when they have struggled to implement changes and why this might be. This data can help to inform the action plan as the coachee works towards achieving their goals.
- Plan how to celebrate successes. It is very easy to plod along with a plan without recognizing both small and larger successes. Plan in milestones including healthy treats to celebrate successes and progress towards goal achievement. These will help to reinforce the good work already done and motivate the coachee to keep with the plan.

Resources

Online four tendencies quiz to identify how you respond to inner and outer expectations: https://quiz.gretchenrubin.com/

Template action plan:

Objective:				
Sub-objective 1:				
Task	Resources needed	When?	Measurement/ accountability	Completed?
Sub-objective 2:				
Task	Resource needed	When?	Measurement/ accountability	Completed?

Sub-objective 3:				
Task	Resource needed	When?	Measurement/ accountability	Completed?
Sub-objective 4:				
Task	Resource needed	When?	Measurement/ accountability	Completed?

This chapter in summary

- A strength of coaching is that it enables coachees to experience clarity about how they can transfer the learning from the coaching sessions back to their work environment.
- Implementation intentions (i.e. when situation x arises, I will perform response y) enables behaviour change by making desirable behaviours easily accessible from our unconscious.
- Individuals vary in how they respond to inner expectations (such as action plans), and, therefore, action plans need to be tailored to the individual to provide them with what works for them to facilitate behaviour change.
- Planning for action and forming implementation intentions should always form part of the coaching conversation. Behaviour change is unlikely to happen without these important steps!

References

Axtell, C. M., Maitlis, S., Yearta, S. K. (1997). Predicting immediate and longer-term transfer of training. *Personnel Review, 26*(3), 201–213.

Baldwin, T. T., & Ford, J. F. (1988). Transfer of training: A review and directions for future research. *Personnel Psychology, 41*(1), 63–105.

Blume, B. D., Ford, J. K., Baldwin, T. T., & Huang, J. L. (2010). Transfer of training: A meta-analytic review. *Journal of Management, 36*(4), 1065–1105.

Campbell, J. P., & Pritchard, R. D. (1976). Motivation theory in industrial and organizational psychology. In M. D. Dunnette (Ed.), *Handbook of industrial and organizational psychology* (pp. 63–130). Chicago, IL: Rand-McNally.

Fitzgerald, R. (2001). The strange case of the transfer of training estimate. *The Industrial-Organizational Psychologist, 39(2)*,18–19.

Glaveski, S. (2019). Where companies go wrong with learning and development. *Harvard Business Review*. Retrieved from https://hbr.org/2019/10/where-companies-go-wrong-with-learning-and-development. Accessed on October 12, 2019.

Gollwitzer, P. M. (1999). Implementation intentions: Strong effects of simple plans. *The American Psychologist, 54*(7), 493–503.

Gollwitzer, P. M., & Brandstatter, V. (1997). Implementation intentions and effective goal pursuit. *Journal of Personality and Social Psychology, 73*, 186–199.

Hawkins, P., & Smith, N. (2013). *Coaching, mentoring and organizational consultancy: Supervision, skills & development*. Berkshire, UK: Open University Press.

Holton, E. F. III., Bates, R. A., & Ruona, W. A. (2000). Development and validation of a generalised learning transfer climate questionnaire. *Human Resource Development Quarterly, 11*, 333–360.

Hooijberg, R., & Lane, N. (2009). Using multisource feedback coaching effectively in executive education. *Academy of Management Learning & Education, 8*(4), 483–493.

Kozlowski, S. W. J., & DeShon, R. P. (2004). A psychological fidelity approach to simulation-based training: Theory, research and principles. In S. G. Schiflett, L. R. Elliott, E. Salas & M. D. Coovert (Eds.), *Scaled worlds: Development, validation and application*. Burlington, VT: Ashgate Publishing.

Lim, D. H., & Morris, M. L. (2006). Influence of trainee characteristics, instructional satisfaction and organizational climate on perceived learning and transfer training. *Human Resource Development Quarterly, 17*, 85–115.

Milne, S., Orbell, S., & Sheeran, P. (2002). Combining motivational and volitional interventions to promote exercise participation: Protection motivation theory and implementation intentions. *British Journal of Health Psychology, 7*(2), 163–184.

Orbell, S., Hodgkins, S., & Sheeran, P. (1997). Implementation intentions and the theory of planned behavior. *Personality and Social Psychology Bulletin, 23*, 945–954.

Powell, K. S., & Yalcin, S. (2010). Managerial training effectiveness: A meta-analysis 1952–2002. *Personnel Review, 39*, 227–241. doi:10.1108/00483481011017435

Royer, J. M. (1979). Theories of the transfer of learning. *Educational Psychologist, 14*, 53–69.

Rubin, G. (2017). *The four tendencies*. London, UK: Hodder & Stoughton.

Salas, E., Tannenbaum, S. I., Kraiger, K., & Smith-Jentsch, K. A. (2012). The science of training and development in organizations: What matters in practice. *Psychological Science in the Public Interest, 13*(2), 74–101.

Sheeran, P., & Orbell, S. (1999). Implementation intentions and repeated behaviors: Augmenting the predictive validity of the theory of planned behavior. *European Journal of Social Psychology, 29*, 349–370.

Smit, B. W. (2015). Successfully leaving work at work: The self-regulatory underpinnings of psychological detachment. *Journal of Occupational and Organizational Psychology, 89*(3), 493–514.

Smith, I. M., & Brummel, B. J. (2013). Investigating the role of the active ingredients in executive coaching. *Coaching: An International Journal of Theory, Research and Practice, 6*(1), 57–71. doi:10.1080/17521882.2012.758649

Taylor, P. J., Russ-Eft, D. F., & Chan, D. W. L. (2005). A meta-analytic review of behavior modeling training. *Journal of Applied Psychology, 90*(4), 692–709. doi:10.1037/0021-9010.90.4.692

Thorndike, E. L., & Woodworth, R. S. (1901). The influence of improvement in one mental function upon the efficiency of other functions. *Psychological Review, 8*, 247–261.

Tubbs, M. E., & Ekeberg, S. E. (1991). The role of intentions in work motivation: Implications for goal-setting theory and research. *Academy of Management Review, 16*(1), 180–199.

Van der Locht, M., van Dam, K., & Chiaburu, D. S. (2013). Getting the most of management training: The role of identical elements for training transfer. *Personnel Review,* 422–439. doi:10.1108/PR-05-2011-0072

Yamnill, S., & McLean, G. N. (2005). Factors affecting transfer of training in Thailand. *Human Resource Development Quarterly, 16*(3), 323–344.

Section Four

The role of the organization

Malcolm Gladwell (2009) famously said 'Who we are cannot be separated from where we're from – and when we ignore that fact, planes crash'. Where we are from, in terms of the organization we reside in, has an impact on who we are. If we are seeking to change who we are, we must consider where we are from. Therefore, it is essential to consider the role the organization plays and in particular the organization's culture, in facilitating sustained behaviour change following coaching. The changes discussed by the coachee during coaching may be drastic, they may be scary, and they may involve a degree of risk and vulnerability. How supportive is the organization's culture to facilitate these changes? This is the focus of this section. Including a section on the role of the organization may seem a strange choice for a coaching text, particularly given that we may assume that a coach has limited influence on their coachees' organizational culture. Or do they? Organizational culture exists because of the people in that organization. These people include our coachees. It is also likely that the coach will be involved with other people within the organization, for example, the coachee's line manager and the HR manager. The coachee him or herself may well be a senior leader within the organization and, therefore, be in a position to influence the organizational culture to a greater degree. Even if this is not the case, it is important to understand the role of the organization as this may also help us to understand when behaviour change has not been sustained, despite the desire and efforts of the coachee. If we can understand these barriers to change presented by the organizational culture, then we can start to work with the coachee to overcome them.

The second aim of this chapter is to help leaders as coaches to understand what they can do to create a culture that facilitates behaviour change. Schein (2010) argues that leaders have a number of 'tools' at their disposal to influence the organizational culture, and these include what leaders pay attention to, measure, and control on a regular basis; how leaders react to critical incidents and organizational crises; how leaders allocate resources; deliberate role modelling, teaching, and coaching; how leaders allocate rewards and status and how leaders recruit, select, promote, and excommunicate members. Therefore, it is important to consider the shared assumptions within our culture and how these may filter through into the leader's behaviour to reinforce the organization's culture. Once we understand this, we are in a position to make changes if we desire.

What is organizational culture?

Schein (2010) defines organizational culture as the set of shared, taken-for-granted implicit assumptions that members of an organization hold and that determines how they perceive, think about, and react to their various environments. The importance of the impact of organizational culture should not be underestimated. For example, in a study of 42 manufacturing companies, Patterson, Warr, and West (2004) found that eight aspects of organizational culture predicted organization productivity when measured by the financial value of net sales per employee divided by the overall sector productivity value. These aspects were:

- Concern for employee welfare – the extent to which the organization values and cares for employees
- Skill development – the extent to which the organization is concerned with developing employee skills
- Innovation and flexibility – the extent to which the organization demonstrates an orientation towards change and the extent of encouragement and support for new ideas
- Performance feedback – the extent to which the organization prioritizes measurement and feedback on job performance
- Supervisory support – the extent to which employees experience support and understanding from their immediate supervisor
- Effort – how hard people in the organization work towards achieving goals
- Quality – the emphasis given to quality procedures
- Formalization – concern with formal rules and procedures

Schein (2010) argues that if we understand organizational culture better, we will understand ourselves better and some of the forces acting within us that define who we are. Culture is not only all around us but within us as well. This is an important point to understand in the context of coaching and behaviour change. Understanding organizational culture can help us to understand our current behaviour and aspects of the culture that may pose barriers or facilitators to the desired change. Schein (2010) argues that culture guides and constrains the behaviour of members of a group through the shared norms or assumptions that are held in that group. These shared assumptions are often below the surface, they are powerful in their impact but invisible and to a considerable degree unconscious. The shared assumptions that form the basis of our organizational cultures define for us what to pay attention to, what things mean, how to react emotionally to what is going on, and what actions to take in various kinds of situations. Organizational culture exists because group members value stability. Culture provides meaning and predictability. Culture provides its members with a basic sense of identity and defines the values that provide self-esteem. Cultures tell their members who they are, how to behave towards each other, and how to feel good about themselves. Understanding this can help us to understand why behaviour change that may challenge the shared assumptions of the organizational culture can be particularly difficult. Any challenge or questioning of the shared assumptions will release anxiety and defensiveness, as a challenge to organizational culture is ultimately a challenge to our sense of identity in that context.

Coupled with this potential challenge to identity is the fact that when we recognize the need to change as individuals, it can produce learning anxiety. Schein (2010) describes learning anxiety as the anxiety associated with the realization that you may not be able to change or that you may be temporarily incompetent during the learning process. According to Schein (2010), learning anxiety may be based on one or more of the following reasons:

- Fear of loss of power or position
- Fear of temporary incompetence – because we have given up the old way and not yet mastered the new
- Fear of punishment for incompetence – if it takes a long time to achieve the change, there may be a period of low productivity
- Fear of loss of personal identity – we may not want to be the kind of people that the new way of working requires us to be
- Fear of loss of group membership – the shared assumptions that make up a culture also identify who is in and who is out of the group. If by developing new ways of thinking or new behaviour, we will become a deviant in our group, we may be rejected or even ostracized

Therefore, to ensure that behaviour change following coaching is successful, it is important to understand the shared assumptions that may present barriers to this change and the associated anxiety that is likely to accompany the challenge to these assumptions. Furthermore, it is important to understand the role of learning anxiety in the context of the individual's organizational culture and explore ways of effectively managing this anxiety. For the leader as a coach, understanding organizational culture is even more pertinent as they are in a position to directly influence this culture in a variety of ways.

Researchers have generally argued that a 'strong' organizational culture is important for the success of the organization. Strong cultures are ones that are clearly understood by those within the organization, with minimal competing sub-cultures. A strong culture provides its members with a strong sense of identity, meaning, predictability, and therefore minimizes anxiety. However, this creates a paradox in today's fast-paced environment. Schein (2010) argues that to cope with the world of tomorrow, leaders and the rest us need to become perpetual learners. If the world is coming more turbulent, requiring more flexibility and learning, does this not imply that strong cultures will increasingly become a liability? Schein (2010) argues that the answer to this paradox lies in a culture that is in its very nature a learning culture. A learning culture is learning-oriented, adaptive, and flexible, thereby stabilizing perpetual learning and change. Rather than the term learning culture, I like to call this type of organizational culture a 'coaching culture' as I believe that many of the underlying principles needed to facilitate behaviour change via effective coaching in individuals can also be applied to understand the type of organizational culture needed to thrive today and in the future. When I use the term 'coaching culture', I do so to describe an organizational culture that is underpinned by many of the principles that are essential to effective coaching in the same way that a leader as a coach does much more than just active listening and asking powerful questioning. The leader as a coach believes in the same principles that an effective coach believes in, that is that they are open, demonstrate unconditional positive regard, have a non-judgmental attitude, adopt a growth mindset, and are authentic. A coaching culture is not just a culture that encourages coaching and has coaching as a training and development tool as part of its corporate strategy (although this may well also be the case). Rather, it is an organization that is characterized by members who are open, demonstrate unconditional positive regard, have a non-judgmental attitude, adopt a growth mindset, and are authentic. The values of the organization reflect these principles, the way they fulfil these values is congruent with these principles including how they measure what they do, and how they celebrate successes and deal with setbacks. Therefore, a coaching culture goes much further than simply embracing coaching. My use of the term coaching culture is, therefore, closely aligned with Schein's (2010) concept of a learning culture; however, I have extended it to more explicitly include the principles of coaching.

The rest of this section will outline these principles along with a discussion of the influence of shared assumptions underpinning organizational culture in four key areas on behaviour change. First, the shared assumptions about the values, mission, and goals of the organization which highlight who we are and what we stand for as an organization. Second, the shared assumptions about the means for achieving the organization's values, mission, and goals which highlight how we fulfil what we stand for. Third, the shared assumptions about measuring results which highlight how do know when we have got where we are heading, and finally, the shared assumptions about rewards and punishments that highlight how do we celebrate when we get to our destination or what do we do when things go wrong.

Shared assumptions about values, mission, and goals

Members of an organization will hold shared assumptions about the values, mission, and goals of the organization. These values, mission, and goals highlight who we are as an organization and what we stand for. Henderson,

Thompson, and Henderson (2006) propose that when members hold values that are aligned with the values of the organization, the organization delivers its values through their cultures via their systems and people. Values provide the only basis for meaningful comprehension of a culture because to make any sense of a culture we need to understand its values. These values and beliefs are expressed through rituals, customs, laws, ceremonies, and systems. Every organizational culture evolves out of a set of values at work. These values might not necessarily be the ones the organization has deliberately chosen, they might, in fact, be a mixture of the values of previous cultures and the personal values that individuals within the organization bring to work.

Barriers to individual change can arise when the coachee is attempting to change their behaviour in a way that contradicts the values, goals, or mission of the organization. For example, a coachee may be seeking to address work-life balance issues; however, a core value of their organization may be responsiveness to clients and colleagues. This value translates into a requirement to respond promptly to email enquiries (the shared assumption about the means to fulfil the value). This value of responsiveness will create the shared assumption that it is important to monitor and respond to emails regularly which can make one individual's efforts to 'switch off' challenging as it will contradict the value of the organization and the shared assumption about the means to achieve this value. If the organization does not value the behaviour that the coachee is attempting to develop, they will need to tap into internal resources, such as their own intrinsic motivation and their own values, to effectively foster this change. The misalignment between the organization's and the individual's values may present additional issues. For example, person-organization fit theory refers to whether the values of the organization are consistent with the values of the individual. A meta-analysis, which amalgamated the results of 21 studies on the topic of person-organization fit, demonstrated that when there was a good person-organization fit (i.e. the organization's and individual's values were aligned) the individuals' job satisfaction and organizational commitment was higher and intention to leave the organization was lower (Verquer, Beehr, & Wagner, 2003). Therefore, it is important to be aware that where an individual's motivation to change involves a misalignment between their own values and the values of the organization, they are likely to find it challenging to execute the change in the short-term as this is likely to contradict the shared assumptions within the organization and in the long-term, this misalignment of values may lead to lower job satisfaction, low commitment to the organization, and higher intentions to leave. Consequently, it is important to discuss explicitly with the coachee any potential challenges that may arise in executing actions based on a potential conflict with organization values, mission, or goals.

For leaders who seek to create a learning or coaching culture, Schein (2010) outlines a number of shared assumptions of a learning culture that should be reflected in the organization's values, mission, and goals. In Table 1, I have built on these shared assumptions, providing an example from a range of organisation's published mission statements and also detailed how this might translate into the means to achieve the organization's values, mission, and goals which I expand on in the next section.

Table 1 Examples of shared assumptions of values, missions and goals for learning or coaching culture (adapted from Schein, 2010)

Shared assumption of a learning or coaching culture to be reflected in the organization's values, mission, and goals	Organizational example of a value, mission, or goal with this underlying shared assumption	How does this translate into shared assumptions about the means to achieve the organization's values, mission, and goals
Members hold the shared assumption that the appropriate behaviour for employees is proactivity and adaptability	'We're always looking to improve. We challenge ourselves to learn about the cutting edge and harness it. We challenge the status quo' Aviva (2019)	Decentralized decision-making
Members hold the shared assumption that learning is a good thing worth investing in and that learning to learn is itself a skill to be mastered	'Leaders are never done learning and always seek to improve themselves. They are curious about new possibilities and act to explore them' Amazon (2019)	Investment in learning for members in terms of time and resources; Reward structure that recognizes learning; Opportunities to safely practise new learning
Members have faith in people and must believe that ultimately human nature is good and malleable	'Caring about individuals and their progress, showing respect, being supportive and responsive' HSBC (2019)	Low levels of monitoring of members daily actions
Members hold the shared assumption that rather than being passively influenced by the environment, the environment can be managed	'We are inspired every day by the genuine belief that we can change the world for the better' Microsoft (2019)	Long-term goals demonstrate that the organization seeks to shape the industry it operates in

Shared assumption of a learning or coaching culture to be reflected in the organization's values, mission, and goals	Organizational example of a value, mission, or goal with this underlying shared assumption	How does this translate into shared assumptions about the means to achieve the organization's values, mission, and goals
Members hold the shared assumption that solutions to problems derive from a deep belief in inquiry and a pragmatic search for 'truth'	'We Face Facts: Look at the facts in a cold-blooded way; admit and learn from mistakes; acknowledge the negatives; have only one truth for all audiences; keep one set of books; get the right people in the room (and the best answers will be found)' JP Morgan Chase (2019)	Decision-making is informed by data
Members hold a shared positive orientation toward the future	'We are optimistic about how technology and connectivity can enhance the future and improve people's lives. Through our business, we aim to build a digital society that enhances socio-economic progress, embraces everyone and does not come at the cost of our planet' Vodaphone (2019)	Meetings are characterized by a discussion of future opportunities
Members hold the shared assumption that communication and information are central to organizational well-being. Everyone must be able to communicate with everyone and everyone must assume that telling the truth is best. This assumption can only be effectively operationalized in a culture that is built on strong levels of trust between members.	'Leaders listen attentively, speak candidly, and treat others respectfully. They are vocally self-critical, even when doing so is awkward or embarrassing. Leaders do not believe their or their team's body odor smells of perfume.' Amazon (2019)	Leaders have an open door policy. Low use of gatekeepers

Leaders play a key role in the development of organizational culture. When considering the leaders actions in relation to the shared assumptions about the organizations values, mission, and goals, leaders as coaches can ask themselves the following questions to self-assess their behaviour. These questions can also be useful for coaches working with coachees on organization culture:

- What is your long-term vision? What is the long-term vision of your organization? Can you identify areas in which these visions align?
- How can you communicate the alignment of your own values to those of the organization to others?
- What specific steps can you take to communicate how your team contributes to delivering the organization's long-term vision? For example, can you map the daily, weekly, or monthly goals for the team onto the organization's goals?
- Consider what would make the organization's long-term vision even more inspiring for your team? How can you communicate this to your team?
- Have you formulated clear and specific expectations for your team in relation to the goals of the organization? What processes can you use to communicate these more clearly to your team?

Shared assumptions about the means to fulfil the organization's vision, mission, and goals

If the shared assumptions regarding the organization's values, mission, and goals set out who we are as an organization, the shared assumptions about the means to fulfil these values, mission, and goals spell out what we do. Schein (2010) argues that some of the most important and most invisible elements of organizational culture are the shared assumptions about how things should be done, how the mission is to be achieved, and how goals are to be met. Leaders usually impose structure, systems, and processes, which if successful, become shared parts of the culture. Once processes have become taken for granted, they become the elements of the culture that may be the hardest to change. Schein (2010) describes how if an assumption comes to be strongly held in a group, members will find behaviour based on any other premise inconceivable. To learn something new in this realm requires us to resurrect, re-examine, and possibly change some of the more stable portions of our cognitive structure. Such learning is intrinsically difficult because the re-examination of assumptions temporarily destabilizes our cognitive and interpersonal world, releasing large quantities of anxiety. Therefore, barriers to individual change following coaching can arise when the organization's existing structure, systems, and processes do not support the desired change. For example, a coachee may be seeking to build trusting relationships within his or her team; however, the organization requires that the leader makes regular checks and conducts frequent monitoring of team members' performance. The close monitoring of employee behaviour is unlikely to be helpful in the context of spreading the message 'I trust you to do your job well'. Consequently, it is important to explore with your coachee any potential barriers to change that the existing structure, systems, and processes may pose and identify ways of overcoming these. The identification of these barriers may be particularly challenging as these structures, systems, and processes may be taken for granted by members of the organization meaning that those members are not even consciously aware of them and their impact. This is where working with an external coach can be particularly beneficial. It is easier to identify these assumptions from the outside looking in; therefore, the external coach provides this outsiders' perspective.

For the leader who wishes to establish a coaching culture, one of the most effective ways to have an impact is in relation to implementing changes around the shared assumptions on how things should be done. I have grouped these shared assumptions for a coaching culture on how things are done into three areas: how we work with others; how we approach tasks; and how we help others to learn.

Creating a coaching culture: how we work with others

A coaching culture holds the shared assumptions of how members work with others including the importance of open communication between members, active listening, high levels of trust, and the importance of teamwork including cross-team collaborations. Therefore, in organizations with a coaching culture, members will hold the shared assumptions that open communication is essential across levels, teams, and departments, and active listening facilitates open communication and members must work together and trust one another to fulfil the values, mission, and goals of the organization. Research on organizational culture that focuses on how we work with others includes a study by Paterson, Luthans, and Jeung (2014) who collected data from 198 employee-supervisor dyads from the United States to investigate the influence of a supportive organizational culture on employee thriving at work. They found that when employees perceived a high supervisor support culture, employees demonstrated higher task focus (for example, 'I focus a great deal of attention on my work'), which in turn led to higher levels of reported thriving at work. They describe how supervisors who create a supportive climate do so by expressing concern for the well-being of their employees, helping employees with their career development, and valuing the work of those who report to them (Zhang, Tsui, Song, Li, & Jia, 2008). These types of supervisor behaviours create a safe environment for employees; consequently, employees are not afraid to take risks or even fail because they are confident that they will be supported by their supervisor. The importance of open communication is highlighted in research by Hartnell, Ou, and Kinicki (2011) who conducted a meta-analysis synthesizing the data of 84 studies on organizational culture. They examined different types of organizational cultures including 'clan' cultures, described as cultures that are based on the assumption that success relies on hiring, developing, and retaining the right people. Clan cultures have a flexible organizational structure, high levels of employee involvement, and open communication. Hartnell et al. (2011) found that there was a large significant relationship between clan cultures, job satisfaction, and organizational commitment indicating that individuals working within clan cultures tending to experience high levels of job satisfaction and commitment to their organization.

Creating a coaching culture: how we approach tasks

My second group of shared assumptions in a coaching culture on how things should be done is around the shared assumptions on how members approach tasks. This includes the importance of proactivity, accountability, and processes that facilitate change including experimenting with solutions. Therefore, in organizations with a coaching culture, members will hold the shared assumptions that a proactive approach that involves experimentation with solutions is the most effective way to complete work tasks and that members should feel accountable for their own role and the role of their team to contributing to achieving the values, mission, and goals of the organization. Research on organizational culture that focuses on how members approach tasks includes a study of 260 Korean companies spread across manufacturing, banking, and non-banking services. Sung and Choi (2014) investigated the influence of a strong innovative organizational culture on the impact of learning on performance. An innovative culture is a culture where employees understand that new ideas are routinely accepted and rewarded rather than rejected and punished (Bowen & Ostroff, 2004). They found that the positive effects of learning practices on innovative performance were stronger for organizations where employees' collective perception of an innovative culture was high than when it was low. This suggests that for learning to translate to performance benefits, employees need to perceive that the organization will embrace experimentation with ideas without fear of being blamed and mutually accept others' risky ideas (West & Richter, 2008).

Creating a coaching culture: how we help others learn

My final group of shared assumptions for a coaching culture on how things should be done is the shared assumptions on how members of the organization help others to learn. This includes asking powerful questions, facilitating learning in others by creating opportunities to raise awareness of the impact of our behaviour, and using goal-setting to facilitate action. Therefore, in organizations with a coaching culture, members will hold the shared assumptions that the most effective way to help others learn is to ask powerful questions, rather than providing solutions, to create opportunities to raise self-awareness and use goal-setting to focus attention and instigate action. This group of shared assumptions has received less attention in the culture literature. However, evidence that is relevant to consider in this context includes research on the role of managerial coaching in the workplace. As already argued, leaders play a key role in the development of organizational culture, therefore, considering the influence of leader's behaviours is an important body of evidence that can help us to understand the wider topic of organizational culture. For example, Ellinger, Ellinger, and Keller (2003) investigated managerial coaching behaviour in an industrial context. They surveyed 438 employees and their managers ($n = 67$). Employees were asked to rate their manager's coaching behaviour while managers rated their own coaching behaviour. The measure of coaching behaviour included items such as 'to help my employees think through issues, I ask questions, rather than provide solutions' and 'I encourage my employees to broaden their perspectives by helping them to see the big picture'. Ellinger et al. (2003) found that when manager coaching behaviours were high, as reported by employees, so was employee job satisfaction (as rated by the employees) and employee performance (as rated by supervisors). A similar study by Dahling, Taylor, Chau, and Dwight (2016) explored the links between managerial coaching skills and frequency to sales goal attainment in a sample of 1,246 sales representatives across 136 teams within a pharmaceuticals organization. Managerial coaching skill was assessed by a third party in a role-play exercise. Managers were assessed on a range of coaching behaviours including behavioural modelling and goal-setting. Results indicated that managerial coaching skill was directly related to employees' annual sales goal attainment; therefore, when managers coaching skill was high so to was employee sales goal attainment. Therefore, while there appears to be a shortage of studies that investigate shared assumptions on how members help others to learn at the organization level, the evidence does indicate the importance of adopting a coaching approach from the perspective of the leader-member level. As we know that culture is a product of those within the organization, it is not an impossible leap to imagine that these results would translate to the positive effects for the organization if these shared assumptions were adopted across the organization.

As with shared assumptions on the values, mission, and goals of the organization, there are a number of questions that leaders wishing to create a coaching culture can ask themselves to assess where they may need to develop in relation to shared assumptions about the means to achieve the organizations' goals. Again, these questions may also be useful for coaches working with coachees on the issue of developing a coaching culture by addressing the shared assumptions about means to achieve organizational values, mission, and goals.

For shared assumptions on how members work with others including open communication between members, active listening, high levels of trust, and the importance of teamwork including cross-team collaborations:

- What actions could you take to encourage a higher level of partnership between team members and yourself?
- Consider how do you personally encourage your team members to be authentic at work? Are there ways in which you can be flexible in ways of working to enhance authenticity? For example, introverts may prefer time and space to consider solutions alone while extraverts may prefer to discuss solutions with others.
- How can you share the responsibility for leading the team? Are there specific tasks or projects that team members could take the lead on?
- What actions do you take to encourage teamwork? Consider the way in which you communicate to the team – for example, do you tend to highlight individual's contribution rather than focusing on team performance? Are there any actions you can take to ensure that organizational policies encourage team cohesiveness?
- What actions do you take to encourage strong bonds between team members? For example, do you provide the time for team members to get to know one another or participate in team-building activities?
- Consider whether there are occasions when you may focus on the influence of individual team members rather than the team as a whole? How can the team as a whole support individual team members who may be struggling?
- What could you do to clearly demonstrate to your team the confidence you feel in their ability to achieve the team's goals? Consider the way in which you communicate verbally, for example during team meetings, your written communication, including the language you use and the way you communicate about your team to others outside of your team.
- What do you do to recognize the contribution of your team? On a one-to-one basis, do you provide feedback to team members that recognizes their contribution? During team meetings, do you focus on the team's contribution to foster teamwork and minimize competition? How can you ensure that you consistently communicate your appreciation to your team?
- What motivates you? By reflecting on and identifying your motivation, you can ensure that you align this with the success of the team. Does

your team know what motivates you? By being open about what motivates us in the workplace we are being authentic with our team. Motivation and passion often inspire motivation and passion in others.

- What stops you from truly listening to others? How can you minimize this interference? How can you demonstrate to others that you are truly listening? Simple actions, such as avoiding interruptions, maintaining eye contact, and using open body language, can have a big impact on ensuring the other person feels listened to.
- Do you find that others have a tendency to misunderstand your point? Can you identify any themes around this – for example, does this tend to happen more frequently during times of high pressure or with particular forms of communication? What actions can you take to minimize the impact of this on your ability to communicate constructively?

For shared assumptions about how members approach tasks including the importance of proactivity, accountability, and processes that facilitate change including experimenting with solutions:

- Reflect on what may be hindering your ability to collaborate proactively across functions, teams, and levels in your organization. What can you do to minimize this interference? How are you communicating your willingness to collaborate proactively across functions, teams, and levels with others? What actions could you take to communicate this more clearly to others?
- What actions do you take to inspire and create energy in others? Do you know what motivates each member of your team and why? What could you do to increase your understanding of what motivates and inspires your team?
- Reflect on why you may feel resistant to change. What barriers may be stopping you from initiating and enabling change? How are you communicating your willingness to respond to, initiate, and enable change with others? What actions could you take to communicate this more clearly to others?
- What actions do you take to positively contribute to the energy of the team? What can you do to manage your own energy or mood when it is low?
- Consider which scenarios might provide an appropriate opportunity to encourage team members to experiment with ideas and solutions? What actions could you take to facilitate this new way of working?
- How can you enhance responsibility among team members? For example, understanding how our actions influence the bigger picture can encourage us to take responsibility for our actions. How can you communicate this clearly and consistently to your team?

- Do your team members understand how they contribute to the organization's long-term vision? Is the organisation's vision aligned with the team member's long-term vision? Wherever possible, recruit team members who share a long-term vision with the organization, as those with a shared vision will automatically experience higher levels of ownership for this vision.

For shared assumptions on how members help others to learn including the importance of asking powerful questions, facilitating learning in others by creating awareness of the impact of our behaviour and using goal-setting to facilitate action:

- In what ways can you increase the level of supportive challenge to team members? How can you challenge your team members to reach their full potential while ensuring that they feel safe and supported to make mistakes? What opportunities can you provide team members to stretch themselves and acquire new skills?
- Which situations might provide a good opportunity to practise using powerful questions to encourage team members to find their own answers rather than providing solutions? What might hinder your ability to use powerful questions? How could you minimize this interference?
- Are you aware of the unique strengths of your team members? How can you enhance your understanding of these strengths – for example, with a team away day aimed at identifying strengths? How can you use this information on a daily basis to structure the allocation of work tasks among the team?
- What opportunities do you provide for your team members to identify their own strengths? What elements of team members' work roles can be flexed to capitalize on their strengths?
- Can you identify ways in which team members can have some degree of flexibility in their goals?
- How can you increase the frequency of opportunities that team members have to review goal progress with you? What processes can support you to achieve this?
- What processes can you put in place to encourage team members to practice new learning – for example, after they have attended a training course? What actions can you take to further support the practice of new skills?
- Do your team members have a development plan? Are they clear on how they need to develop? Individuals who identify their own areas of development are more likely to experience higher levels of motivation and responsibility for pursuing this development.

RESEARCH IN ACTION: A COACH'S EXPERIENCE

We all know of some situations where we have somebody who is trying to change some behaviour, but then the person is still being rewarded for displaying a different type of behaviour. Something is pulling them in one direction even though they want to go in another. For example, typically I would be rewarded for financial results, regardless of how I treat my employees, and yet I am expected to develop my employees but I am not financially rewarded for doing this. Or, I may not get a promotion even if I am doing a fantastic job at developing my people. I may be passed over for promotion by somebody who has just played the political game and has not done such a good job at managing his or her people. This is problematic because there will be a loss of energy related to the frustration that might be experienced around these conflicts, and it will also create, either consciously or unconsciously, dilemmas for the individual regarding how they should behave.

An example of a case where the organizational culture was very supportive of individual behavioural change is from some work that I completed for an international company, with the HQ based in the USA. Here, there was the opportunity to work with the entire system as they wanted to completely revise their leadership development curriculum. After extensive training needs analysis, we designed and delivered a five-day training programme supported by one-to-one coaching for each participant for one year. It was important to the organization that these programmes had impact. Before the launch of the programme, I had the chance to speak with the CEO. I stressed to her that if she was really serious about the programme having an impact, her personal involvement and example would be key to the success of the programme. She would need to speak to the group to highlight the importance of their commitment and engagement in this process. However, it was important that this was not just the usual type of speech from senior management. Instead, I really challenged her to speak at a more personal level about her own personal journey to convey the sense that she not only believed in this but that she is applying this to herself as well. She agreed to this and in fact, she also spoke to every participant after the one-week training programme to ensure that she understood what they had learned from the process and also to understand any learnings that would be useful at the system level. To avoid any inconsistencies between the reward systems in the organization and the behavioural change that was expected of these leaders, she also changed some of the reward systems, to ensure

(Continued)

that everything was aligned as much as possible. This CEO showed real commitment to the programme and she also recognized that to create the right conditions to support the personal development of the leaders the organizational culture needed to change as well. All of these actions combined helped to create the conditions where the organization made it clear that the leadership training and coaching is fully aligned with the organization culture that they wanted to develop. The programme proved to be very effective; in fact, every single leader made some significant progress. For example, in the 360-degree feedback, every leader had made progress when their leadership competencies were assessed by observers a year later. This is an example where organizational culture and in particular, the example set by the CEO really makes a difference to individual behavioural change.

Of course, development can still happen in examples where the organizational culture and senior leaders are not so supportive of change; however, we must be aware of the very real barriers that the organizational culture can present. I do also think that when coachees work in an organizational culture that does not foster learning, our role as coaches is to challenge our coachees to take personal responsibility for instigating a culture change. To ask them: "what can you do to make a difference at your level? Don't wait for the CEO or the others, what is it that you can do at your level of authority or responsibility, with the power that you currently have, what can you do?" Sometimes culture change can start, not at the top, but in some other parts of the organization and those other parts of the organization can set an example for the rest.

For details of the coaches who were interviewed for the 'research in action' vignettes, see page 191.

Shared assumptions about measuring results

So far, we have ascertained that the shared assumptions regarding the organization's values, mission, and goals set out who we are as an organization and the shared assumptions about the means to fulfil these values, mission, and goals spell out what we do. The next important aspect of organizational culture to understand is the shared assumptions about measuring results as this sets out how we will know when we have fulfilled our values, mission, or goals. Schein (2010) argues that all groups and organizations need to know how they are doing against their goals and periodically need to check to determine whether they are performing in line with their mission. This process involves three areas in which the group needs to achieve consensus.

Consensus must be achieved on what to measure, how to measure it, and what to do when corrections are needed. Such measurements are inevitably linked to how each employee is doing in his or her job; therefore, these measurements send important messages to members about what is important in the organization and therefore will create conditions to reinforce certain behaviours. For example, an organizational value that learning is a good thing will be reinforced if the leaders create mechanisms in which learning is measured. On the other hand, if the value states that learning is a good thing, however, the only results that are measured (and therefore implicitly communicated as being important to members) are financial results, then members are likely to place a greater emphasis on achieving short-term goals around financial results, potentially at the expense of other valued but not measured activities such as learning.

The shared assumptions about measuring results are important to understand in the context of the individual coachee's desired behaviour change. If the coachee is seeking to change a behaviour that is not being measured by their organization, it is important to be aware of the impact that this may have on their ability to successfully achieve this change. For example, you may wish to discuss with your coachee, how will they deal with multiple demands on their time if competing tasks include the area that the coachee is aiming to change versus an area which is measured by the organization? Can the coachee discuss with their line manager ways in which the desired behaviour can be measured? Are there any potentially negative consequences to the desired behaviour change on other areas of behaviour that are currently being measured at work? How could these negative consequences be effectively managed to help to facilitate the behaviour change?

For the leader wishing to establish a coaching culture, it is important to consider the shared assumptions around what is measured and how to measure it. What leaders pay attention to via measurement will reflect what is valued by the organization. Therefore, in a coaching culture, leaders should seek to measure open communication, collaborative working, active listening, trusting relationships, proactive working, accountability, and experimenting with solutions.

One important mechanism related to the measurement of results is how feedback is used. Feedback provides a method of providing data related to performance; therefore, effective and constructive feedback is an important process that leaders can use to not only measure results but also to provide information to employees on how they are performing in the areas that matter. The leader wishing to develop a coaching culture can ask themselves:

- When was the last time that you asked for feedback from others? How did you use this feedback? What processes can you implement to ensure that you regularly ask for and use feedback? How can you communicate to others how you have acted upon their feedback?

- How frequently do you seek the opinion and feedback from team members? How could you increase the opportunities to seek opinion and feedback from team members? How can you demonstrate to team members that you value their opinion and feedback? For example, can you communicate to others when you have amended your behaviour or a decision based on the opinion or feedback of others?
- Consider the last few times you have provided feedback to your team. How could you have made this feedback more meaningful to the recipient? How could the feedback have been reframed to further support learning and development? How can you ensure that you apply these principles in the next opportunity to provide feedback?

Shared assumptions about rewards and punishments

What happens when something goes wrong in the organization? What action is taken? How is success (as defined under the shared assumptions regarding measuring results) celebrated and rewarded? The final set of shared assumptions relates to rewards and punishments. Schein (2010) argues that there must be some consensus on what symbolically and actually is defined as a reward or punishment and on the manner in which it is to be administered. Behaviour that is rewarded will be reinforced and encouraged and behaviour that is punished will be discouraged. The antithesis of a coaching culture is a blame culture that implies that whenever something goes wrong, someone is to blame, that individual will be identified and their career will be damaged. Therefore, considering the organization's shared assumptions about what is rewarded and what is punished will be important to understand in the context of the individual coachee's desired behaviour change. Is it likely that the coachee will be rewarded for the new behaviour? Is there a chance that they will be punished in some way? This punishment may be an indirect consequence of the behaviour change. For example, while the coachee is acquiring a new skill, they may have to pull back their efforts in another element of their role, which may have a negative impact on some other aspect of their performance. What are the likely consequences of this? What can the coachee do to manage any potential risk of punishment?

For the leader who wishes to establish a coaching culture, rewards and punishments are one of the most effective ways of encouraging behaviour change. However, it is also important to consider any unintended consequences of rewards (and punishments). For example, earlier, I argued that a shared assumption of a coaching culture is regarding the importance of teamwork. However, many organizations, while relying on teamwork, do not use reward systems that encourage teamwork. Instead, most reward systems encourage competitive behaviours that are more likely to foster distrust and impatience among team members. For example, if my bonus depends on my performance but something you do is holding me up, I am more likely to feel frustrated and resentful and less likely to work with you to explore how I can help you to overcome the hold-up. In his writing on the topic of servant leadership, Greenleaf (1998) proposes that while we uncritically accept competition as being good and consequently deeply embedded in our culture, we will never be able to elicit optimal service from people. Greenleaf (1998) highlights that the Latin origin of the word 'compete' is to *seek or strive together* as opposed to the modern use of the word which is to strive or compete with another. Unfortunately, we see far too much striving against one another, even within our own organizations, rather than striving together towards a common goal and much of this is due to the fact that the organizational process around rewards inherently encourages competitiveness and discourages teamwork.

The leader wishing to develop a coaching culture can ask themselves:

- Do your organization's reward systems foster teamwork or competitiveness? What changes can you make to adjust this balance?
- Many organizations posit that they create an environment where we can learn from error however for how many is this really true? Fear of blame evokes defensiveness and defensiveness reduces awareness. Reflect on the last time an error occurred at work. How was this handled? What could be done differently next time to minimize blame and maximize learning?
- To specifically ensure that we can learn from failures and avoid the fear of failure, it is important to embed learning from failures into part of everyday working life. For example, the use of after-event reviews (AERs), at the end of each workday or on completion of a project are particularly important to discuss successes and what can be learned for the future.

This chapter in summary

- Coaches need to consider their coachee's organizational culture as organizational culture can present barriers to behaviour change. These barriers may be in the form of:
  - When the behaviour change contradicts the values, mission, and goals of the organization
  - When the accepted means to fulfil the values, mission, and goals do not support the desired change
  - When the results that are measured and the methods of measuring results do not support the desired change
  - When the rewards or punishments do not support the behaviour change

- Leaders have the ability to influence and change the culture to one that is conducive to behaviour change
- A coaching culture is one that is learning-oriented, adaptable, and flexible
- A coaching culture is characterized by the following shared assumptions:
  - Proactive and adaptable behaviour is desirable
  - Learning is a good thing worth investing in
  - Human nature is good and malleable
  - The environment can be managed
  - Problems can be solved through inquiry
  - The future is positive
  - To be effective, honest communication and information is essential
- Adopting a coaching culture influences how employees work with others, how employees approach tasks, and how employees help each other to learn

References

Amazon. (2019). Leadership principles. Retrieved from https://www.amazon.jobs/en/principles. Accessed on October 12, 2019.

Aviva. (2019). We fail fast and learn fast, testing and learning at pace. Retrieved from https://www.aviva.com/about-us/never-rest/. Accessed on October 12, 2019.

Bowen, D. E., & Ostroff, C. (2004). Understanding HRM-firm performance linkages: The role of the strength of the HRM system. *Academy of Management Review, 29,* 203–221.

Ellinger, A. D., Ellinger, A. E., & Keller, S. B. (2003). Supervisory coaching behaviour, employee satisfaction and warehouse employee performance: A dyadic perspective in the distribution industry. *Human Resource Development Quarterly, 14*(4), 435–458.

Dahling, J. J., Taylor, S. R., Chau, S. L., & Dwight, S. A. (2016). Does coaching matter? A multilevel model linking managerial coaching skill and frequency to sales goal attainment. *Personnel Psychology, 69*(4), 863–894.

Gladwell, M. (2009). *Outliers: The story of success.* New York: Penguin Group.

Greenleaf, R. K. (1998). *The power of servant leadership.* San Francisco, CA: Berrett-Koehler.

Hartnell, C. A., Ou, A. Y., & Kinicki, A. (2011). Organizational culture and organizational effectiveness: A meta-analytic investigation of the competing values framework's theoretical suppositions. *Journal of Applied Psychology, 96*(4), 677–694.

Henderson, M., Thompson, D., & Henderson, S. (2006). *Leading through values: Linking company culture to business strategy.* New Zealand: Harper Business.

HSBC. (2019). Growing our business in the right way. Retrieved from https://www.hsbc.com/our-approach/our-values. Accessed on October 12, 2019.

JP Morgan Chase. (2019). A commitment to integrity, fairness and responsibility. Retrieved from https://www.jpmorganchase.com/corporate/About-JPMC/ab-business-principles-integrity.htm. Accessed on October 12, 2019.

Microsoft. (2019). Our vision. Retrieved from https://www.microsoft.com/en-gb/about/vision/.

Paterson, T. A., Luthans, F., & Jeung, W. (2014). Thriving at work: Impact of psychological capital and supervisor support. *Journal of Organizational Behavior, 35*, 434–446.

Patterson, M., Warr, P., & West, M. (2004). Organizational climate and company productivity: The role of employee affect and employee level. *Journal of Occupational and Organizational Psychology, 77*, 193–216.

Schein, E. H. (2010). *Organizational culture and leadership.* San Francisco, CA: Jossey-Bass.

Sung, S. Y., & Choi, J. N. (2014). Do organizations spend wisely on employees? Effects of training and development investments on learning and innovation in organizations. *Journal of Organizational Behavior, 35*, 393–412.

Verquer, M. L., Beehr, T. A., & Wagner, S. H. (2003). A meta-analysis of relations between person-organization fit and work attitudes. *Journal of Vocational Behavior, 63*, 473–489.

Vodaphone. (2019). Vodafone is a leader in technology communications through mobile, fixed, broadband and TV. Retrieved from https://www.vodafone.com/about. Accessed October 12, 2019

West, M. A., & Richter, A. W. (2008). Climates and cultures for innovation and creativity at work. In J. Zhou, & E. C. E. Shalley (Eds.), *Handbook of organizational creativity,* (pp. 211–236). New York: Lawrence Erlbaum Associates.

Zhang, A. Y., Tsui, A. S., Song, L. J., Li, C., & Jia, L. (2008). How do I trust thee? The employee–organization relationship, supervisory support, and middle manager trust in the organization. *Human Resource Management, 47*(1), 111–132.

Section Five

Conclusion

In this book, I have sought to bring together the existing research evidence on coaching and related fields and present this in a way that demonstrates how the evidence can be applied in practice. This discussion has not been an exhaustive list of every topic or piece of research relevant to effective coaching. However, I have focused on the key aspects that I believe need to be considered based on the available evidence. You will have noticed that many of the topics I have included in this book are topics that I have argued are central to understand in relation to effective behaviour change from coaching (such as goal-setting and the organizational culture); however, have very little dedicated coaching research. Many of the recommendations I have provided are drawn from evidence from fields related to coaching rather than research that specifically tests these topics in relation to coaching. This, I hope is changing. Even within the last five years, I have witnessed a surge in good quality coaching research. Fortunately, based on the current trends, I anticipate that this will continue to grow, consequently, enabling us to incrementally build our knowledge base as to what makes coaching effective.

As I close this book, I wanted to highlight my own reasons for dedicating my professional life to the pursuit of understanding coaching and behaviour change. One of the reasons that I feel so passionate about the topic of coaching is because I feel passionate about treating people well. I truly believe that if we expect the best of people, then they will achieve this. The world would be a better place if we could all take a moment to treat each other as we wish to be treated – or if we are not very good at treating ourselves well, then treat each other as we wish a loved one to be treated (and improve the way that we treat ourselves in the process!). This is what attracts me to coaching. The principles that underpin coaching that I outlined in Section one: the importance of openness; unconditional positive regard; non-judgmental attitude; growth mindset; and authenticity, are, I believe important qualities that we can all strive to achieve.

Another reason for my passion for coaching is related to my own personal drive for continuous development and my belief in the centrality of continuous development or learning to happiness. After all, one cannot thrive or flourish without growing or developing. Therefore, I was surprised when, in writing Section four on the role of the organization and researching organizations' mission statements, the statement that it took me the longest to find an example for was 'Members hold the shared assumption that learning is a good thing worth investing in and that learning to learn is itself a skill to be mastered'. I had thought that the need to continuously learn was well accepted in today's organizations, and therefore, this need to learn would be reflected in many mission statements. This was not the case. Furthermore, I struggled to find a reference to learning, even on many organizations' recruitment pages. Organizations would often refer to the fact that they would seek to hire the 'right' people for the job; however, little was said about what support and development would be offered to those people once they got there. I guess this indicates my own bias. Because I believe in the centrality of continuous development, I had formed the assumption that this was a commonly accepted, shared belief.

My point is that I believe that this reflects the fact that we still have a very long way to go in how we treat the members of our organizations. Unless an organization is a sole trader, it cannot exist without its employees. The people are how the product or service is delivered. Even in organizations that involve a high degree of automation, the organization is still reliant on its people. Yet why do organizations continue to put the needs of its members at the bottom of the pile? Mission statements talk about customers, of course, they now make reference to sustainability, which is also of course important. Diversity and inclusion came up regularly. Again, very important and I imagine a fairly new inclusion in most organization's mission statements. However, beyond diversity and inclusion, what are organizations doing to treat their members in a way that we would want our loved ones to be treated? To provide the conditions to allow people to reach their full potential, whatever that might be? To challenge people to continually learn and develop in a safe environment free from fear of blame or retribution if the metaphorical foot is taken off the pedal for just a moment in the race for maximum productivity. What I see with the organizations that I work with and the organizations that my MSc students work with, are people continually being asked to do more with less. If we are being asked to do more with less, we become more stressed and at risk of burnout. If we are stressed, we are not in the right place to learn and develop. If we cannot learn and develop, we cannot reach our full potential. Furthermore, we cannot enable our organization to learn and develop. Unfortunately, until leaders of organizations recognize that while profitability is important, maximum profitability is not a necessity, this will not change. Surely earning a fair profit while enabling your members to reach their full potential is a more desirable goal?

This will likely mean taking steps such as hiring more people to provide additional resources, investing in learning and development, and providing safe opportunities for members to practise new skills. These activities take time. Time away from the daily job which is time when that member is not actively contributing to profit-making activities in that moment. Imagine working somewhere where this was the reality. Imagine the relationships you would have with your co-workers. The sense of fulfilment you would have in working hard, doing your job well, and being recognized for this. The weight that would be lifted if you were not pushed to your maximum capacity and beyond, every moment of the day. The influence this would have on your home-life, your relationship with your partner, and with your children. It sounds pretty good to me.

Research in action: Coach biographies

Throughout the book, examples of research in action have kindly been provided by a number of expert coaches. Below (presented alphabetically by surname) are the biographies of these coaches.

Alison Hardingham

Alison Hardingham MA Oxon, MSt, AFBPS, APECS, is Director of Business Psychology at Yellow Dog Consulting, the company which she founded in 2000. She is an executive coach, and a developer and supervisor of other coaches.

Alison is a business psychologist who has worked for over thirty years helping people in organisations to explore and understand their own responses, motives and behaviours so that they can work together more enjoyably and more effectively. She is a Visiting Professor at Henley Business School, where she designed and still teaches on both the Professional Certificate in Coaching and the second year of the MSc in Coaching and Behavioural Change.

Alison is also a qualified psychodynamic psychotherapist, with a private practice which she runs alongside her coaching business.

William McKee

William is the Principal Consultant at North Star Learning and Performance Ltd. Starting out as a Civil Engineer responsible for large infrastructure projects William became fascinated with the people side of business. Now a qualified business psychologist, a training facilitator and an executive coach, William brings a refreshingly practical approach to culture, people and performance. Over the last eight years he's worked with companies like British Airways, the Met Office, Bombardier Transport, University Hospital Leicester and several Local Authorities to train, coach and develop their people's leadership and management capabilities. Having also spent time supporting SME's and start-ups as well as working extensively in the Middle East, he can relate to a wide range of people and organisational contexts. Evidence Based Practice is an important aspect of William's approach, whether coaching, designing and delivering training or working on wider organisational development projects he looks to strike a balance between practical 'rules of thumb' and the latest empirical research.

John Metherell

John is an experienced executive coach, coach supervisor and facilitator, having worked in numerous organisations (large and small) in the UK and internationally. As well as his expertise as a coach he is an experienced leadership development specialist working with senior executives as an internal and external management consultant, and change manager.

John has worked with and coached clients in a broad range of industry sectors (in the UK and in Central Europe and Asia) including Higher Education, Finance, professional services, engineering, retail, management consulting. He works with individuals at all levels from first line managers to CEO and COO, and senior leadership teams. John is an associate tutor and coach at Henley Business School, where he has participated in leadership research projects, and supervises on the MSc in Coaching and Behavioural Change. In addition he has coached on numerous programmes including the part time MBA. John is part of the faculty team for the diploma programme at the Coaching Supervision Academy. He has also contributed to books on Leadership development, and Organisational Stress.

Jonathan Passmore

Jonathan is a chartered psychologist and holds five degrees, including an MBA and a doctorate in occupational psychology, as well as a post-graduate certificate in coaching and two professional qualifications. His doctoral thesis focused on the coaching relationships and behaviours. His current research interests include coaching supervision and ethics, neuroscience of coaching, coach impact evaluation and coaching competences.

Jonathan has published widely with over 100 scientific papers and book chapters. He has edited and written 30 books (including *Excellence in Coaching, Appreciative Inquiry for Change Management and Top Business Psychology Models*) and delivered 200 conference papers. He is series editor of the Wiley-Blackwell Handbook series on organisational psychology.

Jonathan has won several international awards, including the Association for Coaching Global Award (2010), the British Psychological Society Coaching Research Award (2012) and the Association for Business Psychology Chairman's Award for Excellence (2015). He also won Best Article 2019 'Coaching at Work'. Jonathan has held a number of executive and non-executive board roles and worked for global consulting firms, including PwC and IBM Business Consulting. Most recently he was managing director of Embrion, a psychology consulting company with clients such as Technip and HSBC; he has advised professional bodies such as the Institute for Leadership and Management and the European Mentoring and Coaching Council.

Jonathan is Professor Catedratico the University of Évora, Portugal and is Professor of Coaching and Behavioural Change at Henley Business School.

Philippe Rosinski

Professor Philippe Rosinski, MCC, is considered the pioneer of intercultural and global coaching. He is the author of two seminal books, Coaching Across Cultures and Global Coaching, and has contributed to eleven additional books.

His integrated coaching approach leverages multiple perspectives (from the physical to the spiritual) to tackle complex challenges, enabling greater creativity, impact, fulfilment and meaning. Philippe shares his passion for making the most of cultural differences and for learning from multiple disciplines, in order to help unleash the human multifaceted potential. For almost 30 years and across continents, Philippe has helped people and organizations thrive and make a positive difference.

Philippe is a world authority in executive coaching, team coaching, and global leadership development. He is the first European to have been designated Master Certified Coach by the International Coach Federation. He is the author of the Cultural Orientations Framework (COF) assessment.

Philippe is the principal of Rosinski & Company, a consultancy based in Belgium with partners around the globe. A Master of Science from Stanford University, he is also a professor in the MBA program for global managers at the Kenichi Ohmae Graduate School of Business in Tokyo, Japan.

Brian O. Underhill

Brian O. Underhill, Ph.D., PCC, is an industry-recognized expert in the design and management of worldwide executive coaching implementations. He is the Founder and CEO of CoachSource, the world's largest executive coaching provider, with over 1,100 coaches in 100+ countries. Previously, he managed executive coaching operations for Marshall Goldsmith, the world's #1 coach.

Brian's executive coaching work has successfully focused on helping clients achieve positive, measurable, long-term change in leadership behavior. He has also helped pioneer the use of "mini-surveys"—a unique measurement tool to help impact behavioral change over time. He is an internationally sought-after speaker, addressing The Conference Board, ICF, EMCC, and many regional coaching events. Brian is the co-editor of "Mastering Executive Coaching" (Routledge, 2019), author of "Executive Coaching for Results: The Definitive Guide to Developing Organizational Leaders" (Berrett-Koehler, 2007), as well as author of numerous articles and blogs in the coaching field.

Index

acceptance 3–4, 10, 106–107
accountability 157, 159–161, 174, 177, 181
advice 11–12, 15
affective outcomes 30–33, 41, 134
affirmation 78–79
after event reviews 142, 183
agreeableness 55
antagonism 55
antecedent-focused regulation 110, 112
anxiety 31, 67, 69, 104, 121, 167, 172
assertiveness 33
attention 47–48, 68–70, 79, 84, 99–103, 110, 112–115, 123, 130, 148, 151, 165–166, 173, 175, 181
attentional deployment 110
attentional resources 69
attitudes 30, 149
authenticity 2, 8–9, 15, 139–140, 176, 187
autonomy 52–53, 59
avoid goal orientation 67, 69–71, 129

barriers 10, 32, 61, 69, 100–102, 104, 115, 118, 120, 143–144, 155, 165–167, 169, 172–173, 177, 180, 183
behavioural change 2, 10–11, 15, 18, 34, 46, 75, 84, 88, 98–99, 118, 126, 130, 148, 179–180
beliefs 74, 76–77, 81, 85, 106, 116, 124, 127, 129–130, 139, 169
benevolence 107, 140, 144
bias 4, 22, 26, 31, 35, 188
Big Five 24, 56–57
blame 138, 174, 182–183, 188

capability 13, 15, 78, 80, 85, 87, 140, 144
career satisfaction 31
chemistry meetings 50–51, 53

clan cultures 174
clean language 89, 91
climate 3, 37, 173
coaching: as a leadership philosophy 2; behaviour 175; commitment 47, 134–135, 179–180; contract 50–53, 136, 140–141, 144; culture 168, 170, 173–176, 181–184; definition 1, 2, 11–12; questions 48, 75, 79, 84, 93–94, 96, 114, 125, 137–138, 172, 175–176, 178; readiness 47, 49, 57, 60; skills 93, 95, 175; supervisor 9; team 21
cognitive-behavioural 79, 131–132, 137
cognitive change 110–113
cognitive outcomes 30, 32–33, 36, 39, 41, 131
communication 33–34, 68, 86, 90, 114, 144, 171, 173–174, 176–177, 181, 184
confidence 30, 31, 36, 51, 68, 77–80, 120–121, 136, 140, 176
confidential 60, 133, 140
confidentiality 134–136, 140–141
conscientiousness 55
consistency of evidence 20–21, 26, 94, 133
constellations 56, 126
containment 128, 135, 139
counselling 95–96, 133–134, 138
creative 3, 56, 59, 61, 103, 108–109, 123
creative experiment 59
creative language 83, 89
credibility 50–51, 53, 135, 140
cross-sectional 56, 134
culture 53, 70, 107, 165–176, 179–184, 187

decision-making 32–33, 150, 170–171
defence mechanisms 84, 124
delegation 33
depression 31, 121

directness: of the intervention 20–22, 26, 56–57, 94, 133; of the outcome 20, 22, 26, 31, 33, 49, 56–57, 74, 95, 133
disengagement 11
doubt 37, 76–77, 84, 130, 140
drawing 56, 90, 123
Dweck, C. 5, 66

effect size 35–36, 131
emergency reserve 112–113
employee assistance programme (EAP) 134
emotional stability 55
emotion regulation 110–113, 115
empathy 9–10, 51
energy pool 104
evaluation 28, 30–31, 38–41, 120, 192
evidence-based practice 24, 26
experiential learning cycle 84, 124–125
experiential learning theory 84, 123–124
extraversion 55–56

fad 12, 17–19
faulty assumptions 75
five factor model 55, 62
frame of reference 4

gestalt 127
goal: achievement 5, 51–53, 67, 75, 77, 101–102, 115, 129, 154, 160; failure 109–113, 115; focused 10–11, 15, 69; orientation 5, 14, 46, 49, 64–67, 69–71, 99, 129; progression 93
growth mindset 2, 4–10, 12, 15, 66, 139–140, 168, 187

habits 143, 148, 157, 159
habitual behaviours 125
humiliation 84–85, 118, 135

identical elements theory 150
implementation intention 151–154, 156–161
individual differences 46–47, 89, 123, 155–156
Insights Discovery 24
integrity 140–141, 144
intrapersonal 67, 129
introversion 55
intrusive thoughts 122

job satisfaction 31, 38, 169, 174–175

knowledge: declarative 30, 32; procedural 30, 32
Kolb, D. A. 84, 123–124

Latham, G. 31, 52, 99, 101, 104–105, 113–114
leadership skills 33–34, 39
learning agility 33
learning anxiety 167
learning culture 53, 168, 170
learning goal orientation 70
Lego 56
listening 65, 102–104, 118, 133, 168, 173, 176–177, 181
Locke, E. 31, 52, 99, 101, 104, 113–114

mastery goal orientation 49, 66
memory 121–122, 134
mental health 24, 93, 121
mentoring 134, 140
meta-analysis 29, 35–36, 148–149, 169, 174
metaphor 59, 89–91
MBTI 24, 116
mindreading 4
mission 168–176, 180, 183, 188
mood 4, 31, 93, 177
motivational interviewing 79

negative affect 93, 100
neuroticism 55
non-judgmental attitude 2, 4, 15, 139, 144, 168, 187
novel 56, 59, 61, 107

openness 2–3, 15, 53, 55–59, 61, 89–90, 113, 139, 141, 144, 187
openness to experience 55
organizational commitment 31, 38, 174

performance goal orientation 66
personality: assessment 24, 59; profiling 23–25; trait approach 2–3, 24, 55, 58–59, 116; type approach 23–25, 116
persistence 45, 47–48, 53, 66, 77, 99, 104, 108–109, 112–113, 115, 158
person-organization fit 169
placebo effect 22, 31, 95, 139
positive affect 93
positive psychology 100, 126

post shift debriefings 142
problem-focused 93
problem-solving 30, 32–33
psychodynamic 127–128, 137
psychological contract 51
psychological fidelity 149–151, 154
psychometric 56
psychotherapy 3, 95–96, 135, 138

qualitative 20, 26, 35, 48, 119, 131–133, 135, 157
quantitative 20, 26, 66, 131–132, 158

raising awareness 10, 15, 32, 84, 88, 90, 118–119, 127, 130, 137
rapport 50, 94, 134–135
reappraisal 111–112
reflective learning journals 119
reflective practice 9, 50, 83, 87–88, 91, 119–120, 122–124, 142–144
reflective thinking 32, 88, 115
reflective writing 88, 90–91, 122–123, 128
reflexivity 83–84, 123, 142
reframe 71, 80, 84, 100–102, 182
remorse 84
resilience 30, 31, 45, 105
resistance 4, 11, 59, 61, 137
response-focused regulation 110–111
results outcome 29, 34–36, 39, 41, 149
return-on-expectation 37–38
return-on-investment 13, 36–37, 41
Rogers, C. 3
ruminate 67, 129
ruminating 119
rumination 67, 69, 71

safe space 3–4, 10, 135, 144
scientific rigour 19–20, 26
self-awareness 11, 32–33, 74–75, 83–84, 131–133, 160, 175
self-belief 66–68, 71, 74, 77, 81
self-compassion 67–68, 71, 129–130
self-doubt 77, 130
self-efficacy 14, 30, 31, 46, 66–67, 74–81, 93, 129–130, 155
self-fulfilling prophecy 139–140
self-insight 32–33, 131–133
self-judgments 74, 76

self-reflection 9–10, 32, 85, 131–132
self-regulatory resources 67, 129
self-talk 68, 130
sense-making 13
servant leadership 183
shame 84–85, 110–112, 118, 135, 156
situation modification 110
situation selection 110
skill: acquisition 33, 74; enhancement 33
skill-based outcomes 30, 33–34, 39–41, 49, 66, 74, 134
sleep 67, 69
Socratic questions 138
solution-focused thinking 33
storytelling 56, 122
strengths 41, 46, 50, 75–76, 80, 91, 119–120, 126, 129–130, 133, 178
stress 30, 31–32, 37, 40, 67, 69, 121, 133, 159, 188
subconscious 114
subject expert 11–12, 15
supervisory support 166
suppression 111
symbols 89

theoretical underpinning 20, 26, 94, 133
360-degree feedback 21, 180
thriving 173
time-management 33, 121–122
training motivation 47
training transfer 36, 66, 149
transformational leadership 49
trust 4, 9–11, 15, 17, 40, 52–53, 55, 70, 118–119, 128, 133–142, 144, 171–173, 176, 181, 183

unconditional positive regard 2–4, 9, 12, 15, 139–140, 144, 168, 187
unconscious processes 84, 124–125

vision 108, 172, 178
visualization 56
vulnerable 136, 140

well-being 31, 40, 131, 142, 171, 173
Whitmore, J. 75, 98, 108, 125
work-life balance 38, 148, 169

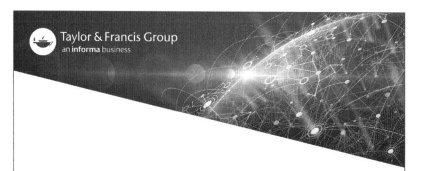

Printed in Great Britain
by Amazon